GOALS 2000

Kathy Finnegan

GOALS 2000:

Restructuring Our Schools . . .
Restructuring Society

Kathy Finnegan

 For information write: Hearthstone Publishing Ltd., 500 Beacon Drive, Oklahoma City, OK 73127.

ISBN 1-57558-003-9

Cover design by Eric Ferguson.

This book is dedicated to
America's endangered Christian families
. . . especially our children.

Acknowledgments

In an undertaking like this, there are many to acknowledge . . .

Above all, I thank God for putting this burden on my heart, and then providing me with all that was needed to bring the task to completion.

I am grateful to my publisher, Hearthstone, and especially to Noah Hutchings who saw the importance of educational restructuring when it was introduced as AMERICA 2000 during the Bush/Lamar Alexander years.

I wish also to acknowledge the many wonderful researchers around the country whose thoughts and writings have been inspirational and of great practical help. Some are quoted extensively, especially in the chronology (Dr. Dennis Cuddy) and the glossary (Dr. Samuel Blumenfeld). I would like to express sincere thanks to numerous obscure and unsung parent/researchers whose commitment to our children and country keeps them at this work. Many have contributed directly or indirectly to this effort. Some are mentioned by name in the book; others, who are not, generously provided material and encouragement.

Finally, I wish to thank my son who helped me obtain documentation materials, my husband who put in many hours assisting me on the computer, and friends who prayed for me and for this work.

Table of Contents

Preface

GOALS 2000, (Public Law 103-227) is the centerpiece federal "education reform" law passed on March 31, 1994, and the successor to the Bush administration plan, **AMERICA 2000**. Because educational restructuring was launched under Bush, then expanded and brought to fruition under Clinton, it should be clear that this has been a broad bipartisan effort. For most Americans, school restructuring became a news item with **AMERICA 2000**, launched in 1991 under then Secretary of Education Lamar Alexander. However, I think people realize that *AMERICA 2000/GOALS 2000* didn't "just happen"—that it wasn't simply a way to codify the six National Education Goals, said to have been formulated at the 1989 National Governor's Conference, nor was it as some said, the long overdue response to the 1983 report, ***A Nation at Risk,*** which pointed out many of the failures of the public school system and contained the oft-repeated quote: "If an unfriendly foreign power had attempted to impose on America the mediocre educational performance that exists today, we might well have viewed it as an act of war." The next sentence, "As it stands, we have allowed this to happen to ourselves," is not as often quoted. Maybe this is because we don't want to believe that's the case—or maybe it's blame unfairly assigned. What is the history of educational restructuring that culminated in *GOALS 2000*?

The seeds of "the problem" in education, set forth in ***A Nation at Risk,*** were sown—and "the solution" (*GOALS 2000*) was cultivated over a long period of time by forces beyond the sight or knowledge of most Americans, including parents using the system and teachers working in it. While it may be true that most of us have been asleep (wanting to believe that because we went through the public schools and turned out "O.K.," this will still be the case for our children), and we may have been too complacent and trustingly left things in the hands of educational "experts," but to blame the civilian equivalent of "an act of war" on parents and other ordinary citizens is grossly unfair. It's more than unfair; it's **blaming the victims.**

To trace the roots of the problem, and to learn who is proposing the solutions and what they are, we must go back many decades. If you accept the premise that events and (largely) unseen hands are propelling us rapidly into what President Bush, and many before him, called the New World Order (NWO), then (and only then) will you be able to understand that what is happening to our schools is part of that larger scenario.

What we have finally gotten with *GOALS 2000* is a national—soon to be international—school system, as dreamed of and patiently planned for by socialists, one-worlders, and their fellow-traveler Utopians. **Appearances to the contrary, ours is not a system run amuck; it's a system very much on track if viewed from an historical (and especially) a prophetic perspective.** We are, at last, where those who have tried for decades to control education, hoped that we would one day be.

This book was written to show Christian parents what is contained in the *GOALS 2000* legislation, and through the commentary to provide **an interpretation in plain English** of some of the more convoluted, ambiguous, or misleading language and ideas contained in this law. I have attempted to decipher as a layman (for laymen) what I think the language of the law means and how it will likely be applied in our homes, schools, and communities. This information is for Christian parents, grandparents, and others who have a loving concern for America's school children. My conclusions are alarming—and **I would like to be wrong** about them, but I believe the schools have passed a point of no return and the hour is very late for America.

GOALS 2000* is raw social engineering, intended to restructure all of American society and not just the schools.** The schools, in fact, are just a medium (though a very important one) for the restructuring to occur. *GOALS 2000* sets up a "framework" for the desired changes, just as the ***Elementary and Secondary Education Act (ESEA) thirty years ago set up a similar framework to engineer racial and economic equity in the schools.

This book is not light reading, and I don't imagine from the title you expected it to be. The subject is a very serious one, and the legal language, quoted extensively, can get you lost in a thicket of words. It may help as you read through this commentary to keep your eyes on some themes that run throughout the law. **The themes are also the "paradigm" (whole system) shifts** that make *GOALS 2000* such a radical piece of legislation.

The first alarming paradigm shift seeks to make **parents "just partners" in a "whole village" of educators, health care providers, job counselors, social service personnel, and others who presumably have a vested interest in your child.** Some programs begin at birth and come right into your home.

Another theme is the **shift away from a broad, general education that graduates can apply where and how they wish—to a much narrower, vocationally-focused "training" that has as its end point a planned niche in a planned economy.** Other federal work force legislation tied to *GOALS 2000* locks this in.

Still another shift is **the way schools are to be managed at all levels:** federal control, state control, and control of the local school. Usurping local control is a necessary first step toward national control.

The **nationalization of standards and tests,** packaged deceptively to appear "bottom-up" and voluntary, is the next shift. *GOALS 2000* introduces three kinds of new standards: Content, Performance, and Opportunity-to-Learn. Tests are called "Assessments."

Just when you've realized what nationalization of curriculum and tests will mean for local control, you learn of an **even bigger paradigm shift**—that standardization at the national level is only the opening salvo—and that these areas are being **internationalized.**

For internationalization to occur, another shift, **"leveling," must take place—leveling of the individual, of schools, and the nation.** Many strategies and techniques will be used to accomplish this—whole language, OBE, equity suits, and more. (We'll get into the specifics.)

The next shift follows logically from internationalization: **children must be trained to be world citizens with the right attitudes, values, and beliefs for the NWO that's being created.**

And all of these shifts are to occur in your home, local school, or community (with your tax dollars—**and the government hopes, your**

approval) under a new unifying control concept called **"lifelong learning."**

In addition to these themes, **keep your eye on four recurring words: "all," "partnerships," "challenging," and "voluntary."** Their repeated use is not accidental.

We begin with **"A Seventy-Year Trail,"** a chronology of significant events in American education because **it's impossible to understand the law (or to believe the direction we're being taken) without seeing the historical context of restructuring.** You may be surprised at the role of key nongovernmental organizations (NGOs), and especially of the wealthy foundations, and of UNESCO in shaping our educational policies. The entries are numbered and frequent references in the text will refer you back to related past events. **Follow this trail of money and ideology and see if you do not agree that we have arrived educationally where we were being taken all along.** Most of these entries have been extracted (with some changes) from Dr. Dennis L. Cuddy's longer work, ***A Chronology of Education with Quotable Quotes,*** which covers a 200-year period. **(See resources.)**

Each of the **ten titles** of ***P.L.103-227*** and the law's introductory section is arranged as a **separate chapter.** Enough of the actual language *of* ***GOALS 2000*** *(printed in italics)* has been included, followed by my comments, to show what I feel is its intent or likely application. Not every word of this **155-page** law is reprinted because much of the text is either repetitive or otherwise of little note. For those wishing to read ***P.L.103-227*** in its entirety, you may obtain it from the GPO, Superintendent of Documents (while it remains in print), in government depository libraries, or from Citizens for Academic Excellence. **(See resources.)**

Each title in ***GOALS 2000,*** and the law's introductory section begins with a **summary overview** to explain briefly what the chapter covers. This was done because even with the commentary, ***GOALS 2000*** is not the easiest reading, partly because laws are cast in arcane legalese, and partly because it's easy when reading through a long title to lose sight of the "big picture" or where that section is heading. It will help to keep your eyes on the **eight paradigm shift/themes** outlined above and the **four oft-repeated words.**

A **glossary** of expanded entries defines twenty-three terms, organizations, or concepts used either in *P.L.103-227* or the commentary that parents may not be familiar with.

A list of **resources** that may be purchased will help you to further research the information contained in this book and to learn more about related issues. Investigate school restructuring for yourself, but with a sense of urgency, please. Time is running out.

May God bless you with wisdom in applying this information.

A Seventy-Year Trail of Significant Events and Telling Quotes

Leading to the Passage in 1994 of the Goals 2000: Educate America Act

Emphasis has been added to statements and quotes.

105 of these entries were extracted (with some changes) from Dr. Dennis L. Cuddy's complete work of almost 700 entries, ***A Chronology of Education with Quotable Quotes***, covering from about 1790 to the present.

A Seventy-Year Chronology of Education Related to Goals 2000

1925

1. **The International Bureau of Education (IBE),** formerly the Institut Jean-Jacques Rousseau, begins with a **grant from the Rockefeller Foundation.** IBE is the first intergovernmental organization in the field of education.

1930

2. The **"Dick and Jane"** basal reading series, using the **"look-say"** or **"whole word"** method of reading instruction begins. The consequences of using this method of the "progressive educators" (instead of the highly successful intensive phonics method) will prove disastrous.

1930s

3. The influence of **John Dewey,** "father" of **Progressive Education** (who started his career in the 1890s) is felt in classrooms across America. Dewey founded the "Lab School" at the University of Chicago, and went on to teach for many years at Teachers College, Columbia University in New York City. His enormous influence on education was twofold: on the two generations of students he taught, and throughout the entire field via the numerous books and articles he authored. His writings are still read by college education majors. Dewey was also the founder of the Progressive Education Association (1919); a cofounder of the New School for Social Research (1919); honorary president of the National Education Association (1932); and coauthor of the first *Humanist Manifesto* (1932). Largely because of the latter, he remains a revered figure among liberals.

4. A new "discipline," **social studies,** is introduced. Watered down

civics, geography, economics, and history (especially American) are subsumed under this heading. In 1929 the American Historical Association sponsored a **Commission on the Social Studies in the Schools.** This commission published ***A Charter for the Social Studies in the Schools*** in 1931, and in 1934, their ***Conclusions and Recommendations (CAR).*** In the preface to this latter work, the commission acknowledges its indebtedness to the **Carnegie Corporation** whose financial aid made possible the five-year investigation of social science instruction in the schools, culminating in the ***CAR.*** In chapter 1 of ***CAR,* "The Obligations and Procedure of the Commission"** we read:

> 1) The social sciences, more than any other division of the school curriculum, are concerned immediately with the life, the institutions, the thought, the aspirations, and the far-reaching policies of the nation in its world setting. 2) In view of this fact, the Commission could not limit itself to a survey of textbooks, curricula, methods of instruction, and schemes of examination, but was impelled to consider the condition and prospects of the American people as a part of Western civilization **now merging into a world order.** 3) The Commission was also driven to this broader conception of its task by the obvious fact that American civilization, in common with Western civilization, is passing through one of the great critical ages of history, **is modifying its traditional faith in economic individualism, and is embarking upon vast experiments in social planning and control which call for large-scale cooperation on the part of the people.** It is likewise obvious that in corresponding measure the **responsibilities and opportunities of organized education, particularly in the social sciences, are being increased.**

1932

5. ***Toward Soviet America*** by William Z. Foster (head of the American Communist Party) is published. Measures called for that have (at least in part) been realized are: schools to be coordinated under a national department of education; studies to be cleansed of religious, patriotic, and other features of "bourgeoisie" ideology, with God banished from the schools, and with students taught on the basis of internationalism, and the general ethics of the new socialist society.

1934

6. *The New World Order* is written by Fabian Socialist **H. G. Wells**. In it he declares:

> The organization of this that I call the **Open Conspiracy**, the evocation of a greater sounder fellow to the first Communist essay, an adequately implemented **Liberal Socialism**, which will ultimately supply teaching, coercive, and directive public services to the whole world, is the immediate task before all rational people. **I believe this idea of a planned world-state is one to which all our thought and knowledge is tending**. . . . It is appearing partially and experimentally at a thousand points. . . . When accident finally precipitates it, its coming is likely to happen very quickly. . . . Sometimes I feel that generations of propaganda and education may have to precede it. . . . **Plans for political synthesis seem to grow bolder and more extensive**. . . . The New Plan in America to the New Plan in Russia and how are both related to the ultimate World-State? . . . **There must be a common faith and law for mankind**. . . . Only after a huge cultural struggle can we hope to see the world-state coming into being. The Open Conspiracy has to achieve itself in many ways, but **the main battle before it is an educational battle.**

1939

7. **"Theory of Valuation,"** an essay by John Dewey is published. This work concerns the **formation of values** and will form a partial basis upon which Louis Raths will develop (in the late 1950s) his seven-part valuing process which he calls **"values clarification."**

1942

8. The American Institute for Character Education is incorporated. **AICE's program will not be based exclusively upon Judeo or Christian values, but rather upon ethical concepts shared by major world religions and cultures. "Clarifying values" is a familiar term used in an AICE handbook.**

1945

9. The **United Nations** is established by international charter. The

United States is one of fifty signatory nations. More than one hundred others will join later.

1946

10. The United States formally joins the United Nations Educational, Scientific, and Cultural Organization **(UNESCO)** on July 30.

11. *NEA Journal* (Jan.) publishes, **"The Teacher and World Government"** by its editor, Joy Elmer Morgan, in which he states:

> In the struggle to establish an adequate world government, the teacher . . . can do much to prepare the hearts and minds of children for global understanding and cooperation. . . . **At the very top of all the agencies which will assure the coming of world government must stand the school, the teacher, and the organized profession.**

12. *NEA Journal* (Apr.) prints **"National Planning in an International World,"** by I. L. Kandel of Teachers College, Columbia University, who comments:

> The establishment of the United Nations Educational, Cultural and Scientific Organization (sic) marks the culmination of a movement for the creation of an international agency for education which began with Comenius. . . . **Nations that become members of UNESCO accordingly assume an obligation to revise the textbooks used in their schools. . . . Each member nation, if it is to carry out the obligations of its membership, has a duty to see to it that nothing in its curriculum, courses of study, and textbooks is contrary to UNESCO's aims.**

13. The NEA sponsors a World Conference of the Teaching Profession. Representatives from twenty-eight nations attend. A constitution for a **World Organization of the Teaching Profession (WOTP)** is drafted. They hold their first regular meeting in 1947 and in the words of NEA's William Carr who is also WOTP's secretary-general, WOTP will be **"a mighty force in aiding UNESCO."** In 1951, the organization expands to include elementary and secondary teaching associations and changes its name to **World Confederation of Organizations of the Teaching Profession (WCOTP).**

1947

14. The U.S. Supreme Court delivers its ***Everson v. Board of Education*** decision in which, for the first time, the court declares a **separation of church and state** to exist in the First Amendment to the Constitution.

15. *NEA Journal* (Oct.) carries an article by NEA official, William Carr, **"On the Waging of Peace."** In it he says:

> As you teach about the United Nations, lay the ground for a stronger United Nations by developing in your students a sense of world community. The United Nations should be transformed into a limited world government. **The psychological foundations for wider loyalties must be laid. . . .** Teach about the various proposals that have been made for strengthening the United Nations and the establishment of world law. **Teach those attitudes which will result ultimately in the creation of a world citizenship and world government. . . .** We cannot directly teach loyalty to a society that does not yet exist, **but we can and should teach those skills and attitudes which will help to create a society in which world citizenship is possible.**

16. In volume 8 of a report by President Truman's Commission on Higher Education is found the following recommendation:

> **The role which education will play officially must be conditioned essentially by policies established in the State Department in this country, and by ministries of foreign affairs in other countries. Higher education must play a very important part in carrying out in this country the program developed by UNESCO. . . . The United States Office of Education must be prepared to work with the State Department and with UNESCO.**

1948

17. *UNESCO: Its Purpose and Its Philosophy* is written by Sir Julian

Huxley (the first director-general, 1946–48). In it he declares:

> The general philosophy of **UNESCO** should be **a scientific world humanism, global in extent and evolutionary in background. . . . In its education program it can stress the ultimate need for world political unity and familiarize all peoples with the implications of the transfer of full sovereignty from separate nations to a world organization.** . . . Political unification in some sort of world government will be required. . . . Tasks for the media division of UNESCO (will be) to promote the growth of a common outlook shared by all nations and cultures . . . **to help the emergence of a single world culture.** . . . Even though it is quite true that **any radical eugenic policy will be for many years politically and psychologically impossible, it will be important for UNESCO to see that the eugenic problem is examined with the greatest care, and that the public mind is informed of the issues at stake so that much that now is unthinkable may at least become thinkable.**

18. ***Education for International Understanding in American Schools—Suggestions and Recommendations*** is produced by the NEA (with partial funding by the **Carnegie Corporation**), and contains the following statements:

> The idea has become established that **the preservation of international peace and order may require that force be used to compel a nation to conduct its affairs within the framework of an established world system.** The most modern expression of this doctrine of collective security is in the United Nations Charter. . . . Many persons believe that enduring peace cannot be achieved so long as the nation–state system continues as at present constituted. It is a system of international anarchy—a species of jungle warfare. **Enduring peace cannot be attained until the nation–states surrender to a world organization the exercise of jurisdiction over those problems with which they have found themselves unable to deal singly in the past.**

1949

19. **UNESCO** publishes a series of booklets titled ***Towards World Un-***

derstanding. In volume l, we read that children should be taught "... **those qualities of citizenship which provide the foundation upon which international government must be based if it is to succeed."** In volume 5, one reads:

> **The kindergarten** ... **has a significant part to play in the child's education.** Not only can it **correct many of the errors of home training,** ... it can prepare the child ... for membership in the world society. ... The success of the teacher in bringing up his pupils to be good citizens of the world. ... **As long as the child breathes the poisoned air of nationalism, education in world-mindedness can produce only precarious results.** ... For the moment, it is sufficient to note that **it is most frequently in the family that the children are infected with nationalism** by hearing what is national extolled and what is foreign disparaged. ... The activity of the school cannot bring about the desired result unless, repudiating every form of nationalism ... may usher in the revolution.

1952

20. F. A. Magruder's textbook, ***American Government,*** contains the attitude and philosophy of "progressive educators" taught to millions of American students. Statements about the UN include the following:

> Give the UN absolute power to regulate international trade and commerce. ... Immigration control now handled by each country would be relinquished to the UN along with the power to arbitrarily remove people from one part of the world and settle them in a place a UN planner determines their skills, etc. are needed. ... Place control of the Panama Canal under the United Nations. ... Establish an international police force strong enough that no nation can resist its orders. ... Give the UN power of taxation. ... Place control of broadcast stations, press, speech, etc. under UN control to insure development of "cooperative" public opinion. ...

1954

21. ***Education in the New Age,*** by influential occultist Alice Bailey, is

published posthumously. In it she noted that the "science of meditation should influence the field of education in the new age" and that it is:

> a subsidiary science preparatory to the science of the *antahkarana.* This is the means of building between the personality and the soul. This is the true science of bridging unconsciousness. It relates the individual mind eventually to the higher mind and later to the universal mind. It will eventually dominate the new educational methods in schools and colleges.

Alice Bailey will be credited in the preface to Robert Muller's 1986 ***World Core Curriculum.*** **(See entry 84.)**

1955

22. ***Why Johnny Can't Read and What You Can Do About It,*** by Rudolph Flesch is published. It's a stinging criticism of the "look-say" reading method. **(See entry 2.)**

1962

23. The U.S. Supreme Court rules in ***Engel v. Vitale*** that government cannot compose **prayers** or require them to be recited by public school students.

1963

24. The SAT scores begin a nose-dive which does not begin to level off till 1981. The educational and moral decline of America, **dating from the removal of school prayer**, is documented in David Barton's book, ***America: To Pray or Not to Pray*** (1988).

25. The Thomas Jefferson Research Center (name changed to the Thomas Jefferson Center in 1989) is founded and begins producing **character education materials.** This center will be linked to the earlier (1942) American Institute for Character Education by the presence of the AICE chairman on TJRC's senior advisory board. The center will be listed in the ***Eupsychian Network*** by Abraham Maslow, a founding father of humanistic "Third Force" psychology, Humanist of the Year

in 1967, and originator of "the hierarchy of needs" toward self-actualization (still taught in educational psychology classes). TJRC will also be listed as a resource in a number of New Age/globalist directories. In 1985, TJRC is awarded $80,000 by the U.S. Department of Education. **(See entry 8.)**

1964

26. ***Visions of Order*** by Richard Weaver is published. He describes **"progressive" educators** (those formed in the John Dewey mold) as a "revolutionary cabal" engaged in:

> a systematic attempt to undermine society's traditions and beliefs. . . . The world for which the progressivists are conditioning their students is not the world espoused by general society, but by a rather small minority of radical doctrinaires and social faddists. . . . They have no equal as an agency of subversion. **Their schemes are exactly fitted, if indeed they are not designed, to produce citizens for the secular communist state, which is the millennial dream of the modern gnostic.**

27. ***The Journal of Marriage and the Family*** publishes an article by Elizabeth Force, in which she writes about her paper, **"The Role of the School in Family Life Education,"** presented at a July 1963 **UNESCO** Conference of the International Union of Family Organizations. The editor of the journal comments: "We think the paper performs **an important service for family life teachers in the United States by linking them and their efforts to a movement which is worldwide in scope."**

28. **UNESCO** convenes an International Symposium for **Health Education, Sex Education and Education for Home and Family Living in Hamburg, Germany.**

29. **The Sex Information and Education Council of the United States (SIECUS)** is founded. Dr. Mary Calderone, former medical director of Planned Parenthood–World Population, will serve as a SIECUS president. SIECUS adopts the plan for universal sex education devel-

oped at the UNESCO Hamburg meeting three months earlier. In addition to promoting **comprehensive sex education** in schools, SIECUS position statements say:

> It is the position of SIECUS that **contraceptive services should be available to all**—including minors who should enjoy the same rights of free and independent access to . . . contraceptive care as do others. . . . It is the position of SIECUS that **the use of explicit sexual materials** (sometimes referred to as **pornography**) **can serve a variety of important needs in the lives of countless individuals. . . .**

30. ***Taxonomy of Educational Objectives, Handbook II: Affective Domain,*** a textbook used extensively in the training of teachers, is published. The "affective domain" is that area connected with attitudes, values, and beliefs. In his *Taxonomy,* author **Benjamin Bloom** states: "A large part of what we call **'good teaching'** is the teacher's ability to attain affective objectives through **challenging the student's fixed beliefs."**

31. **The Carnegie Corporation** appoints the Committee on Assessing the Progress of Education (Ralph Tyler, chairman) "to explore the possibility of obtaining **census-like data** on what Americans in several age groups (up to 30 years of age) know in (ten) given fields." The project is funded by the **Ford Foundation** and **Carnegie Corporation** and will **in 1969 become the National Assessment of Educational Progress (NAEP).**

1965

32. President Lyndon Johnson introduces the **Planning, Programming, Budgeting System (PPBS)** throughout the federal government. It was first used by Robert McNamara at the Department of Defense, as a control mechanism for the Vietnam War. PPBS was developed by Charles Hitch, comptroller of the U.S. Defense Department. Hitch's prior employment had been as research director at the Rand Corporation.

33. ***The Elementary and Secondary Education Act (ESEA)*** is passed by

Congress. Introduced as a "War on Poverty" program by President Johnson, the **ESEA** will be reauthorized every five years. This landmark legislation brought massive amounts of federal money, experimental programs, record-keeping, regulations, and other intrusions into a domain (education) reserved by the Tenth Amendment of the U.S. Constitution to the states, or to the people.

1966

34. ***Values and Teaching: Working with Values in the Classroom,*** an influential **"values clarification"** text by Louis Raths, Merrill Harmin, and Sidney Simon is published. The authors comment:

> As the family changed, and as new influences came into the family, the impact of the church began to wane. . . . (There was also) a weakening of the authority of parents with no substitute authority to fill the vacuum beyond the temporal standards of the boys and girls themselves. . . . Also there is the idea that the child needs to be really free to choose. . . . **Moralizing has not worked in the past; do not be afraid to abandon it as a classroom practice. . . . We are primarily concerned with the process that a person uses to get at a value, not with what value he chooses at any one time and place—we are concerned with the process of valuing and not particularly with the product.**

35. **The Education Commission of the States (ECS)** is established with foundation funding. State governors will take turns chairing the commission.

1967

36. ***Role-Playing for Social Values*** by Fannie and George Shaftel is published in which the authors explain:

> Once values are out in the open, they can be looked at, considered, compared with alternate values. **Only then can one criticize, evaluate, deny, or confirm and reconstruct one's value system. Children can be helped to . . . develop an explicit set of values.** In group discussions, in role-playing enactments . . . **they can explore**

> **their values and learn the process of criticizing and reconstructing them . . . under skilled guidance.**

37. The Bureau of Research, U.S. Office of Education, spends $1.5 million for design proposals for teacher colleges and universities **"to completely restructure their teacher education programs."** Eight universities and a federal regional lab receive funding. One of these, Michigan State, develops the Behavioral Science Teacher Education Program **(B-STEP).** The teacher is referred to as a **"change agent"** or **"clinician"** and the B-STEP manual addresses the importance of **"an Evaluative Data Collection System"** and "a key feature of B-STEP is its use of **behavioral objectives emphasizing performance criteria,"** one of the earliest large-scale experiments with **outcome-based education.**

38. *Educational Leadership* (May) publishes **"A Plan for Self-Directed Change in an Educational System"** by **Carl Rogers** (1964 Humanist of the Year, and with Abraham Maslow, and others, founder of "Third Force" psychology, and the Association for Humanistic Psychology). In the article he states:

> . . . the goal of education must be to develop individuals who are open to change. . . . **The goal of education must be to develop a society in which people can live more comfortably with change than with rigidity. In the coming world the capacity to face the new appropriately is more important than the ability to know and repeat the old.**

1968

39. **Carl Rogers** (again), speaking at the Esalen Institute's symposium entitled **"U.S.A. 2000"** projects the future thus:

> If we consider the incredible difficulties in bringing about change in . . . education, and religion, . . . it seems likely that schools will be greatly de-emphasized in favor of a much broader . . . **environment for learning.** . . . The teacher or professor will have largely disappeared. **His place will be taken by a facilitator of learning** . . . focusing his major attention on the prime period for learning—**from**

> **infancy to age six or eight.** . . . (The student's) unhappiness with parents or with other children—all these will be an open part of his curriculum, as worthy of exploration as history or mathematics. . . . Because he has discovered the world to be a fantastically changing place, he will wish to continue his learning . . . and **the student will never be graduated.** . . . By the **year 2000**, institutionalized religion already on the wane as a significant factor in everyday life, will have faded to a point where it is of only slight importance in the community. Theology may still exist as a scholastic exercise, but **in reality the God of authoritative answers will be not only dead but buried.**

40. Educrat/change agent John Goodlad, in his book *Curriculum Inquiry* (1979) tells us of Benjamin Bloom:

> Bloom was invited by UNESCO in 1968 to submit a proposal for a six to nine week training program which would partially fulfill recommendations made at **UNESCO's Moscow meeting dealing with the formation of national centers for curriculum development and research.** . . . His program was ultimately approved by the UNESCO General Council. . . . The **International Association for Evaluation of Educational Achievement** was invited to take full responsibility for developing and conducting programs in 1971 at Granna, Sweden. **(See entry 30.)**

1969

41. The International Bureau of Education (IBE), founded in 1925 as the first intergovernmental organization in the field of education, joins forces with **UNESCO** to prepare for the upcoming International Education Year (1970). **(See entry 1.)**

42. The Joint Commission on Mental Health of Children issues its report to Congress, in which it states:

> As the home and the church decline in influence . . . schools must begin to provide adequately for the emotional and moral development of children. . . . **The school . . . must assume a direct respon-**

> **sibility for the attitudes and values of child development.** The child advocate, psychologist, social technician, and medical technician should all **reach aggressively into the community, send workers out to children's homes, recreational facilities, and schools. They should assume full responsibility for all education, including pre-primary education.**

43. ***Pacesetters in Innovation,*** a project funded under Title III of the *ESEA* (OE-20103-69) is published. **Its purpose is to sensitize/change teachers**. Projects under ***Pacesetters in Innovation*** include: 001-783: laboratory human relations, sensitivity training, and the role of teachers as in-house change agents; 001-996: teachers from model schools to serve as change agents; 002-010: change agents (emphasis placed on effecting change in teacher behavior/attitude); 002-060: vehicle for change (to facilitate the fifteen-year leap into the age of cybernation); 002-172: sex education in all academic subjects; and 002-230: "Forces which block the adoption of new ideas will be identified and ways to overcome them will be explored."

44. **The National Assessment of Educational Progress (NAEP)**, which grew out of a foundation-funded committee is given its new name and transferred to the Education Commission of the States. **(See entries 31 and 35.)**

45. *Phi Delta Kappan* publishes **"Education Planning–Programming–Budgeting: A Systems Approach"** by Harry Hartley. Seven years later (Sept. 1976), on the same subject, Hartley will state:

> **PPBS may simply disappear from sight but the mode of thinking that PPBS supports will probably continue to increase.** Even though the initials PPBS are likely to self-destruct in the near future, the need for better planning and control systems will increase. **(See entry 32.)**

46. ***How to Plan a Drug Abuse Education Workshop for Teachers*** is published by the **National Institute for Mental Health** as a "model" for training teachers. In the booklet's introduction, it is stressed that

"at all grades, a factual, **nonmoralizing** presentation is essential." An objective is that **"changes in teachers' knowledge, insights, attitudes, skills"** will be achieved. And the type of teachers desired are "open-minded individuals, as opposed to those known to have fixed or hostile positions, (who) would preferably be selected except where in-service training might change an attitude or where an individual is included as a foil demonstrating the disadvantage of inflexibility." The booklet also emphasizes that **"diametric 'good' and 'bad' approaches are not helpful to drug education."**

1970

47. **UNESCO** declares this the **International Education Year**. By year's end, **UNESCO** and **IBE** have determined that **lifelong education is to be the master concept for the restructuring of schools throughout the world. (See entry 41.)**

48. The White House Conference on Children and Youth resolves that:

> **Society has the ultimate responsibility for the well-being and optimum development of all children. . . . The time has come to reexamine such fundamental issues as the extent to which a child is entitled to seek medical and psychiatric assistance, birth control information and even abortion, without parental consent or over parental opposition.**

It recommends "sex education—including family planning, birth control, contraception, abortion, venereal disease, homosexuality and lesbianism," and also recommends "repeal of laws on fornication, adultery, homosexuality, lesbianism, and so-called unnatural acts."

49. **NEA president** George Fischer tells NEA representatives that:

> a good deal of work has been done to begin to bring about uniform certification controlled by the unified profession in each state. A model Professional Practices Act has been developed, and work has begun to secure passage of the Act in each state where such legisla-

tion is needed. **With these new laws, we will finally realize our 113-year-old dream of controlling who enters, who stays, and who leaves the profession. Once this is done, we can also control the teacher training institutions.**

50. *Educational Leadership* (Dec.) publishes "**Sensitivity Training and Education: A Critique**" by Clifford Edwards, who explains that in the early stages of a student's value development, **if the student's home, family, religion, attitudes, or beliefs are criticized by the group, this "produces disillusionment and value disintegration and encourages acceptance of group values.** . . . The person may then suffer disassociation from parents and others as a consequence of his altered beliefs."

1971

51. The White House Conference on Youth endorses **universal sex education** for elementary and secondary schools. **(See entries 27, 28, and 29.)**

52. *Towards a Conceptual Model of Lifelong Education* (Education Studies and Documents, No. 12) is written by George W. Parkyn. This study was commissioned and published by **UNESCO.** The Secretariat asked Parkyn to: "outline a possible model for a(n) (education) system based on the ideal of **a continuous educational process throughout the lifetime of the learner,**" and to develop "**a means for bringing an existing national school system into line with lifelong learning.**" **(See entry 47.)**

1972

53. *Working with Parents* is published by the National Public School Relations Association and tells teachers that **using a citizen advisory committee** at each stage of planning a sex education program ". . . **can be a strong force in quieting parent protests,**" but some parents and citizens ". . . whose personal attitudes are warped, may complain or may try to sabotage the program."

54. *Values Clarification: A Handbook of Practical Strategies for Teach-*

ers and Students by Sidney Simon, et al, is published. The authors ask: "How does the young person choose his own course of action from among the many models and many moralizing lectures with which he has been bombarded? **Where does he learn whether he wants to stick to the old moral and ethical standards or try new ones?**" And in the ***Handbook,*** strategy number 77 is:

> **Diaries** . . . enable the students to bring an enormous amount of information about themselves into class to be examined and discussed. . . . For a whole week or longer, students (and the teacher) keep their own individual diaries. If they have chosen a Religion Diary, they record all thoughts, conversations, and actions having to do with religion. **(See entries 7, 8, 30, 34, 36, and 50.)**

55. Kurt Waldheim, secretary-general of the UN, addresses the executive board of **UNICEF**:

> Until fairly recently, in most societies, the responsibility for child development rested entirely with parents or in the immediately surrounding community. This is still largely true but it is changing. . . . **The process of child development has to be the concern of society as a whole—on the national and international level.** From the very beginning, the leaders of **UNICEF**—both Board and Secretariat—clearly understand this, and I congratulate them for their foresight and their vision.

56. ***Learning to Be: The World of Education Today and Tomorrow,*** a best-seller for **UNESCO** by Edgar Faure, et al, is published. The authors say they're in search of a "new educational order . . . based on scientific and **technological training**, one of the essential components of **scientific humanism.**" Instead of God and religious standards, one reads that **"relativity and dialectical thought would appear to be a fertile ground in which to cultivate the seeds of tolerance.** . . . An individual should avoid systematically setting up his beliefs and convictions . . . his behavior and customs as models or rules valid for all times. . . ." **(See entries 8 and 25.)**

57. The U.S. Supreme Court rules in ***Wisconsin v. Yoder*** that there

should be **no values inculcation** in public schools.

58. The **National Institute of Education (NIE)** is established as a "separate, coequal administrative unit alongside the Office of Education within a new Division of Education in the Department of Health, Education, and Welfare (DHEW)." At the request of DHEW, the Rand Corporation prepares ***National Institute of Education: Preliminary Plan for the Proposed Institute*** (R-657-HEW, Feb. 1971). The NIE will become responsible for millions of dollars spent on the National Diffusion Network (NDN), Educational Laboratories and Centers, and will fund many objectionable programs brought into classrooms around the nation. NIE will be absorbed into the Office of Educational Research and Improvement (OERI) within the U.S. Department of Education in the mid-1980s.

1973

59. ***The Change Agent's Guide to Innovation in Education*** by Ronald Havelock is published. Portions of the book have been developed under federal Office of Education Contract OEC-0-8-080603-4535(010). In this "guide," one reads: **"It must be admitted that sometimes collaboration just will not work and, when it fails, there are a number of alternatives (e.g., a 'fait accompli' strategy) that should be considered, ranging . . . to complete deception."**

1975

60. ***Phi Delta Kappan*** (Apr.) publishes **"World Order Education: What Is It?"** by William Boyer, who explains:

> . . . the National Council for the Social Studies has recognized peace education and world order education as a legitimate part of the social studies program. Yet few educators and fewer of the general public know what "world order education" means. **World order education is an upgraded form of political education. It . . . transcends the nationalistic . . . values of the old citizenship education. . . . World order education . . . is an instrument of social-cultural change. Its first and continuing commitment is to aid . . . the creation of global institutions. . . . (See entries 4, 6, 10–13, 15–20, 26, 40, 41, 47, 52, 55, and 56.)**

61. *Phi Delta Kappan* (Dec.) publishes **"The Failure of Our School Drug Abuse Programs"** by Bernard Bard. While critical of drug abuse programs, the article refers to **"solutions"** such as **"responsible" use of "small" quantities of drugs**. The article cites Edward Brecher's statement in *Licit and Illicit Drugs:* ". . . I believe our drug education goal should be to teach young people to use drugs just a bit more skillfully and responsibly, and a bit less hazardously than their parents do." **(See entry 46.)**

1976

62. *The American School Board Journal* (Mar.) publishes **"The Case for Having the Public Schools Teach Our Youngsters How to Drink,"** by Lee Hames. The author proclaims: **"Youngsters should be taught how to drink** . . . (and alcohol) can be integrated into a balanced lifestyle." Hames believes the main obstacle to his proposal "is **parental resistance**. Parents must be given to understand that the real hazard of alcohol comes from not knowing . . . what is entailed in establishing a lifestyle that accommodates the sensible use of alcohol. . . . No one can prove that his way of living and doing is sacrosanct. And that is why **adults must maintain an open mind about juvenile drinking. . . .**"

63. **UNESCO** publishes ***Foundations of Lifelong Education,*** a master text of education reform and restructuring, containing chapters on the philosophical, historical, sociological, psychological, anthropological, economic, and practical aspects of **lifelong learning. (See entries 46 and 60.)**

64. *Phi Delta Kappan* (Sept.) prints **"America's Next 25 Years: Some Implications for Education"** by Harold Shane, who advises:

> Rather than adding my voice to those who urge us to go "back to the basics," I would argue that we need to move ahead to **new basics**. . . . Certainly, cross-cultural understandings and empathy have become fundamental skills of human relations and intercultural rapport . . . the arts of **compromise** and reconciliation, of **consensus building,** and of **planning for interdependence**, a command of these talents

> becomes "**basic.**" . . . As young people mature, we must help them develop . . . **a service ethic** which is geared toward the real world . . . **the global servant concept** in which we will educate our young for **planetary service** and eventually for some form of **world citizenship.**

65. The **NEA** describes its chosen theme of "**world interdependence**" for the Bicentennial of the United States and states that "educators around the world are in a unique position to help bring about a harmoniously interdependent global community."

66. ***The Scientific and Technological Revolution and the Revolution in Education*** by Vladimir Turchenko is published in Russian, translated into English, and imported into the U.S. Many interesting parallels exist between the "revolution" (restructuring) of Russian education and the restructuring of American schools. The book jacket indicates that this work

> **examines the fundamental directions that the revolution in education will take: introduction of teaching machines, instruction from a younger age, linking instruction with productive labour, "continuous" education, and so on. . . . Under socialism, education has become not only the personal affair of every individual, but also a concern of society as a whole.**

Emphasized is the socialization of children: ". . . The first thing that distinguishes education from all other processes connected with the reception of information is that it is functionally geared to shaping personality." Equally important is the preparation of a skilled labor force for the national economy: ". . . . the principle of combining schooling with productive labour is one of the first principles in the Marxist-Leninist theory of communist education." (See resources: Citizens for Academic Excellence)

1977

67. Newly appointed **U.S. Commissioner of Education Ernest Boyer** declares **global education a top priority**, and sets up a federal Task Force on Global Education. Boyer will leave the Office of Education

to become the head of the highly influential Carnegie Foundation for the Advancement of Teaching **(CFAT)**, a position he held for eighteen years till his death in December 1995.

68. U.S. Assistant Secretary of Education Mary Berry delivers an address at the University of Illinois, **"The Chinese Experience in Education: What America Stands to Learn,"** in which she reveals that **the U.S. Office of Education is developing lifelong learning programs modeled after the Chinese communist programs,** and she expects these programs to meet the "needs for intellectual fulfillment and social growth. It is here that the Chinese have set the pattern for the world to follow, and **it's here that American higher education may have its last, best opportunity for growth." (See entries 47, 52, and 63.)**

1978

69. Senator Orrin Hatch (R-UT) is successful in having the ***Protection of Pupil Rights Amendment*** added onto the General Education Provisions Act **(GEPA)**. The **"Hatch Amendment"** is a family protection measure destined to be more honored in the breach than in the observance.

1979

70. Despite opposition from various quarters, President Carter establishes a separate **cabinet level U.S. Department of Education** which is signed into law on October 17 (P.L.96-88).

1980

71. The Foundation for Critical Thinking is established to implement critical thinking instruction at **all levels of education**. The foundation is affiliated with the National Education Association, the Association for Supervision and Curriculum Development (an NEA spinoff), and the American Federation of Teachers.

72. ***The Aquarian Conspiracy,*** by New Age networker Marilyn Ferguson, is published. The book will become a best seller. In it, the author points out the many venues through which the "conspiracy" is being carried out, school curricula being a prime example. She states that of conspirators surveyed, **more were involved in education than any other single category of work**. She comments:

> Educators are belatedly examining a holistic Greek concept, the *paidea* . . . in which the community and all its disciplines generated learning resources for the individual, whose ultimate goal was to reach the divine center in the self. . . . Educators engaged in transpersonal and humanistic methods have begun linking in national networks and centers. . . . The new school community is very close, more a family than a school. . . . Virtually no subject is too difficult, controversial, or offbeat to think about. . . . **Altered states of consciousness** are taken seriously: centering exercises, meditation, and fantasy are used. . . . Education is a **lifelong journey**. . . . Part of the transformative process is becoming a learner again, whatever your age . . . . openness to **lifelong learning**. . . . A major ambition of the curriculum is autonomy. This is based on the belief that **if our children are to be free, they must be free even from us—from our limiting beliefs**. . . . A top-level government policymaker for education speculates that we may eventually have the equivalent of the GI Education Bill in lieu of compulsory curricula—**an allotment to be spent by the individual for whatever learning, specialized or general, he seeks** "funding the student and not the institution."

On pages 289–91, Ferguson compares side-by-side the assumptions of **the old and new paradigms of education and learning. (See entries 21, 38, 39, 54, 63, 68, and 75.)**

73. John Goodlad, who has been serving on the governing board of UNESCO's Institute for Education, publishes ***Schooling for a Global Age.*** In the preface he says: "Parents and the general public must be reached also. Otherwise, children and youth enrolled in globally oriented programs may find themselves in conflict with values assumed in the home. And then the educational institution frequently comes under scrutiny and must pull back." **(See entry 40.)**

1981

74. The **National Institute of Education** produces a working paper,

"**Measuring the Quality of Education,**" which makes plain the link between the National Assessment of Educational Progress **(the NAEP)**, the Carnegie Foundation for the Advancement of Teaching **(CFAT)**, and the Educational Testing Service **(ETS)**, a private organization which administers the SATs. The paper states that "along with the work toward a centralized computer bank and the funding arrangement to make it all happen . . . **achievement data are not the primary focus of the studies, which also collect data on educational attainment, student characteristics and attitudes, parent attitudes, and school programs.**" The database for the supercomputer is to include pupil files containing personal information about "**home environment and family characteristics,**" which will be linked to personnel files on teachers. Everyone can be tracked from kindergarten into the job force. According to Beverly Eakman who commented extensively on the NAEP in ***Educating for the New World Order,*** "**NAEP is not about mere academic testing, but, rather, is a first step toward a permanent, interlinkable dossier and databank on the nation's citizens—and a way of imposing a national curriculum." (See entries 31, 44, and 58.)**

1982

75. In a clear admission by a highly placed educrat that **federal subsidies in the form of vouchers, etc. will bring federal control** is the following statement by **Chester E. Finn**, assistant secretary of education (1980s). In the March ***NASSP Bulletin*** in his article **"Public Service, Public Support, Public Accountability,"** Finn says:

> Some, to be sure, **like to think they can have it both ways**; i.e., can obtain aid without saddling themselves with unacceptable forms of regulation. But most acknowledge the general applicability of the old adage that he who pays the piper calls the tune, and are more or less resigned to amalgamating or **choosing between assistance and autonomy. (See entry 72.)**

1983

76. ***A Nation at Risk*** by the National Commission on Excellence in Education is published. In this report, the commission states:

> The educational foundations of our society are presently being eroded by a rising tide of mediocrity that threatens our very future as a nation and a people. What was unimaginable a generation ago has begun to occur—others are matching and surpassing our educational attainments. **If an unfriendly foreign power had attempted to impose on America the mediocre educational performance that exists today, we might well have viewed it as an act of war.** As it stands, we have allowed this to happen to ourselves. . . . The world is indeed one global village. . . . **(See entries 1–75 and 77–129!)**

77. Chester Finn, acting as an advisor to the U.S. delegation to a UNESCO conference on education held in Paris in April 1982, comments unfavorably about U.S. membership in this UN agency. His remarks appear in an article entitled **"How to Lose the War on Ideas"** in the August *Commentary*:

> At UNESCO, the United States subsidizes the erosion of intellectual freedom, the degradation of democratic values, the redefinition of human rights, and the manipulation of education into an instrument of political indoctrination by those who wish us ill. . . . UNESCO has become, in the main, an instrument of destruction that is wielded to chip away at the idea of freedom and the practice of democracy. . . . The Western democracies lack the votes to prevail against the combined forces of the Third World nations (the latter known as the "G-77," though there are now many more than seventy-seven of them). And those forces are generally combined, because **Moscow takes UNESCO very seriously indeed, recognizing it as an important theater in the war of ideas** and in the competition for Third World favor. Accordingly, **the Soviets assign to UNESCO duty senior people with great skill in ideological combat. . . . They have a UNESCO strategy,** and in recent years it has been notably successful. The Western democracies have no such strategy . . . within the intellectual communities, UNESCO is, for obvious reasons, rarely criticized from the left. **(See entries 10, 12, 13, 16, 17, 19, 27–29, 40, 41, 47, 52, 56, 60, 63, 67, 68, and 73.)**

78. Former commissioner of education and longtime head of CFAT,

Ernest Boyer, in his book ***High School***, calls for a new Carnegie unit of **120 hours of mandatory community service**, ". . . involving volunteer work in the community or at school. . . . The goal of service in the schools is to teach values . . . to help all students understand that **to be fully human one must serve." (See entries 64 and 67.)**

79. A letter is written, showing the **open collaboration** between the highest official of the U.S. Department of Education, the highest official of a state Department of Education, and an important private contractor (Bill Spady, "father" of OBE) **to get OBE into the nation's schools**. The letter is dated July 27, 1984, and is addressed to T. H. Bell, the U.S. secretary of education; it's from G. Leland Burningham, the state superintendent of public instruction for Utah, who writes:

> I am forwarding this letter to accompany the proposal which you recommended Bill Spady and I prepare in connection with Outcome-Based Education. This proposal centers around the **detailed process by which we will work together to implement Outcome-Based Education using research verified programs. This will make it possible to put Outcome-Based Education in place, not only in Utah but in all schools of the nation.**

80. Seven days of hearings are held in seven locations around the country to obtain testimony from parents, teachers, and other concerned citizens regarding proposed regulations to make the ***Protection of Pupil Rights Amendment ("Hatch Amendment")*** enforceable. The Hatch Amendment is really two amendments to the General Education Provisions Act **(GEPA)**. GEPA was originally set up in 1968 to provide general housekeeping rules for the *ESEA* of 1965. The first amendment (part A) was added in 1974 and the second (part B) was added in 1978. The problem was that years after passage of the Hatch Amendment, the Department of Education refused to issue regulations providing for enforcement, and had not established procedures for citizens to file their complaints, or obtain remedy for violations. The written record of the testimony at the hearings ran to more than 1,300 pages. When the Department of Education failed to publish the transcript of the hearings, Phyllis Schlafly of Eagle Forum edited and published it herself under the title *Child Abuse in the Classroom.* Three weeks after the book was published, the Department of Education finally issued the regulations. **(See entry 69; and resources: Eagle Forum.)**

1985

81. U.S. Secretary of State George Shultz signs the **Soviet-American Exchange Agreement (negotiated by the Carnegie Corporation).** The agreement is for the development and exchange of curricula and other teaching materials for elementary and secondary students.

1986

82. **The Carnegie Task Force on Teaching as a Profession** releases its report, *A Nation Prepared: Teachers for the 21st Century.* The report calls for "sweeping changes in education policy," especially **the creation of a national teacher certification board.** The report also calls for prominence in decision-making to be given to "lead teachers" and for **states to take over local school systems that do not meet state educational standards. (See entry 49.)**

83. *The Washington Post* (Nov. 26) carries an article, **"Reading Method Lets Pupils Guess"** in which one finds the following:

> **The most controversial aspect of whole language is the de-emphasis on accuracy.** . . . American Reading Council President Julia Palmer, an advocate of the approach, said it is acceptable if a young child reads the word house for home, or substitutes the word pony for horse. . . . "Accuracy is not the name of the game." **(See entries 2 and 22.)**

84. *The Robert Muller School World Core Curriculum Manual* is published. The Robert Muller School (est. 1980) is located in Arlington, Texas, and is named for the former assistant secretary general to the United Nations, who is currently chancellor of the University of Peace in Costa Rica. The authors say in the preface:

> The world is indebted to Dr. Robert Muller . . . for the formulation of the World Core Curriculum in its skeletal form. It is upon that

> scaffold combined with the **Ageless Wisdom** teachings that this present work has precipitated. **The underlying philosophy upon which the Robert Muller School is based will be found in the teachings set forth in the books of Alice A. Bailey by the Tibetan teacher, Djwhal Khul (published by Lucis Publishing Company)** . . . and the teachings of M. Morya as given in the Agni Yoga Series books. . . .

The Robert Muller School was fully accredited by the Southern Association of Colleges and Schools in 1985 and is certified as a United Nations Associated School "providing education for international cooperation and peace." (Djwhal Khul is reputed to be the spirit guide that channeled Bailey's writings to her and Lucis Publishing was first established as Lucifer Publishing.) **(See entry 21.)**

85. Muller's **World Core Curriculum** is endorsed by Gordon Cawelti, the executive director of the influential Association for Supervision and Curriculum Development, in an article entitled ***"Toward a World Core Curriculum"*** in the Dec. 1986/Jan. 1987 issue of *ASCD's journal, **Educational Leadership.*** In it Cawelti says: "The long-term goal of a universal or world core curriculum is to assure peaceful and cooperative existence among human species on this planet. To accomplish this goal, the curriculum elements originally proposed by United Nations Assistant Secretary-General Robert Muller provide a useful model."

86. While William Bennett is secretary of education, a character education grant is awarded to the Thomas Jefferson Research Center by the U.S. Department of Education. Commenting on this grant and **"character education"** in her book ***The Great American Con Game,*** author Barbara Morris says:

> **So-called "character education" in U.S. schools does not have an ethical basis rooted in absolutes and it certainly cannot have a Christian basis.** Most of what we have seen is a conglomeration of Humanistic situation ethics, Skinnerian behavior modification, assorted psychological theories and techniques, and some New Age

occult practices (guided imagery, for example) that result in students displaying (they hope) acceptable **"character traits" i.e. behavior that will benefit the state. The Russians speak about character education in relation to economic activity. It can serve the same purpose here. We must have people with the correct "character traits" that benefit a planned, full employment economy.** And it is here that Mastery Learning (previously discussed) fits into the "full employment" picture. **(See entries 8, 25, 56, and 66.)**

1987

87. **The National Board for Professional Teaching Standards** is established. This board is the brainchild of the **Carnegie Forum on Education and the Economy**, and a majority of the board members are with the NEA or AFT unions. The board wants to **nationally certify teachers**, and not simply on the basis of academic competence, but also on such things as how they would teach students with different religious backgrounds. Correlated with the formation of the board is a 1986 grant **(from Carnegie)** to Stanford University's Education Policy Institute to develop new forms of teacher assessment materials that would be the basis of standards adopted by a national teacher certification board. **(See entries 49 and 82.)**

1988

88. **The National Center on Education and the Economy (NCEE)** is formed to carry on the policy development work begun by the **Carnegie Forum on Education and the Economy** (founded in 1985). **"To Secure Our Future: The Federal Role in Education,"** the NCEE's first publication (1989), will **play an important role in framing the issues and shaping the agreements that are made at the Governor's Education Summit held in Charlottesville, Virginia, in the fall of** 1989. The **NCEE's president, Marc Tucker,** was executive director of the earlier group **(Carnegie Forum)**. Prior to his Carnegie affiliation, Tucker had two federal jobs as an associate director at the National Institute of Education and before that at the Northwest Regional Laboratory—a typical career pattern of a "revolving door" educrat. **NCEE** will have three major **"programs": the New Standards Project (NSP)—(see entry 107); the National Alliance for Restructuring**

Education (NARE)—(see entries 97 and 110); and **the Commission on the Skills of the American Workforce (see entries 92, 96, 98, 102, 110, 111, 112, 126, 127, and 128)**.

1989

89. The **Carnegie** Council on Adolescent Development publishes *Turning Points: Preparing American Youth for the 21st Century.* Focusing exclusively on the middle-grade schools, the report recommends **schools-within-schools with students and teachers grouped together in teams. "Critical thinking" and education for "citizenship in a pluralistic society,"** along with **"youth service," "cooperative learning,"** and **"access to health and social services" (school-based clinics)** are also recommended. **Bill Clinton** is a *Turning Points* task force member.

90. President Bush convenes a **Governor's Education Summit** at the University of Virginia in Charlottesville, Virginia. An agreement is made there to establish **National Educational Goals.** Sitting governors who are instrumental in this work include: **Tom Kean** of New Jersey; **Lamar Alexander** of Tennessee; **Richard Riley** of South Carolina; **Bill Clinton** of Arkansas; and **Roy Romer** of Colorado. **(See entry 88.)**

91. **Lamar Alexander** speaking at the Governor's Conference on Education in Wichita, Kansas, says that he envisions America will go through "its own *perestroika*" (restructuring/reform) and form a "brand new American school" that would be open year-round from six a.m. to six p.m. He also says: "I would go down to the maternity ward of the local hospital . . . and find out how many babies are born out of wedlock." (His wife has been a volunteer worker for Planned Parenthood.) And he adds: "These schools will serve children from age three months to age eighteen. That may be a shocking thought to you, but if you were to do an inventory of every baby in your community, and think about what the needs of those babies were for the next four or five years, you might see that those needs might not be served any other way."

1990

92. The U.S. Department of Labor **Secretary's Commission on Achiev-**

ing Necessary Skills (SCANS) is established. Composed of representatives of education, business, labor, and state government, it is charged with **"defining a common core of skills that constitute job readiness in this new economic environment."**

93. ***The Keys of This Blood*** is published by Vatican insider Malachi Martin. In it, the author critically describes the transnationalists' goal that "ideally the same textbooks should be used all over the world in both the hard sciences and the soft curricula. And sure enough, a concrete initiative in this direction has been under way for some years now, undertaken by Informatik, a Moscow-based educational organization, and the **Carnegie Endowment Fund.**" He names **Ernest Boyer, head of CFAT** as one of the transnationals and goes on to say:

> **The Transnationalist education formula is in essence one step in a drive to build a worldwide human infrastructure upon which an effectively working global economy can base itself with some security. The emphasis is on homogeneity of minds, on the creation and nourishing of a truly global mentality. . . . We must all become little Transnationalists. (See entries 67, 78, and 81.)**

94. **The National Education Goals Panel (NEGP)** is formed. Governor **Bill Clinton** will head the initial work leading to the six **National Education Goals.**

95. **The World Conference on Education for All** meets in Jomtiem, Thailand. The conference is convened by The Inter-Agency Commission and is cosponsored by **UNESCO, UNICEF,** the UN Development Program **(UNDP),** and the **World Bank,** and is attended by some 1,500 participants from around the world. Two documents, ***The World Declaration on Education for All*** and ***Framework for Action to Meet Basic Learning Needs,*** including six international education goals, are revised and then adopted at the closing plenary session. **The six international goals bear a striking resemblance to the six National Educational Goals being worked on by the National Education Goals Panel.** These National Educational Goals will be formally introduced to the American public in 1991 as part of **AMERICA 2000.**

96. *America's Choice: High Skills or Low Wages!* is published by the **Carnegie-initiated** National Center on Education and the Economy (NCEE). This report recommends that "**a new educational performance standard should be set for all students, to be met by age 16. This standard should be established nationally and benchmarked to the highest in the world." Hillary Rodham Clinton** is one of the notables on the NCEE's board of trustees and two years later will co-authors an article of nearly identical title. **(See entry 111.)**

97. **David Hornbeck, lawyer/change agent,** presents his draft proposal, **The Iowa Initiative for World-Class Schools.** His proposal includes outcome-based education, working in groups, and testing related to feelings, behaviors, values, opinions, and attitudes. Like Ernest Boyer and other highly placed change agents, Hornbeck is a **"revolving door" educrat, one who leaves an influential job in the private sector or academia to take another at a similar level in government and goes back and forth between these spheres of influence throughout a professional career.** Hornbeck has been the **state superintendent of schools for Maryland** (twelve years); **chairman of the board for CFAT; president of the Council of Chief State School Officers; senior advisor to the Business Roundtable; has traveled around the country as a consultant to state departments of education**; and has been affiliated with the **National Center on Education and the Economy, acting (with Marc Tucker) as co-director of its National Alliance for Restructuring Education** (one of the eleven NASDC Design Team winners). He's currently **head of the Philadelphia school system**, where he's expected to do a major overhaul of their schools. **(See entry 110.)**

1991

98. **David Hornbeck** and Lester Salamon (professor of political science and director of the Institute for Policy Studies at Johns Hopkins University) coedit ***Human Capital and America's Future,*** a collection of essays. In his chapter, **"New Paradigms for Action,"** Hornbeck calls for an outcome-based, comprehensive system overhaul, complete with staff development, site-based shared decision making, interaction between independent agencies, a "Board of Children and Families" to

look after health and "well being" issues and sanctions and rewards for achieving desirable outcomes. He enthusiastically recommends legal remedies to make these changes happen—not altogether surprising since he is an attorney. In commenting on what's needed, Hornbeck states:

> . . . Demonstration projects and charismatic leaders can be useful, but there is little evidence that alone they can sustain the type of change that is required. Additional money spread around differently will be critically important, but it too cannot do the job alone from a substantive point of view, and for political reasons it will not be abundantly available to do the job. **Court orders and/or legislation (I subsume contracts under legislation since they define required outcomes and activities), must be our primary vehicles to provoke and sustain the magnitude and kind of change that is necessary. . . . Court orders can be exceptionally good vehicles for creating a sufficient sense of crisis and an imperative to act so that supporting court legislation can be enacted. . . . Wars, natural disasters, and large-scale public movements such as the civil rights movement are also capable of producing sweeping change; a court order can constitute a controlled societal counterpart to these forces. When sweeping, sustained change occurs, however, it generally happens through legislation.**

In the end notes, Hornbeck mentions his involvement in key legislation—the 1990 **Kentucky Education Reform Act (KERA)**, a clean slate/start from scratch approach enacted after **the entire educational system in the state of Kentucky was declared illegal**. He acknowledges the "generous support" of the **Carnegie Corporation of New York** which allowed him to develop the thoughts in his chapter of ***Human Capital and America's Future.***

99. Lamar Alexander, former governor of Tennessee, is appointed U.S. secretary of education. (See entry 91.)

100. Chester Finn publishes ***We Must Take Charge: Our Schools and Our Future.*** Finn was **head of OERI** at the Department of Education, and Lamar Alexander's trusted adviser. After reading ***We Must Take Charge***, Alexander told Finn, "You saved me six months in organizing the president's education initiative." In the book, not only does Finn **advocate a national curriculum**, but he also writes:

> **The school is the vital delivery system, the state is the policy setter (and chief paymaster) and nothing in between is very important. This formulation turns on its head the traditional American assumption that every city, town, and county bears the chief responsibility for organizing and operating its own schools as a municipal function. That is what we once meant by "local control," but it has become an anachronism no longer justified by research, consistent with sound fiscal policy or organizational theory, suited to our mobility patterns, or important to the public.**

Every student must meet a core learning standard or be penalized, according to Finn, who says:

> **Perhaps the best way to enforce this standard is to confer valuable benefits and privileges on people who meet it, and to withhold them from those who do not. Work permits, good jobs, and college admission are the most obvious, but there is ample scope here for imagination in devising carrots and sticks. Drivers' licenses could be deferred. So could eligibility for professional athletic teams. The minimum wage paid to those who earn their certificates might be a dollar an hour higher.**

101. *AMERICA 2000: An Education Strategy,* is published by the U.S. Department of Education, and introduced with considerable fanfare by the new secretary, **Lamar Alexander**. **Chester Finn is identified as the primary architect of this educational restructuring strategy.** The first DOE publication on *AMERICA 2000* is a 66-page booklet with a red cover, quickly replaced by a virtually identical 62-page booklet with a white cover. Thousands of free copies were handed or mailed out during the remainder of Bush's tenure. Highlights of *AMERICA 2000* include: **coverage of the six National Education Goals and**

four tracks or strategies to accomplish them; the creation of 535 "Break the Mold" New American Schools (one for each congressional district); the creation of AMERICA 2000 communities; national achievement tests (with the assurance that these don't mean a national curriculum will follow); expanding the data collecting function of the NAEP so that comparative records can be kept on schools, districts, and states; issuing state and national report cards; business and labor collaboration to establish skill standards; and comprehensive lifelong learning. (See entries 31, 35, 44, 47, 52, 63, 68, 74, 92, 95, 96, 102, 105–108, 110–112, 115, 117, 122, 124, and 126–128.)

102. *What Work Requires of Schools: A SCANS Report for AMERICA 2000* is published by the U.S. Department of Labor **Secretary's Commission on Achieving Necessary Skills (SCANS)**. The report elaborates on the **five identified "competencies"** of effective workers and the **three "foundations"** necessary to achieve them. The **Competencies** are:

> **Resources**—allocation time, money, materials, space, and staff; **Interpersonal Skills**—working on teams, teaching others, serving customers, leading, negotiating, and working well with people from culturally diverse backgrounds; **Information**—acquiring and evaluating data, organizing and maintaining files, interpreting and communicating, and using computers to process information; **Systems**—understanding social, organizational, and technological systems, monitoring and correcting performance, and designing or improving systems; and **Technology**—selecting equipment and tools, applying technology to specific tasks, and maintaining and troubleshooting technologies.

The **Foundation** consists of:

> **Basic Skills**—reading, writing, arithmetic and mathematics, speaking, and listening; **Thinking Skills**—thinking creatively, making decisions, solving problems, seeing things in the mind's eye, knowing how to learn, and reasoning; **Personal Qualities**—individual re-

sponsibility, self-esteem, sociability, self-management, and integrity. **(See entry 92.)**

103. ***The Unfinished Agenda: A New Vision for Child Development and Education*** is published by the **Committee for Economic Development (CED)**, including a section titled **"Removing the Barriers to Change,"** which states:

> Public education itself is difficult to change because it is not one corporate entity but many. Public education in the United States is a $210 billion industry with 50 independent state bureaucracies that have jurisdiction over 16,000 quasi-independent local school districts, 84,000 schools, and 4.2 million employees serving nearly 50 million pupils. **The public schools are not the only societal institutions that need to be restructured.**

The document **emphasizes preschool and early childhood education,** favorably mentioning the **Parents as Teachers (PAT) program, and using schools as bases for delivering social services.**

104. ***Ready to Learn: A Mandate for the Nation*** by **Ernest Boyer, head of CFAT,** is published. In its preface, Boyer tells how he concluded from a CFAT study entitled **"The Early Years"** that **"vast numbers of children are at risk, not just the poor."** Boyer calls for "a national network of Ready-to-Learn Clinics . . . **'one stop shopping' health and education centers** . . . (which) would integrate health, education, and social services." He supports both **PAT** and **HIPPY,** a program very similar to PAT used in Arkansas (and elsewhere) endorsed by **Hillary Clinton,** and states that **"without a 'conspiracy of protection,' today's children are socially, emotionally, and educationally at risk." (See entries 67 and 78.)**

105. ***AMERICA 2000: Excellence in Education Act,*** the Republican bill supporting the ***AMERICA 2000*** restructuring effort is introduced. A similar piece of legislation will also be introduced by the Democrats. In the year and a half remaining in Bush's tenure, these and other pieces of "reform" legislation are debated at length, but after prolonged

wrangling by Republicans with a Democrat-controlled Congress, Bush leaves office with none of the major restructuring legislation in place and his campaign promise to be the "Education President" unfulfilled. **(See entry 101.)**

106. The New American Schools Development Corporation (NASDC) is set up at the request of President Bush. Composed of business leaders and guided by the six National Education Goals, they issue a request for proposals for **"Break the Mold—New American Schools." (See entry 101.)**

107. The New Standards Project (NSP), a joint program of the **Learning Research and Development Center at the University of Pittsburgh (Lauren Resnick)** and the **National Center on Education and the Economy (Marc Tucker)** is established through **foundation grants.** Commenting on the need for a national exam and the work of the NSP, Colorado governor **Roy Romer (who is also chair of the National Education Goals Panel and cochair of the National Council on Education Standards and Testing)** says there needs to be a group **outside government** willing to take the lead and show how this can be done. In an **NSP** press release, Lauren Resnick states: **"Standardized tests are outdated,"** and Marc Tucker comments, **"These tasks are tied to the world-class standards that all students will need to meet." (See entry 88.)**

108. The United States Coalition for Education for All holds a conference on ***"Learning for All: Bridging Domestic and International Education,"*** with **Barbara Bush** as the honorary chair. This gathering evolved out of the 1990 World Conference on Education for All in Jomtiem, Thailand. The coalition **(USCEFA)** is part of a 156-nation network working to "reform" education worldwide. One of the conference programs is ***"Education for a New World Order"*** with keynote speaker Elena Lenskaya, deputy to the minister of education of Russia. **(See entry 95.)**

109. The International Consultative Forum on Education for All, another spinoff of the Jomtiem conference, sponsored by **UNICEF,**

UNESCO, UNDP, and the **World Bank** convenes in Paris, France.

1992

110. The New American Schools Development Corporation (NASDC) selects from 686 proposals submitted, **eleven design teams** to produce **"New American Schools."** Winners and initial sites for testing of these programs are: **ATLAS Communities:** Lancaster, Pa.; Norfolk, Va., Prince George's County, Md., Gorham, Me.; **Roots and Wings:** four elementary schools in St. Mary's County, Md.; **Audrey Cohen College:** selected schools in Alexandria, Va., Chicago, Il., Hollandale, Ms., N.Y.C., N.Y., Phoenix, Az., San Diego City Schools, Ca., Washington, D.C., and selected schools in Florida and Texas; **the National Alliance for Restructuring Education:** Kentucky (one district, three schools), New York (Rochester district, three schools), Vermont (one district, three schools); **Odyssey Project:** Gaston County, N.C.; **Los Angeles Learning Center:** Los Angeles County, Ca. (approx. 3,200 children); **the Bensenville Community Design:** Bensenville, Il.; **Community Learning Centers:** Minnesota (Rothsay School District, North Branch, and St. Cloud); **Expeditionary Learning:** Portland, Me., Boston, Ma., N.Y.C., N.Y., Decatur, Ga., Douglas County, Co.; **the Co-NECT School:** Boston and Worcester, Ma.; **the Modern Red Schoolhouse:** Indiana (Indianapolis, Columbus, Beech Grove, and Greentown), Charlotte, N.C., Kayenta, Az. **The Modern Red Schoolhouse** concept came from a collaboration of Hudson Institute "education experts" and included former U.S. Secretary of Education **William Bennett**, as well as Assistant Secretary **Chester Finn**. Because of the involvement of Bennett and its emphasis on "classical education," hopes were initially high about this program. However, every child is to have an Individual Education Contract (the IEP useful for tracking), there is to be a new way of assessing mastery (OBE), and the SCANS project (labor-education linkup) is to form part of the core curriculum. So although the focus of each experimental school differs, **all have been selected for adherence to basic AMERICA 2000 principles,** as spelled out in the U.S. Department of Education's publication, ***AMERICA 2000: An Education Strategy. Education Week*** (6/9/93) will report that two of the NASDC winners, **Odyssey** (Gaston County, N.C.) and **the Bensenville Community Design** (Bensenville,

Il.) have lost NASDC support. **(See entries 101 and 106.)**

111. *Educational Leadership* (Mar.) publishes **"Will America Choose High Skills or Low Wages?"** by Ira Magaziner and **Hillary Rodham Clinton**, in which they recommend:

> A new educational **performance standard** should be set for all students, **to be met at or around age 16.** This standard should be **established nationally** and benchmarked to the highest in the world. Students passing a series of **performance-based assessments** that incorporate this new standard would be awarded a **Certificate of Initial Mastery.** Possession of the certificate would qualify a student to choose among going to work, entering a college preparatory program, or studying for a Technological and Professional Certificate. **(See entries 88 and 96.)**

112. In a congratulatory letter dated November 11 from **Marc Tucker of the NCEE (see entries 88, 96, 107, and 111) to his old friend, Hillary Clinton,** Tucker states that in a meeting in David Rockefeller's office those present were "literally radiating happiness at Bill Clinton's victory." Tucker goes on in this 18-page letter to lay out an aggressive plan for moving ahead with their educational strategy. He speaks of remolding the schools into a "national human resources development system . . . guided by clear standards that define the stages of the system for the people who progress through it, and regulated on the basis of outcomes that providers produce for their clients." He envisions a "seamless web" that "literally extends from cradle to grave and is the same system for everyone—young and old, poor and rich, worker and full-time student." He calls for a national employment service in which "all available frontline jobs, whether public or private, must be listed in it by law." He recommends: "A system of labor market boards is established at the local, state, and federal levels to coordinate the systems for job training, postsecondary professional and technical education, adult basic education, job matching and counseling." The "new general education standard" (Certificates of Mastery in lieu of diplomas) will become a "prerequisite for enrollment in all professional and technical degree programs." Schools will be required to provide information "to government agencies in a uniform format." The letter makes even clearer than the SCANS report, the intent of the change agents to merge education with labor and to have the government managing both. **(See entry 102; and resources: miscellaneous—Parents Involved in Education.)**

113. The *Higher Education Amendments of 1992, Public Law 102-325,* is passed and **includes a $20 million appropriation (Oct. 1992–Sept. 30, 1997) for the Carnegie-spawned National Board for Professional Teaching Standards** to "be used for research and development activities directly related to the development of **teacher assessment and certification procedures for elementary and secondary school teachers." (See entries 49, 82, and 87.)**

114. ***The Brownsville Herald*** (Texas) published on November 21 the text of a pledge recited by students in a Brownsville school. Not "the pledge" all U.S. citizens are familiar with, it is the **United Nations World Pledge** and reads: **"I pledge allegiance to the world, to cherish every living thing, to care for the earth and sea and air, with peace and freedom everywhere."**

115. ***The New York Times International*** of March 16, 1992, reports that the Chinese government keeps a **lifelong dossier called a *dangan*** on every citizen. The article explains that the *dangan* is a file opened on each urban citizen when he or she enters elementary school, and it shadows the person throughout life, moving on to high school, college, employer. . . . The *dangan* contains political evaluations that affect career prospects and permission to leave the country. . . . The file is kept by one's employer. The *dangan* affects promotions and job opportunities. . . . Any prospective employer is supposed to examine an applicant's *dangan* before making hiring decisions." **(See entries 31, 32, 44, 45, 52, 63, 66, 68, 74, 112, 122, and 127–129.)**

1993

116. Richard Riley, former governor of South Carolina, is appointed by President Bill Clinton as the new U.S. **secretary of education**.

117. GOALS 2000, the Clinton/Riley version of *AMERICA 2000* is announced by Secretary Riley. Michael Cohen, Riley's assistant, is said to be the chief architect. The legislation to make school restructuring a reality is introduced: **S.1150** (in the Senate) and **H.R.1804** (House version).

118. ***USA Today*** (Feb. 25) carries a story by John Hillkirk on Total Quality Management (TQM), **"Toppling Top-down Culture: TQM Sweeps White House."** He writes:

> The Clinton administration's TQM philosophy is largely based on the bestselling 1991 book ***Reinventing Government: How the Entrepreneurial Spirit Is Transforming the Public Sector.*** The authors say the single most influential figure behind the book is Peter Drucker, the business management expert. The book draws heavily on the teachings of **W. Edwards Deming. . . . In Arkansas, Clinton studied TQM** under Asa Whittaker, quality director at Eastman Kodak's chemical plant in Batesville. **Nearly 90 percent of Arkansas' 36,000 workers have been trained in TQM.** Clinton learned more about customer service and TQM in one-on-one discussions with Xerox CEO Paul Allaire and the late Sam Walton who founded Wal-Mart. **Hillary Rodham Clinton served on Wal-Mart's board.**

The article mentions that **Clinton has created "teams," including a health-care task force headed by wife, Hillary.**

119. Education International (EI) is formed as the international affiliate of the National Education Association (known as World Confederation of Organizations of the Teaching Profession [WCOTP]) and the American Federation of Teachers (known as International Federation of Free Teachers Unions) join together. **Mary Futrell**, former head of the **NEA** and current head of WCOTP is **president**. Creation of this organization causes speculation about a future merger of the NEA and AFT in the U.S. **(See entry 13.)**

120. The **Character Education Partnership, Inc.**, is incorporated. Its organizational members include, among others, the Institute for Global Ethics, Jefferson Center for Character Education, National Education Association, Quest International, and Focus on the Family. **(See entries 8, 25, 56, 57, and 86.)**

121. ***Update,*** a newsletter of the Association for Supervision and Curriculum Development **(ASCD)**, reports in its May issue that:

> ASCD has joined a national coalition that hopes to provide leadership in the effort to develop **civic virtue and moral character in students. The Character Education Partnership (CEP)**, officially incorporated in February . . . grew out of a 1992 meeting on K–12 values and character education programs . . . which ASCD cosponsored. . . . CEP anticipates a national clearinghouse of education and community programs. . . . **CEP will stress consensus building.** . . . Thirty representatives of education and youth groups last summer adopted **"six pillars of character"** as part of the ***Aspen Declaration on Character Education.*** And the CEP is helping to link academic leaders and practitioners in the field. The Aspen agreement, the result of a conference in Aspen, Colorado, is **designed to replace the values clarification approach with programs that advocate respect, responsibility, trustworthiness, caring, justice and fairness and civic virtue and citizenship.** The declaration states that such values **"transcend cultural, religious, and socioeconomic differences."** Michael Josephson, president of the Josephson Institute of Ethics, which organized the Aspen conference that produced the declaration, says, **"we're just entering a whole new generation of curriculum development. . . . In the next five years, we're literally going to see hundreds of individual experiments created."** . . . The Child Development Project established in 1980, is considered the most well-researched values education program in the country. It blends cooperative learning, literature-based language arts, and a discipline approach that doesn't rely on a system of rewards and punishments in an effort to create "caring communities." **(See entries for 120 above.)**

122. ***Field Restricted Use Data Procedures Manual*** is published by the National Center for Education Statistics **(NCES)**. In it **"individually identifiable information"** is defined as including an **"individual's**

education, financial transactions, medical history, and criminal or employment history" with some **"identifying particular assigned to the individual"** (e.g., name, fingerprint, voiceprint, etc.). NCES indicates that the bulk of its data files containing such information on individuals is maintained by Boeing Computer Services. On January 6, 1994, NCES will provide a list of **twenty-nine companies, contractors, and organizations which have access to restricted use National Assessment of Educational Progress (NAEP) databases that contain individually identifiable information.** Some of them are: Rand, Inc., CTB/MacMillan/McGraw-Hill, Economic Policy Institute, Westat, National Computer Systems, Educational Testing Service, North Central Regional Educational Laboratory, Texas Education Agency, University of Michigan School of Education, Montana State Attorney-General, etc. **(See entries 31, 32, 44, 45, 52, 63, 66, 68, 74, 112, 115, 122, and 127–129.)**

123. The Clinton administration unveils its proposal for the upcoming five-year **reauthorization** of the **Elementary and Secondary Education Act (ESEA)**. This is presented in the Senate as **S.1513**, and in a longer House version as **H.R.6. (See entry 32.)**

124. **The New American Schools Development Corporation (NASDC)**, whose future has been in question, is given a new lease on life by the contribution of $50 million by the Annenberg Foundation. The total Annenberg donation is $500 million to improve education and reduce school violence. $15 million will go to the Education Commission of the States, and another $50 million to Theodore Sizer's National Institute for School Reform (which they rename the Annenberg National Institute for School Reform). **(See entries 35, 101, 106, and 110.)**

1994

125. *Education Week* (Feb. 16) publishes **"Distance-Learning Network Launched"** by Peter West, in which he announces: "The founding of the satellite-based Interactive Distance Education Alliance Network, or **IDEANET**. . . . The network will serve schools in thirty-three states and the District of Columbia when it begins broadcasting in

the fall." IDEANET will provide instructional and staff development programs to two thousand schools nationwide.

126. In an article in the December/January 1994 issue of ***Oregon Education***, author Bruce Adams (president of the Oregon Education Association) tells of his trip to Lower Saxony, Germany, to study the German educational system, **particularly the apprenticeship system**. He says:

> We wanted to see what we could learn that might be useful to Oregon since **the German system was used as a model when Oregon created the Education Reform Act with the components of the Certificate of Initial Mastery (CIM) and the Certificate of Advanced Mastery (CAM)**. . . . Is the German system better than ours? That depends on what you value. Do you value a well-ordered society where everyone has a place, where workers are well-trained and training is well-defined? Where no one can open a small business without doing an apprenticeship, passing tests and then becoming a master by passing more tests? . . . This system fosters quality and consistency more than creativity or innovation. . . . Their respect for education and training cannot be overstated. **They come from a tradition that allows them to be more comfortable with tracking than are we**. . . . German laws require apprenticeships in many fields, and **businesses cooperate to enforce the system.**

Despite some reservations about the German system, the author concludes that the German idea can be adapted to our system if there is sufficient business support. He says: "**This would almost certainly require laws or tax incentives that would motivate businesses to participate in great numbers." (See entries 88, 92, 96, 101, 102, 107, 110–112, 115, 122, 127, and 128.)**

127. *GOALS 2000: Educate America Act, Public Law 103-227* (the marked up version of H.R.1804, totaling 156 pages, and having had several other bills rolled into it) is approved by a conference committee of the House and Senate and signed by Bill Clinton on March 31. **It will become the law of the land on July 1, 1994. (See entries 105 and 117.)**

128. ***The School-to-Work Opportunities Act, Public Law 103-239,*** becomes law on May 4. This establishes a formal partnership between the U.S. Departments of Education and Labor, with collaboration on an OBE-based apprenticeship program, complete with "portable credentials" (Certificates of Mastery). The grant money for this education-labor linkup is tied to compliance with requirements outlined in the ***GOALS 2000*** legislation. **(See entries 88, 92, 96, 102, 111, 112, 126, and 127.)**

129. Improving America's Schools Act of 1994, Public Law 103-382, the marked-up version of **H.R.6,** the **ESEA reauthorization bill** is signed into law on October 20, 1994. The final product is a massive 544 pages. Like the **School-to-Work Opportunities Act,** this **ESEA** reauthorization will have strings attaching it to **GOALS 2000.** Because of the many overlapping areas covered by both laws, this **ESEA** reauthorization functions almost as a companion to **GOALS 2000. (See entries 33, 123, and 127.)**

Summary of Themes

As you begin the text of *P.L. 103-227*, keep your eyes on the eight main paradigm shifts/themes outlined in the preface:

1. Partnerships (with reduced authority for parents)

2. Work force training (away from broadly educating)

3. New management models for schools (away from local control/accountability)

4. Nationalized curriculum and tests (short term goal—almost in place)

5. Internationalized curriculum and tests (ASAP—mid-range goal)

6. Leveling (individuals, schools, the nation)

7. Global citizenship training (not U.S.)

8. Lifelong learning (the gatekeeper of jobs and services)

. . . and the four recurring words: "all," "partnerships," "challenging," and "voluntary."

Introductory section preceding the text of *P.L. 103-227*

In which you will find:

1. The popular name of the law, *"To improve learning . . ."*
2. The enactment clause, *"Be it enacted . . ."*
3. **Section 1.**
   (a) the short title: ***Goals 2000: Educate America Act*** and
   (b) the Table of Contents
4. **Section 2.**
   covering the purpose of (rationale behind) *GOALS 2000* and ending with definitions of six terms used in the law.

Public Law 103-227—March 31, 1994
103rd Congress

An Act

To improve learning and teaching by providing a national framework for education reform; to promote the research, consensus building, and systemic changes needed to ensure equitable educational opportunities and high levels of educational achievement for all students; to provide a framework for reauthorization of all Federal education programs; to promote the development and adoption of a voluntary national system of skill standards and certification; and for other purposes.

Be it enacted by the Senate and House of Representatives of the United States of America in Congress assembled,

Sec. 1. Short Title; Table of Contents.

Title 4. PARENTAL ASSISTANCE
Title 5. NATIONAL SKILL STANDARDS BOARD
Title 6. INTERNATIONAL EDUCATION PROGRAM
Title 7. SAFE SCHOOLS
Title 8. MINORITY-FOCUSED CIVICS EDUCATION
Title 9. EDUCATIONAL RESEARCH AND IMPROVEMENT
Title 10. MISCELLANEOUS

SEC. 2. PURPOSE

The purpose of this Act is to provide a framework for meeting the National Education Goals established by title 1 of this Act by—

A framework is something to be built upon and added to, thus we may expect that ***GOALS 2000,*** as outlined here, is not the last word on education reform, but rather a "work in progress." Another "framework" piece of education legislation is the ***Elementary and Secondary Education Act (ESEA)*** brought in in 1965, reauthorized and enlarged every five years since.

(1) promoting coherent, nationwide, systemic education reform;

"Systemic" is the operative word. ***The New Lexicon Webster's Dictionary (NLWD),*** 1990, defines systemic as: "of or relating to a system, esp. (physiol.) of or relating to the entire bodily system." For example: The whole body is infected so we must treat the disease systemically.

(2) improving the quality of learning and teaching in the classroom and in the workplace;

(3) defining appropriate and coherent Federal, State, and local roles and responsibilities for education reform and lifelong learning.

There is no *"appropriate"* federal role in education reform. Our U.S. Constitution long ago settled that matter. Education is one of the responsibilities delegated to the states and to the people. Recall that the Tenth Amendment reads:

> **The powers not delegated to the United States by the Constitution, nor prohibited by it to the States, are reserved to the States respectively, or to the people.**

Therefore, if states or localities wish to reform or otherwise modify their educational practices, *they already have that power,* and a grave mistake is made in allowing the federal government to illegally redefine who's in charge of what. This is a thinly disguised encroachment into an area where the federal government has no legal right to be.

Further, the Bible entrusts the role and responsibility of educating (training up) children to the parents, not to the state (Caesar) (Prov. 22:6; Mark 12:17). Parents who allow the federal government to usurp a God-given and constitutionally protected role are doubly delinquent in their duty—first as parents and secondarily as citizens.

"Lifelong learning" (LL) is a central concept in ***GOALS 2000.*** See LL glossary entry and decide if you want the federal government (or other central planners) determining what you and your children will learn from cradle to grave. **(See also chronology: 47, 52, 63, and 68)**

> *(4) establishing valid and reliable mechanisms for—*
>
> *(A) building a broad national consensus on American education reform;*

Wasn't the time for building *"consensus"* **before** passing this legislation? Shouldn't there have been (at a minimum) a series of nationally televised programs and debates about the substance of the *GOALS 2000* legislation before even thinking about bringing this up on the floor of the House and Senate? To call for consensus **after** this is a done deal is typical of the hypocrisy and deceit that has characterized the entire *AMERICA 2000/GOALS 2000* effort. The framers and promoters of this legislation anticipated some opposition from alert parents, so they have prepared for both damage control and phony consensus building. **(See glossary entries: Community Action Tool Kit, Delphi Technique, and Facilitator/facilitation.)**

> *(B) assisting in the development and certification of high-quality,*

internationally competitive content and student performance standards;

In order to know how standards compare internationally, it is necessary to study what other countries are doing. Presumably this will call for a realignment of what we are currently doing to get in step with other nations. This is a big departure for the United States—a country that has always set **the standard** or at least our own standards without looking over our shoulders to see what other nations are doing.

This new approach makes sense if one of the paradigm (total system) shifts implicit in *GOALS 2000* is the internationalization of education with the desired end point or "outcome" a global labor pool of interchangeably trained workers. **The international dimensions of *GOALS 2000* are extremely significant though frequently overlooked by parents who are, rightfully, alarmed about the federal takeover of their schools. The international connection in this legislation, primarily through the outworkings of UNESCO, is a true hidden agenda, and an even greater threat than the federal takeover because if we lose our national sovereignty, federal, state, and local control becomes a moot point. (See glossary: UNESCO; and chronology: 10, 12, 15–20, 28, 40, 47, 52, 55, 56, 63, 73, 77, 95, 108, and 109.)**

(C) assisting in the development and certification of opportunity-to-learn standards; and

See the definition of *"opportunity-to-learn"* in section 3, item 7 below. Briefly, "opportunity-to-learn" (O-T-L) is a euphemism for a set of stringent standards applied in such a way that the net effect is to "level" the schools. In leveling, the standards of some schools are raised, but others are **lowered.** If *"all"* students and schools must have the same *"resources, practices, and conditions,"* it follows that schools less well funded than those with a healthy tax base will have to be given more money to raise their level of resources, practices, and conditions. Where will this money come from? One answer is from the wealthier districts (the Robin Hood plan). Those districts obviously will then have less money available to them, the net effect being a leveling of all districts with each having approximately the same per pupil expenditure. **This leveling is a very important and intentional effect of the *GOALS 2000* legislation.** O-T-L standards are but one leveling device. The text of ***P.L.103-227*** contains others as we shall see.

> *(D) assisting in the development and certification of high-quality assessment measures that reflect the internationally competitive content and student performance standards;*

"Assessment measures" is jargon for testing usually associated with outcome-based education (OBE). Here we are told that the federal government intends to not only develop and certify (officially sanction) student tests, but that these will be developed to reflect what they consider *"internationally competitive"* standards. Few parents are aware that both the curriculum and testing of U.S. students is being **internationalized at the same time it's being federalized.** Evidence of this has been increasingly overt since the restructuring movement picked up steam in the 1980s. Some may recall the U.S.–Soviet agreements entered into in 1985 for the exchange of textbooks and software. Or you may have noticed in your local papers that teachers from your schools are traveling to Russia or other foreign countries to observe and learn about practices outside the U.S. Exchanges of teachers, teaching methodologies, and content (curriculum) back and forth have become very commonplace, and even logical, as we move closer to an internationalized education system. **(See glossary: U.S./Soviet Agreements; and chronology: 66 and 81.)**

The United States is not the only country experiencing a radical restructuring of its education system, nor are all these exchanges a sudden goodwill impulse brought on by *glasnost.* The Russian word *perestroika* means reform/restructuring. Curious that the two superpowers, so long at odds, have chosen the same word for their transformational reform efforts. If the educational systems of developed countries around the world are being merged into an international educational system, the American people have a right to know this is happening—and why. **One of the driving forces behind restructuring is that an interchangeably trained work force is required to serve the needs of a one-world government and global economy.**

> *(5) supporting new initiatives at the Federal, State, local, and school levels to provide equal educational opportunity for all students to meet high academic and occupational skill standards and to succeed in the world of employment and civic participation;*

The word ***"initiatives"*** may sound like friendly persuasion, but one of its definitions is: "the power or **right** to introduce a policy or measure" **(NLWD).** The phrase **"equal educational opportunity"** like **"opportunity-to-learn,"** is more leveling jargon. Equal educational opportunity, also known as finance equity, is currently being decided in many courts around the country. A common tactic is for the court to find the existing school funding formula illegal because it does not provide equal amounts for all students. Parents have often chosen to move into a particular school district (and pay higher taxes there) because the district has a reputation for good schools that sometimes, though not always, accompanies a healthy tax base and high per pupil expenditure. Under various ***"equal educational opportunity"*** guises and legal maneuvers, the state may function as a modern-day Robin Hood, stealing from the rich to give to the poor. Those in more affluent areas who protest about the loss of money for their schools, are shamed into silence by blistering newspaper and TV editorials, scolding them for their niggardly, mean-spirited attitude.

"All students" is used for the first time here. References to **"all"** children or students will appear more than fifty times throughout this law.

"Occupational skill standards" are very central to ***GOALS 2000*** because to a large extent **this law is labor-driven.** The skill standards and skills certification called for are presented as "voluntary." However, once they are widely adopted by schools and industries, they will be first highly desirable—then quickly nonvoluntary. The compulsory aspects of ***GOALS 2000*** are always cloaked with an assurance they are voluntary and entirely at the discretion of each state. While this may be true of skill standards initially, it won't be for long. We will look closely at these in Title 5.

> *(6) providing a framework for the reauthorization of all Federal education programs by—*

A *"framework"* is "a basic structure which supports and gives shape, or a broad outline, plan, etc. . . ." **(NLWD).** It's important to keep in mind that *GOALS 2000* is only a framework. It's not a finished structure; it's a work in progress. *"Reauthorization"* indicates that *GOALS 2000* will have to be refunded periodically, so this is not a one-time infusion of seed money. Moreover, *GOALS 2000* is so important, so central to the direction that American education is being moved, that **this law is to be tied to the reauthorization of "all" existing federal education programs.**

> *(A) creating a vision of excellence and equity that will guide all Federal education and related programs;*

Here ***"equity"*** is used instead of "equal educational opportunity," the term used in point 5 above. The term ***"related programs"*** is highly significant in this act as we see many programs, etc. never formally linked to education before that have become part of the national agenda. **(See glossary: Partnerships.)**

> *(B) providing for the establishment of high-quality, internationally competitive content and student performance standards and strategies that all students will be expected to achieve;*

This brings us back to the international thrust of curriculum and testing under *GOALS 2000.* During the twentieth century, the United States set **the standard** in education, technology, manufacturing, medicine, and other areas. Shouldn't we again determine our own "personal best" standards without looking over our shoulders to see what the rest of the world is doing? Anyone doing a superior job will be competitive. Shouldn't we be trying to determine how and why we lost our competitive edge? **The exchange of curriculum and teaching methodologies from country to country will tend only to produce a standardized product—not excellence.** This is what was meant in the earlier Bush/Alexander plan, ***AMERICA 2000,*** by the phrase **"world class standards"—no better and no worse than any other country is doing.** People assumed "world class" meant "first class," but international curriculum and testing standards will tend not toward the

"high quality" implied here, but simply toward **"educational equity" on a global scale,** "standards . . . that **all** students will be expected to achieve." ***GOALS 2000*** is replete with leveling, internal and international.

> *(C) providing for the establishment of high-quality, internationally competitive opportunity-to-learn standards that all States, local educational agencies, and schools should achieve;*

Comments for (B) apply here as well; simply more leveling off.

> *(D) encouraging and enabling all State educational agencies and local educational agencies to develop comprehensive improvement plans that will provide a coherent framework for the implementation of reauthorized Federal education and related programs in an integrated fashion that effectively educates all children to prepare them to participate fully as workers, parents, and citizens;*

"Encouraging and enabling" is a euphemistic way of saying **rewards and punishments**—financial rewards for compliance (positive reinforcement) and no federal funds and other sanctions (negative reinforcement) for state departments of education and local educational agencies (districts) that fail to develop comprehensive ***GOALS 2000*** State Improvement Plans (SIPs). For the first time, getting the ***Elementary and Secondary Education Act (ESEA)*** money (that 30-year-old federal program that every state has become dependent upon) is tied to also showing that you are (or are in the process of becoming) a ***GOALS 2000*** state. For example, the 1994 ***ESEA*** requires that states submit to the U.S. Department of Education a State Improvement Plan that includes the adoption of challenging content standards and aligned assessments for Title I students. **(See chronology: 33 and 129.)**

The last three words, *"workers, parents, and citizens,"* are interesting. School has always been, in part, about preparing students for some niche in the work force, and it has always been about creating literate, informed citizens able to participate in the body politic. Also until quite recently one of the functions of state schools was to produce uniquely "American" citizens—to take from the mix of America's ethnic groups, races, and religions everyone, male and female, and to train them all to subsume their differences under the covering of U.S. citizenship—**to think of themselves as American first and foremost.** Anyone who attended a state school and graduated prior to the mid-late 1960s will recognize this **"melting pot"** notion underlying the public schools' mission. Oddly, references to **U.S. citizens,** or **American citizens,** to make clear the importance of teaching the uniqueness, blessing, and responsibilities of **U.S. citizenship** are noticeably lacking from ***GOALS 2000.*** Citizens will be trained; that's a given in any school system. But where will the loyalty and allegiance of these brave new ***GOALS 2000*** students be? Will it be to the great Republic of the United States of America or simply to their own ethnic, racial, or religious identity first, and perhaps secondarily to a consciousness that they are **world citizens?** Something very different from the "melting pot" is going on here. **(See chronology: 2, 6, 9–12, 15–20, 55, 56, 60, 63, 64–68, 73, 84, 85, 93, 95, 108, and 109.)**

And what about educating all children to ***"prepare them to participate fully as parents"?*** Do we want the schools preparing students for parenthood? What does that mean and encompass? If the family is the primary conduit of culture and values from one generation to the next, is the culture and value system in a state school harmonious with what is passed on at home? The alleged (but legally enforced) "wall of separation of church and state" precludes any but secular values from being discussed during classes, including "preparation for parenthood" classes. Even secularists would have a hard time agreeing on the fine points of culture and values. This is an area that belongs to the family and to the church precisely because it is totally predicated on attitudes, values, and beliefs. It is not the domain of state schools and should not be part of the curriculum. **Parenthood training is one of the seemingly innocuous, but actually very radical elements in this law.** We'll see more of what the government means by parenthood training in the National Education Goals, and especially as we look at Title 4. **(See chronology: 27–29 and 48.)**

> *(E) providing resources to help individual schools, including those serving students with high needs, develop and implement comprehensive improvement plans; and*

"High needs" though not spelled out, usually encompasses geographic areas with large concentrations of poor students, can include children with disabilities or bilingual children and could include any child deemed by authorities to be **"at risk."** As with other vague language in this act, *"high needs"* could be, over time, **anything the government decides it is** in order to increase their authority.

> *(F) promoting the use of technology to enable all students to achieve the National Education Goals;*

The increased use of technology is a very important component of restructuring the schools. We'll take a closer look at this under Title 2, Part C.

> *(7) stimulating the development and adoption of a voluntary national system of skill standards and certification to serve as a cornerstone of the national strategy to enhance workforce skills; and*

The word ***"voluntary"*** appears 101 times in ***P.L.103-227.*** The repeated use of **"voluntary"** is, of course, to convey the strong impression that many aspects of this law are only guidelines or suggestions. We will see as we proceed through ***GOALS 2000*** how adoption is tied to rewards and punishment. As of early 1996, four states (Virginia, New Hampshire, Montana, and Alabama) have backed away from ***GOALS 2000*** money, hoping to avoid the strings that **always** accompany federal dollars.

We will look more closely at national skill standards and federalized skill certificates under Title 5.

> *(8) assisting every elementary and secondary school that receives funds under this Act to actively involve parents and families in supporting the academic work of their children at home and in providing parents with skills to advocate for their children at school.*

This represents a radical move toward statism (planning and control by a centralized government). Christian parents are not going to happily submit to having social workers and other agents of the government provide them with such training. ***"Skills to advocate for their children at school,"*** is an example of the preposterous double-talk found in ***GOALS 2000***. Parents have been, are now, and forever will be advocates for their children. **If not the parents, who?** They need no "skills" provided by the government to speak up for their own children. This is co-option by the state of a right and responsibility parents are already entrusted with. Any parent who willingly goes along with this intrusion into their family and God-given responsibilities has been duped. **(See also goal no. 8 of the National Education Goals and Title 4.)**

SEC. 3. DEFINITIONS.

(a) TITLES 1, 2, 3, and 10—As used in titles 1, 2, 3, and 10 of this Act—

(1) the terms "all students" and "all children" mean students or children from a broad range of backgrounds and circumstances, including disadvantaged students and children, students or children with diverse racial, ethnic, and cultural backgrounds, American Indians, Alaska Natives, Native Hawaiians, students or children with disabilities, students or children with limited-English proficiency, school-aged students or children who have dropped out of school, migratory students or children, and academically talented students and children;

Who's been left out here? No one! They probably mean that the law is aimed particularly (or first) at all the special categories of students in this list. The use of the words *"students **or** children"* is interesting because it makes a distinction between the two. This definition encompasses the entire U.S. population, womb-to-tomb, when we take into account prenatal programs, early childhood education, and the lifelong learning called for by ***GOALS 2000***.

(2) the term "Bureau," unless otherwise provided, means the Bureau of Indian Affairs;

(3) the terms "community," "public," and "advocacy group" in-

> *clude representatives of organizations advocating for the education of American Indian, Alaska Native, and Native Hawaiian children and Indian tribes;*

What about other obvious (and maybe not so obvious) definitions of these terms, e.g., the Black community, the Islamic community, the Hasidic community, the Hispanic community, etc.? Aren't these all valid "communities" in certain geographic areas? There are numerous **advocacy groups** not listed above: groups from the Christian right, environmental advocacy groups, the ACLU, gay and lesbian student advocates, etc. Much in this law invites lawsuits as one group after another scrambles to ensure their interests are represented. **Whatever happened to the "melting pot"?**

> *(4) the term "content standards" means broad descriptions of the knowledge and skills students should acquire in a particular subject area;*

Translation: A national (federalized) curriculum based on subject area standards. The ***"broad descriptions"*** are not very "broad" either. The push for content standards predates ***GOALS 2000*** by several years. Detailed model curricula have been prepared by committees of "subject experts" and are now available in the following fields: mathematics, the arts, civics, foreign languages, geography, physical education, social studies, English, and history. The last two have been very controversial: history because of its revisionist, politically correct content, and English because of its PC tone and vagueness. Both were extensively reworked and still came out poorly. The only area not yet completed is economics; their standards are expected by the end of 1996. This is an example of how **much of the restructuring work called for in *GOALS 2000* is already in place in our schools.** In many ways ***GOALS 2000*** is simply the government seal of approval (and dollars) for the many parts of restructuring that have been coming in quietly and piecemeal (to avoid detection and resistance) over the years.

> *(5) the term "Governor" means the chief executive of the State;*

(6) the terms "local educational agency" and "State educational agency" have the meaning given such terms in section 1471 of the Elementary and Secondary Education Act of 1965;

Section 1471 of the ***ESEA*** defines a **local educational agency** as: ". . . a public board of education or other public authority legally constituted within a State for either administrative control or direction of, or to perform a service function for, public elementary or secondary schools in a city, county, township, school district, or other political subdivision of a State, or such combination of school districts or counties as are recognized in a State as an administrative agency for its public elementary or secondary schools. Such term includes any other public institution or agency having administrative control and direction of a public elementary or secondary school."

Section 1471 defines a **state educational agency** as: ". . . the officer or agency primarily responsible for the State supervision of public elementary and secondary schools."

(7) the term "opportunity-to-learn standards" means the criteria for, and the basis of, assessing the sufficiency or quality of the resources, practices, and conditions necessary at each level of the education system (schools, local educational agencies, and States) to provide all students with an opportunity to learn the material in voluntary national content standards or State content standards;

I have commented on O-T-L standards above in Section 2, 4.C. No wonder some have called O-T-L **"opportunity-to-litigate."** Lawyers must be lining up to take O-T-L challenges on behalf of the less well-funded school districts. Remember, **all** O-T-L standards must be equal: school to school; district to district; and state to state. **(See glossary: Opportunity-to-Learn.)**

(8) the term "outlying areas" means Guam, American Samoa, the Virgin Islands, the Commonwealth of the Northern Mariana Islands, Palau (until the effective date of the Compact of Free Association with the Government of Palau), the Republic of the Marshall Islands, and the Federated States of Micronesia;

> *(9) the term "performance standards" means concrete examples and explicit definitions of what students have to know and be able to do to demonstrate that such students are proficient in the skills and knowledge framed by content standards;*

The words ***"performance standards"*** and the phrase ***"what students have to know and be able to do to demonstrate"*** are both jargon associated with outcome-based education (OBE). **The actual term "outcome-based education" is not to be found anywhere in *GOALS 2000*.** The writers knew better. Nevertheless, the use of the above euphemisms and other OBE buzzwords found throughout the law show that **the national curriculum/testing package is outcome-based.**

> *(10) the term "related services" has the same meaning given such term under section 602 of the Individuals with Disabilities Education Act.*

Section 602 of the ***IDEA*** defines **related services** as:

> . . . transportation, and such developmental, corrective, and other supportive services (including speech pathology and audiology, psychological services, physical and occupational therapy, recreation, including therapeutic recreation and social work services, and medical and counseling services, including rehabilitation counseling, except that such medical services shall be for diagnostic and evaluation purposes only) as may be required to assist a child with a disability to benefit from special education, and includes the early identification and assessment of disabling conditions in children.

Look closely at all that's covered. What exactly is meant by ***"a child with a disability"*** or ***"disabling conditions"?*** Identification and assessment of "disabilities" in children may lead directly to "help" that is not wanted by parents especially in the areas of counseling and social work services.

> *(11) the term "State assessment" means measures of student performance which include at least 1 instrument of evaluation, and may*

include other measures of student performance, for a specific purpose and use which are intended to evaluate the progress of all students in the State toward learning the material in State content standards in 1 or more subject areas;

Translation: State tests. "Assessments" (frequently used with OBE) will consist of at least one particular type of test (*"instrument of evaluation"*) and will compare students' knowledge of the state curriculum in at least one subject area. Examples of different kinds of measures might be a "live performance" to test how well students are achieving the outcomes of the music standards or could be a machine-graded, multiple-choice math test to measure against the math standards. The idea is to have all subjects standardized so scores can be compared.

(12) the term "school" means a public school that is under the authority of the State educational agency or a local educational agency or, for the purpose of carrying out section 315(b), a school that is operated or funded by the Bureau;

Although the definition says ***"a public school,"*** in some states even home schools are considered to be ***"under the authority of the State educational agency,"*** (State Department of Education) or (more commonly) under the ***"local educational agency,"*** (school district). How this will be interpreted in the future remains to be seen. Court challenges to home schoolers are possible with this ambiguous language.

(13) the term "Secretary," unless otherwise provided, means the Secretary of Education, and;

(14) the term "State," unless otherwise provided, means each of the 50 States, the District of Columbia, the Commonwealth of Puerto Rico, and each of the outlying areas.

(b) Titles 4, 5, 6, 7, 8, and 9.—For the purpose of titles 4, 5, 6, 7, 8, and 9—

(1) except as provided in paragraph (3) and unless otherwise pro-

vided, the terms used in such titles have the same meanings given such terms in section 1471 of the Elementary and Secondary Education Act of 1965;

(2) the term "Bureau," unless otherwise provided, means the Bureau of Indian Affairs; and

(3) the term "Secretary," unless otherwise provided, means the Secretary of Education.

This is the end of the introductory material that precedes the ten titles or main text of the law. Before moving into the titles, let's take another look at the very first part of ***GOALS 2000***, the popular title:

An Act to improve learning and teaching by providing a national framework for education reform; to promote the research, consensus building, and systemic changes needed to ensure equitable educational opportunities and high levels of educational achievement for all students; to provide a framework for reauthorization of all Federal education programs; to promote the development and adoption of a voluntary national system of skill standards and certification; and for other purposes.

Though brief and broad, it doesn't seem quite so innocuous the second time it's read, does it? We need to avoid being lulled to sleep as we read through the ten titles of this law. Defining terms and giving the bland, reassuring rhetoric a "reality check" will enable us to see the way the *GOALS 2000* "framework" is to be filled in.

Restructuring is a process, not a product. An organization (school district or school) never reaches the final state of being restructured. The process is dynamic. (*Developing Leaders for Restructuring Schools*, p.7)

Title 1—
National Education Goals

In which you will find details of the eight National Education Goals. Abbreviated they are:

1. School Readiness
2. School Completion
3. Student Achievement and Citizenship
4. Teacher Education and Professional Development
5. First Internationally in Math and Science
6. Adult Literacy and Lifelong Learning
7. Safe, Disciplined, and Alcohol and Drug-Free Schools
8. Parental Participation

Perhaps these should be called the "international education goals" as six of the eight correlate with international goals formulated in 1990 at a UNESCO sponsored conference.

TITLE 1—
NATIONAL EDUCATION GOALS

SEC. 101. PURPOSE.

The purpose of this title is to establish National Education Goals.

SEC. 102. NATIONAL EDUCATION GOALS.

The Congress declares that the National Education Goals are the following:

(1) SCHOOL READINESS.—(A) By the year 2000, all children in America will start school ready to learn.

This sounds like a worthwhile goal, but what does it actually mean? Aren't young children by their very nature curious, ready, and eager to learn? For the vast majority of children this is **not** a problem. So what does the federal government mean by ***"ready to learn"***? Read on.

(B) The objectives for this goal are that—

(i) all children will have access to high-quality and developmentally appropriate preschool programs that help prepare children for school;

In other words, the government will enter the preschool business. If ***"all children"*** are to have access to these preschool programs then the government has just added an enormous new foundational layer to their current K–12 offerings which have up to this time been limited to half or full-day kindergarten programs—with attendance at parent's discretion. Government agents will determine what is ***"developmentally appropriate"*** and what needs to be taught to ***"prepare children for school."*** This will be a growth industry for those in the "developmentally appropriate" preschool field and, who knows, parents too busy to look closely at the programs may welcome the "help."

> *(ii) every parent in the United States will be a child's first teacher and devote time each day to helping such parent's preschool child learn, and parents will have access to the training and support parents need; and*

I hope this one jumped off the page at you! There's a world of difference between acknowledging that parents are a child's first teacher, with most as a matter of course, devoting time each day to helping their children learn—and in having the government tell parents they ***"will be"*** a child's first teacher and that they ***"will have access"*** to the training and support (the government obviously feels) ***"parents need."*** There is no way the government could effect such a takeover of parent's rights and responsibilities without monitoring parents in their own homes. And just such a surveillance system, the **Parents as Teachers (PAT)** program, in fact, already exists. PAT will be discussed in detail under **Title 4—Parental Assistance.** That this has been made part of a national education strategy and codified as a National Education Goal should be cause for alarm and indignation to every parent who knows the government has no right defining what a good parent is or does. **(See glossary: Parents as Teachers; and chronology: 42, 55, 66, 103, and 104.)**

> *(iii) children will receive the nutrition, physical activity experiences, and health care needed to arrive at school with healthy minds and bodies, and to maintain the mental alertness necessary to be prepared to learn, and the number of low-birthweight babies will be significantly reduced through enhanced prenatal health systems.*

Again the use of that coercive sounding ***"will receive,"*** etc. Good physical, spiritual, and emotional care for children is a wonderful objective that needs to be accomplished one family at a time, but is hardly the province of the government. If the ***"number of low birthweight babies will be significantly reduced through enhanced prenatal health systems,"*** does this mean pregnant women will be forced to participate in government-sponsored prenatal programs to ensure this occurs? The basic question that parents need to settle in their own minds is: **Who owns the children?** Are they yours? Does the state (government) own them? Or **are you willing to share custody of your children with the state?** This is a foundational question to ask again and again as you read through ***GOALS 2000.*** **(See chronology: 91.)**

> *(2) SCHOOL COMPLETION.—(A) By the year 2000, the high school graduation rate will increase to at least 90 percent.*
>
> *(B) The objectives for this goal are that—*
>
> *(i) the Nation must dramatically reduce its school dropout rate, and 75 percent of the students who do drop out will successfully complete a high school degree or its equivalent; and*

Lowering the dropout rate sounds like a reasonable and worthwhile goal, but how is this to be accomplished? You can't force students to stay in school. Or can you? The mandatory attendance age, varying from 16 to 18 years from state to state, is an acknowledgment that at some point in young adulthood, citizens are free to decide if they wish to continue their education, join the work force, the military, or—though it's a sad choice—do nothing and become a drain on their families or the public through tax-supported welfare programs. How does the government intend to go after students who have dropped out to ensure the 75 percent completion rate? A fairly high percentage of students who drop out do go on to completion later when their motivation or circumstances change. The General Equivalency Diploma (GED) is perhaps the best known "second chance" program. This is widely available to those who want it enough to put in the necessary time and effort. What more should be provided? Since **"life-long learning" (LL)** is mentioned numerous times throughout ***P.L. 103-227,*** perhaps one of the hidden agendas is that the mandatory school attendance age is being changed to **"the rest of your life."** Knowing that the LL concept comes out of UNESCO and has already had a long run in China and the Soviet Union, we need only look at those totalitarian states to see where this idea takes us. **(See glossary: Lifelong Learning; and chronology: 39, 47, 52, 63, 66, 68, 72, and 101.)**

> *(ii) the gap in high school graduation rates between American students from minority backgrounds and their non-minority counterparts will be eliminated.*

With statist policies of the last thirty years on how to do this increasingly unpopular and being successfully challenged in the courts, what new strategies does the government have? This is where leveling mechanisms like O-T-L standards will be used. Vast amounts of money will be poured into schools with large proportions of minority students in an attempt to obtain "equity." **Equity always ends up a leveling process.**

> *(3) STUDENT ACHIEVEMENT AND CITIZENSHIP.—(A) By the year 2000, all students will leave grades 4, 8, and 12 having demonstrated competency over challenging subject matter including English, mathematics, science, foreign languages, civics and government, economics, arts, history, and geography, and every school in America will ensure that all students learn to use their minds well, so they may be prepared for responsible citizenship, further learning, and productive employment in our Nation's modern economy.*

"Having demonstrated competency" is OBE testing jargon and is a reference to the National Assessment of Educational Progress (NAEP), given in grades 4, 8, and 12 (with some variation from state to state). Notice that *"responsible citizenship"* is mentioned without any reference to the United States of America. An oversight? Also *"further learning"* (lifelong learning) and *"productive employment"* are listed as the desired end result (outcome) of studying the ten subjects over a twelve-year period. Since *GOALS 2000* is a labor-driven plan, coordinated closely with the U.S. Department of Labor, it should not be surprising that the final outcome of twelve-plus years of learning is to be a productive

worker primed for further learning. David Hornbeck, one of the important figures in school restructuring (and currently superintendent of the Philadelphia public schools) has edited a book about "an economic strategy for the '90's" whose title accurately reflects this thinking: ***Human Capital and America's Future.*** And in case there's any doubt about the meaning of that phrase, the **"human capital"** are your children. **(See chronology: 31, 44, 74, and 98.)**

> *(B) The objectives for this goal are that—*
>
> *(i) the academic performance of all students at the elementary and secondary level will increase significantly in every quartile, and the distribution of minority students in each quartile will more closely reflect the student population as a whole;*

Quartiles are four-part divisions (quarters), in this case used for testing purposes. One way to raise test scores is by making the tests easier, or to so completely change the way tests are designed and scored that it becomes impossible to make meaningful comparisons with former test scores. An example of this is the new Scholastic Achievement Test, the SAT I. According to an article entitled **"When All Else Fails; Restructure: Interpreting the New SAT Scores,"** by Gary L. Bauer of the Family Research Council, ". . . SAT I has fewer questions. And allows students 30 more minutes to take the test. And permits calculators, and throws out antonyms, one of the most difficult verbal sections on the test." I think it's safe to predict higher test scores with what the FRC calls the "SAT-lite." The second clause *"and the distribution . . ."* sounds like "norming" to level everyone out. Norming or artificially elevating scores for particular groups does not produce academic excellence; the net effect is simply to lower the overall standard for everyone. When this is done everyone loses, but especially those—when a day of reckoning comes, as it eventually does—whose scores have been inflated.

> *(ii) the percentage of all students who demonstrate the ability to reason, solve problems, apply knowledge, and write and communicate effectively will increase substantially.*

These skills *"to reason, solve problems, apply knowledge"* all sound admirable. How can anyone argue with the need for this? However, these very terms are used to describe one of the current classroom fads, **"critical thinking skills,"** also known as **"higher order thinking skills."** The basic problem with "thinking skills," by whatever name, is its remarkable similarity to the old values clarification which swept through classrooms in the late 1960s and 1970s. Parents resisted VC when they realized their children were being manipulated into exchanging values brought from home for new values the children were told were "their own values, freely arrived at, after group discussion and personal reflection." **(See glossary: Higher Order Thinking Skills; and chronology: 7, 30, 34, 36, 50, 54, 56, 57, 71, 80, and 89.)**

> *(iii) all students will be involved in activities that promote and demonstrate good citizenship, good health, community service, and personal responsibility.*

Is this U.S. *"citizenship"*? Global? Again, note this is not specified. What sort of activities ***"demonstrate"*** that you are a ***"good citizen"***? How do you demonstrate *"good health"*? Or exhibit *"personal responsibility"*? How easily politicized all of these will be. *"Community service"* (a.k.a. service learning) is an idea that's catching on in a big way. Seventy-five hours of this are now required for high school graduation in Maryland. Many parents would like their children out in the community doing volunteer work for worthwhile causes. Such service has benefits to the individual and to the community at large. The difference is that serving others loses most of its value if it's coerced (threat of not graduating). Also the student and his parents should be the ones to decide what volunteer work has value to them. What will the schools decide is worthwhile? Volunteering at a crisis pregnancy center? Volunteering at the local Planned Parenthood office? The very choice of work will be subject to the shifting winds of political correctness and, most importantly, the whole thing is **unconstitutional**; the government has no right to compel free citizens to work. It may seem a small matter, but by just such small blows our liberties are being chipped away and we are conditioned to serve the state. **(See chronology: 64 and 78.)**

> *(iv) all students will have access to physical education and health education to ensure they are healthy and fit;*

Don't all children get physical education already? It has been a part of the curriculum anywhere I have lived. We don't need *GOALS 2000* to get phys ed into America's schools. **Comprehensive *"health education"*** is what this is about. Under that name, or "family life education" (and various other euphemisms) many schools now present graphic sexuality without any reference to the biblical context, or even the context of heterosexual marriage; offer information on contraceptives, and in some districts hand out condoms and offer abortion referrals. This is all part of being **"comprehensive."** The emergence of HIV/AIDS as a health problem instead of causing educators to rethink "comprehensive" sex ed has provided promoters with a new justification for getting these programs into the schools beginning with younger and younger children. **(See chronology: 27–29, 34, 48, 50, 51, and 53.)**

Drug "awareness" programs that are anything but drug "prevention," and/or self-esteem programs that delve into the personal areas of a student's values and attitudes can be found in most of the nation's schools. Parents are given alarming statistics concerning substance abuse and teen suicide and assured that these programs are absolutely necessary—the sooner the better. The government is now calling for **thirteen years of "comprehensive health education,"** beginning in kindergarten and continuing through twelfth grade. **(See chronology: 46, 61, and 62.)**

> *(v) the percentage of all students who are competent in more than one language will substantially increase; and*
>
> *(vi) all students will be knowledgeable about the diverse cultural heritage of this Nation and about the world community.*

This is the multiculturalism approach (many cultures maintaining their distinct identities) as opposed to the former melting pot (subsuming one's cultural identity under the overarching identity of being an American). **Nationalism is not presented as a positive, but as a**

detriment to world cooperation and peace. By presenting the U.S. as just one country among many in the larger "world community," a **"world citizen," global mindset is gradually formed.** We know that frogs floating in a slowly heated kettle of water lose their natural ability to get out of harm's way. In much the same way, students steadily indoctrinated during the thirteen years spent in state schools will not be able to detect the danger and avoid enslavement in a one-world government. **(See chronology: 4, 6, 9–12, 15–20, 55, 56, 60, 63–68, 73, 84, 85, 93, 95, 108, and 109; and glossary: Infusion Model.)**

> *(4)* TEACHER EDUCATION AND PROFESSIONAL DEVELOPMENT.—
>
> *(A) By the year 2000, the Nation's teaching force will have access to programs for the continued improvement of their professional skills and the opportunity to acquire the knowledge and skills needed to instruct and prepare all American students for the next century.*

This fourth goal is not one of the original six formulated under *AMERICA 2000* (the Bush/Alexander version of *GOALS 2000*). An obvious oversight in the earlier plan was how to bring the teachers "on board" for all the restructuring changes. There is at present no shortage of continuing education programs for teachers desiring access to them. What is at issue here is that *"the knowledge and skills needed to instruct and prepare all American students for the next century"* is something so radically different from teacher training as it now exists that entire new programs have been and are being created to do the job. A brave new student requires a brave new teacher. **(See chronology: 37, 43, 49, 59, 82, 87, and 113.)**

> *(B) The objectives for this goal are that—*
>
> *(i) all teachers will have access to preservice teacher education and continuing professional development activities that will provide such teachers with the knowledge and skills needed to teach to an increasingly diverse student population with a variety of educational, social, and health needs.*

"Preservice teacher education" is whatever an individual state requires for certification (entry into the field). *"Continuing professional development"* would include training after someone is already teaching, e.g., in-service training, workshops, summer courses, work toward advanced degrees, etc. *"Diverse student population"* indicates that teachers will be trained in multiculturalism. (See Title 8.) *"Social and health needs"* means there will be an increased emphasis on teachers functioning as social workers. This is not going to sit well with many experienced teachers who want a no-frills, no-nonsense approach to academics. Those who cannot "go along to get along" will be weeded out.

> *(ii) all teachers will have continuing opportunities to acquire additional knowledge and skills needed to teach challenging subject matter and to use emerging new methods, forms of assessment, and technologies;*

What is ***"challenging"*** subject matter? It must be something pretty central to ***GOALS 2000*** because the word **"challenging" appears more than thirty times throughout the law.** Is it subjects taught at a more difficult level or in a more interesting way? I think that's what we're supposed to conclude, but I don't think that's it at all. I believe the writers of ***GOALS 2000*** have played with the word in a sly, deceptive way and this is another paradigm shift—from the old facts/knowledge model, employing the cognitive domain—to the new model of attitudes/values/beliefs, in the affective domain. The second definition of **"challenge"** listed in the ***NLWD*** is: **"a calling in question (of the truth of statements, rights, authority, etc.)"** And that comes close to what's actually meant throughout ***P.L.103-227*** by *"challenging."* I also base this conclusion on the way Benjamin Bloom uses the word in his ***Taxonomy of Educational Objectives, Handbook II.*** In it he says: "A large part of what we call 'good teaching' is the teacher's ability to attain affective objectives through **challenging** the student's fixed beliefs." If ***GOALS 2000*** is deceptive about OBE (and it is), it seems likely this is more semantic deception. The *"emerging new methods, forms of assessments . . ."* is **an acknowledgment that OBE is now a classroom reality.** In 1993, the National Association of State Directors of Teacher Education and Certification (NASDTEC) adopted **outcome-based standards** and portfolio assessments **for elementary and**

middle school teachers and drafted a similar document for high schools. Teachers are now to be evaluated in the same manner they are expected to "assess" their students. The *"technologies"* include distance learning and, of course, greatly expanded use of computers in the classroom (another paradigm shift from the teacher-led classroom). **(See glossary entries: NASDTEC and Distance Learning.)**

> *(iii) States and school districts will create integrated strategies to attract, recruit, prepare, retrain, and support the continued professional development of teachers, administrators, and other educators, so that there is a highly talented work force of professional educators to teach challenging subject matter; and*

The framework is in place for entry-level teachers through the NASDTEC outcome-based standards. All those passing through teacher training programs in colleges will be taught content and methodology compatible with *GOALS 2000*. The *"teachers, administrators, and other educators"* already out there (a large work force) present the real challenge to *"retrain."* The *"integrated strategies"* of the state departments of education and individual districts will ensure that **all** teachers meet the new standards.

> *(iv) partnerships will be established, whenever possible, among local educational agencies, institutions of higher education, parents, and local labor, business, and professional associations to provide and support programs for the professional development of educators.*

"Partnerships" are one of the **key** concepts behind *GOALS 2000*. Like other oft-repeated key words, **"partnerships"** is used more than forty times in *P.L.103-227*. A seamless cloth is being woven to integrate education at all levels with business, with social services, with health services, and with the home. A trend that emerged in the 1980s was to ask businesses to pick up the tab on various public education expenses. The "sell" for this was that business has a vested interest in the product (the student/eventual worker), so assistance could be viewed as a sound investment and not a donation. **(See glossary: Partnerships and Lifelong Learning.)**

> *(5)* Mathematics and Science.*—(A) By the year 2000, United States students will be first in the world in mathematics and science achievement.*

Sounds good, but why were math and science singled out? Isn't this where we should be in every academic area?

> *(B) The objectives for this goal are that—*

> *(i) mathematics and science education, including the metric system of measurement, will be strengthened throughout the system, especially in the early grades.*

Does it strike you as strange that something as specific as "*the metric system of measurement*" is spelled out in a sketchy "framework" like this one? It makes sense if you accept the premise that we are heading for a global work force with interchangeably trained workers, and with most of the world using the metric system, the U.S. is out of step. Attempts made by schools in the 1970s to "go metric" were a big failure. Metrics will be pushed harder in the 1990s.

> *(ii) the number of teachers with a substantive background in mathematics and science, including the metric system of measurement, will increase by 50 percent; and*

The economic planners must be projecting a great need for workers with strong math and science backgrounds.

> *(iii) the number of United States undergraduate and graduate students, especially women and minorities, who complete degrees in mathematics, science, and engineering will increase significantly.*

There is no easy, quick way to increase the numbers of women and minorities completing degrees in these areas. There is, however, an easy, though unfair and unwise way to accomplish this; it's called quotas and affirmative action.

(6) ADULT LITERACY AND LIFELONG LEARNING.—*(A) By the year 2000, every adult American will be literate and will possess the knowledge and skills necessary to compete in a global economy and exercise the rights and responsibilities of citizenship.*

When the charge is made that ***GOALS 2000*** is not just about restructuring the public schools, but is, in fact, about restructuring society, one thinks of this goal. Once U.S. citizens have attained the legal age to drop out of school, what business is it of the government whether they are literate or have *"the knowledge and skills necessary to compete in a global economy"*? And if they aren't literate by the time they drop out or graduate, haven't the schools totally failed them? With this sixth goal, we're back to the overriding concern seen throughout ***P.L.103-227***—that of producing workers prepared for a global economy. **(See glossary: Lifelong Learning; and chronology: 47, 52, 63, 66, 68, and 72.)**

(B) The objectives for this goal are that—

(i) every major American business will be involved in strengthening the connection between education and work.

A great deal of education/labor coordination has already been accomplished. In 1991 (during the Bush years), the U.S. Department of Labor came out with a report, ***What Work Requires of Schools,*** put together by the Secretary's Commission on Achieving Necessary Skills (SCANS). Several passages in the SCANS report acknowledge that these "necessary skills" have been coordinated with ***AMERICA 2000*** (the never-adopted forerunner of ***GOALS 2000***). This part of the sixth goal will also be accomplished by Title 5 where we will see a National Skill Standards Board setting standards for the training and certification of workers. **(See chronology: 88, 92, 93, 96, 102, 107, 111, 112, 126, and 128.)**

(ii) all workers will have the opportunity to acquire the knowledge and skills, from basic to highly technical, needed to adapt to emerging new technologies, work methods, and markets through public

> *and private educational, vocational, technical, workplace, or other programs;*

This will be discussed more fully when we look at Title 5. As with teacher training, workers already have the opportunity to acquire knowledge and skills for workplace entry, advancement, or to change fields. However, **with the coming national skill standards and work cards (Certificates of Initial Mastery and Certificates of Advanced Mastery—CIMs and CAMs), people will be required to acquire government-approved training in order to enter or advance in various fields.** Does this sound closer to communism/socialism than a free market economy? Lifelong learning is not optional under a planned and centralized global economy. **Workers will be constantly retrained, reindoctrinated, and recycled according to the dictates of the central planners.**

> *(iii) the number of quality programs, including those at libraries, that are designed to serve more effectively the needs of the growing number of part-time and midcareer students will increase substantially;*

Libraries (including those in schools) will be used in lifelong learning centers.

> *(iv) the proportion of the qualified students, especially minorities, who enter college, who complete at least two years, and who complete their degree programs will increase substantially;*

This has been happening steadily since the mid-1960s. Will the process now be artificially accelerated?

> *(v) the proportion of college graduates who demonstrate an advanced ability to think critically, communicate effectively, and solve problems will increase substantially; and*

The SCANS report, ***What Work Requires of Schools,*** lists these skills as among the most sought after in the twenty-first century worker. Schools are de-emphasizing content and emphasizing instead how to think Socratically (posing a series of questions about problems), how to access knowledge (using technology), how to work effectively in groups (reaching consensus), how to communicate well, and how to adapt to change. **(See chronology: 102.)**

> *(vi) schools, in implementing comprehensive parent involvement programs, will offer more adult literacy, parent training and life-long learning opportunities to improve the ties between home and school, and enhance parents' work and home lives.*

"Comprehensive" or "all inclusive" parent involvement programs will do more than *"offer"* parent training, adult literacy, and lifelong learning opportunities. They will intrude into American homes, evaluate what they find there, and then prescribe "remedies" for perceived inadequacies. Whatever happened to the Fourth Amendment and "the right of the people to be secure in their persons, houses, papers, and effects, against unreasonable searches and seizures . . ."? Does the language here leave any doubt that this law goes far beyond restructuring the schools and moves every American regardless of age into a collectivist/socialist system and mindset.

> *(7) Safe, Disciplined, and Alcohol and Drug-Free Schools.—*

> *(A) By the year 2000, every school in the United States will be free of drugs, violence, and the unauthorized presence of firearms and alcohol and will offer a disciplined environment conducive to learning.*

What a laudable goal. We know, however, that absent a heart-change, this can only be accomplished by Draconian means. Money that should be spent on academic programs will be poured into "beefing up security." The substance abuse programs that have been in place in our schools for the last twenty years have not been successful or this goal wouldn't have been included. What then is the plan? More of the same? Under the guise of protecting innocent children from gun play, it seems likely that gun laws will be made more restrictive, further encroaching on the Second Amendment rights of citizens. Clearly, this will not keep guns out of the hands of gang members or anyone determined to be armed.

> *(B) The objectives for this goal are that—*

> *(i) every school will implement a firm and fair policy on use, possession, and distribution of drugs and alcohol;*

Alcohol use by minors is against the law and use of "street" drugs is illegal for everyone, so it's hard to imagine this hasn't already been done.

> *(ii) parents, businesses, governmental and community organizations will work together to ensure the rights of students to study in a safe and secure environment that is free of drugs and crime, and that schools provide a healthy environment and are a safe haven for all children;*

This is more **partnershipping**—creating the seamless societal cloth that everyone is woven into. Putting aside academic considerations for a moment, why would any parent send their child to a school (or anywhere) where their safety was in question? The ***"rights of students"*** sounds like a new entitlement and the basis for more lawsuits. The term ***"safe haven"*** is sometimes used in connection with schools that provide a "homophobia" free environment for homosexual students. Physical harm is not the only damage children may suffer in state schools.

> *(iii) every local educational agency will develop and implement a policy to ensure that all schools are free of violence and the unauthorized presence of weapons;*

With metal detectors at school entrances, students wearing bar-coded ID badges, "guards" patrolling the halls, and security personnel with walkie-talkies on the playground, many children must feel they are daily entering a fortified prison. **(See also Title 10—Part B.)**

(iv) every local educational agency will develop a sequential, comprehensive kindergarten through twelfth grade drug and alcohol prevention education program;

Unless the schools begin adopting tough, "Just say no!" prevention programs instead of the "drug awareness" programs that are currently offered, the problem is not going to go away or even diminish. Allowing for elaboration on three basic points—followed by a transparent bottom line—the message schools should be conveying is a very simple one: **"It's harmful to your body, mind, and spirit; it's illegal; it will prevent you from doing and being all you can be. Now what part of 'NO' don't you understand?"** Surely it doesn't take thirteen years to get that message across. **(See resources: McLemore on DARE.)**

There's a hidden agenda in these *"comprehensive"* health programs. Most of the substance abuse programs, including the best known and trusted, are equal parts of drug **information** (not the same as **prevention**); self-esteem; deciding what your own values are regarding drug and alcohol use (values clarification); group therapy (being encouraged to talk about yourself and others and discussing problems and feelings); assertiveness skills; and counseling and referrals for those the leader feels need additional therapy. **Drug and alcohol awareness is a whole package that involves a student's personal attitudes, values, and beliefs. The schools want access to those areas.** That's the **hidden agenda** and **that's why these programs must be "comprehensive" and extend over thirteen years.**

(v) drug and alcohol curriculum should be taught as an integral part of sequential, comprehensive health education;

Recall that ***"health education,"*** aka "family life education," is the misleading name for today's explicit sex education. This is a call to get sex ed and drug and alcohol ed integrated into one unified *"health education"* curriculum and to have it taught sequentially (one part building on the next) over the entire course of the school years. Like substance abuse ed, sex ed works perfectly as an instrument to probe the student's attitudes, values, and beliefs and the ***"comprehensive"*** aspect gives the state thirteen years to work on molding those values.

(vi) community-based teams should be organized to provide students and teachers with needed support; and

More **partnershipping** as people outside the school system (and unaccountable to parents) *"support"* the drug/alcohol/sex ed programs. Will this include groups such as Planned Parenthood coming into a school and making classroom or student assembly presentations? Will there be equal time for opposing points of view? And will the parents even know what is presented by people outside the school system?

(vii) every school should work to eliminate sexual harassment.

This is a political hot potato and few people could even agree on a definition of what sexual harassment is. Probably sexual harassment will be defined very broadly because that's a way of promoting a pro-feminist, pro-homosexual agenda and attacking the traditional family. **Strong families are a bulwark against totalitarian governments; that's why they're under such attack.** Sexual harassment should fit right into the attitudes, values, and beliefs being worked on in the "comprehensive" K–12 "health education."

8. Parental Participation.—

(A) By the year 2000, every school will promote partnerships that will increase parental involvement and participation in promoting the social, emotional, and academic growth of children.

The eighth goal, like the fourth (Teacher Education), is not one of the original six goals from the ***AMERICA 2000*** proposal. Along with Title 4 (the Parents as Teachers program), it has been added to the Clinton/Riley plan **to ensure that parents will be held accountable to standards set by the state.**

(B) The objectives for this Goal are that—

(i) every State will develop policies to assist local schools and local educational agencies to establish programs for increasing partner-

ships that respond to the varying needs of parents and the home, including parents of children who are disadvantaged or bilingual, or parents of children with disabilities;

See Title 4, the PAT program. I assume *"disadvantaged"* means economically disadvantaged, but because it is not spelled out, it could include many other categories that meet the government's evolving criteria. During the "melting pot" decades, having parents whose first language was something other than English was not considered a "risk" category, or even anything very unusual. Presumably *"disabilities"* means physical disabilities that would make it difficult for a student to participate in a "mainstream" (regular) classroom. But again, because it is vague, this could be interpreted in broad and novel ways. I have commented on the use of "disabilities" labeling paired with Medicaid in **Title 3 under (10)(D).**

(ii) every school will actively engage parents and families in a partnership which supports the academic work of children at home and shared educational decisionmaking at school; and

The use of the verb *"engage"* (which has a number of meanings) turns up frequently in the writing of sociologists and social workers. Two definitions of "engage" found in the *NLWD* are 1) to occupy the time of or compel the attention of; 2)(in warfare or other dispute) to come to grips with, attack; v.i. to join battle. Some combination of these two definitions probably comes closest to the actual intent of the school/home partnerships. **Parents who become "engaged" in a partnership with a school (or social service agency) have just entered into a potentially adversarial relationship with binding legal ramifications** and need to realize in the event of a difference of opinion, they are going to find themselves "up against the system." When asked to join a program, sign a contract, etc., parents need to ask themselves that key question: **To whom do these children belong?** To you or to the state? We can expect to see an increase in agreements, contracts, covenants, and other formal pieces of paper spelling out what you, as parents, agree to do and requiring your signature. This is not like signing for your child's report card or giving your permission for a field trip. These "partnership" devices may look innocent; they may even look like something you agree with and are already doing, but **you should not sign away (or even verbally assent to giving up) any basic rights and authority you have in your home,** making it easy for the government to enlarge its authority over you and your children. The government (and its many representatives) doesn't really want to "take" this authority from you; **they're hoping you will surrender it willingly.** Home/school partnerships should meet with many legal challenges from parents. As for *"shared educational decisionmaking at school,"* ask any parent who has ever been involved in a serious dispute with their child's school how much weight their opinion carried and if it was easy getting a fair hearing and satisfactory resolution.

> *(iii) parents and families will help to ensure that schools are adequately supported and will hold schools and teachers to high standards of accountability.*

This is the second time *"parents and families"* are treated as two separate entities. See (ii) above. Is this an acknowledgement of the many new definitions of "families," or does this simply mean that birth or custodial parents plus children, grandparents, and others living in the home and considered part of the family are all to be included in these partnerships? The centralization of power at the federal level and the many mandates resulting from this federalization of education will make it increasingly difficult for parents to hold schools, teachers, or anyone at the local level accountable. The stock answer to parent complaints will be, "We're just complying with Title such-and-such of the new *GOALS 2000* (or other federal) legislation and we really have no control over this." That answer will be, for the most part, truthful. The partnerships are a one-way street. Parents will be held accountable ***"to ensure that schools are adequately supported,"*** but exacting accountability from the schools will be another matter, as it already is.

Title 2—
National Education Reform Leadership, Standards, and Assessments

In which you will learn of two new school restructuring entities:

1. **The National Education Goals Panel (NEGP)**, whose primary function is to review and sit in final judgment on the new national content standards, the performance standards, opportunity-to-learn (O-T-L) standards, and state assessments. You will see that the NEGP is especially interested in looking at Early Childhood Assessment. The NEGP issues an annual "report card" and makes nominations to the President for appointments to the second (and closely related) restructuring body, the National Education Standards and Improvement Council.
2. **The National Education Standards and Improvement Council (NESIC)**, if funded by Congress, will "certify" the three new standards: Content, Performance, and O-T-L, as well as the state Assessments before passing them back to the NEGP for final approval. The NESIC will periodically review standards and assessments to identify areas that need development or change.

The third area covered in Title 2, is **Leadership in Educational Technology**, in which you will learn of the plan to develop a coordinated national strategy to infuse technology into all educational planning, programs, and functions at the state and local level.

TITLE 2— NATIONAL EDUCATION REFORM LEADERSHIP, STANDARDS, AND ASSESSMENTS

PART A—NATIONAL EDUCATION GOALS PANEL

SEC. 201. PURPOSE.

It is the purpose of this part to establish a bipartisan mechanism for—

(1) building a national consensus for education improvement;

The consensus on what needed (and still needs) to be done for *"education improvement"* should have been a lengthy national debate, **with the public invited.** Since that was not the case, there will be instead a considerable public relations effort to "sell" what the government has decided to go ahead and do. **(See glossary: Community Action Toolkit.)**

(2) reporting on progress toward achieving the National Education Goals; and

The so-called annual "national report card."

(3) reviewing the voluntary national content standards, voluntary national student performance standards and voluntary national opportunity-to-learn standards certified by the National Education Standards and Improvement Council, as well as the criteria for the

> *certification of such standards, and the criteria for the certification of State assessments certified by the National Education Standards and Improvement Council, with the option of disapproving such standards and criteria not later than 90 days after receipt from such Council.*

If they can "disapprove," they obviously can approve as well. This is set up to be a powerful panel; the buck stops here on the national curriculum, performance standards (benchmarking), assessments, and O-T-L standards. This is the first time in our nation's history we have permitted the federal government to set the entire philosophy and direction of public education. In a diverse country like ours, will **anyone** be entirely pleased with the result? With a history of ignoring the concerns and complaints of Christian parents at the local level, the prospect of being under federal directives is extremely discouraging. If parents have concerns, there will be no local official they can go to; they will have to address their complaints to unelected panel members or other faceless bureaucrats in Washington.

As this goes to press (early 1996) the National Education Standards and Improvement Council (NESIC) has failed to get funding and no members have been appointed. However, the NEGP may simply absorb the "essential" work of NESIC—which is the likely short-term scenario.

> SEC. 202. NATIONAL EDUCATION GOALS PANEL.

Under this part the National Education Goals Panel (NEGP), an organization created in 1990 as a presidential advisory body (serviced by DOE), is set up as an official entity of the federal government. Almost five pages (sections 202–207) are devoted to the composition, appointment rules, duties, powers, rules for meeting, appointment of a director and other paid staff, and there is a final section on Early Childhood Assessment.

Facts about the NEGP

Composition

Eighteen members from both political parties. The current panel consists of eight governors (five Republicans and three Democrats), two members appointed by the President, including the secretary of education; four members of Congress (two R and two D); and four state legislators (two R and two D).

Duties

Those spelled out in Section 201 above. The annual report is to be in a form *"understandable to parents and the general public."* The NEGP will also submit to the President nominations for appointment to the National Education Standards and Improvement Council.

Powers

Conduct hearings *"to receive reports, views, and analyses of a broad spectrum of experts and the public"* on the establishment of content, performance, and opportunity-to-learn (O-T-L) standards and state assessments. They may make contracts to compile and analyze data for the panel's use.

Meetings

NEGP to meet on a regular basis (not spelled out). The public is to have access to transcripts of proceedings (other than personnel and internal management matters) at a reasonable cost.

Director and Staff

Provision is made for a director paid at a *"rate not to exceed the rate of basic pay payable for level V of the Executive Schedule"* ($108,200 per annum). In addition, the director may appoint four staff employees to be paid a rate that does not exceed *"the maximum rate of basic pay payable for GS-15 of the General Schedule"* (assuming step 1: a minimum of $67,941 per annum). The director is empowered to appoint *"additional employees to serve as staff"* (no number given), may procure *"temporary and intermittent services of experts and consultants"* and upon request of the panel may detail any personnel of any federal department or agency to assist the panel in its duties.

Early Childhood Assessment

Within the panel are Resource and Technical Planning Groups on

School Readiness (**"Groups"**) *"to improve the methods of assessing the readiness of children for school that would lead to alternatives to currently used early childhood assessments."* Activities the groups will engage in are listed as:

> *(1) develop a model of elements of school readiness that address a broad range of early childhood developmental needs, including the needs of children with disabilities;*
>
> *(2) create clear guidelines regarding the nature, functions, and uses of early childhood assessments, including assessment formats that are appropriate for use in culturally and linguistically diverse communities, based on model elements of school readiness;*
>
> *(3) monitor and evaluate early childhood assessments including the ability of existing assessments to provide valid information on the readiness of children for school; and*
>
> *(4) monitor and report on the long-term collection of data on the status of young children to improve policy and practice, including the need for new sources of data necessary to assess the broad range of early childhood developmental needs.*

Since the National Education Goals have been formulated (at least for now), and this is the only "agenda item" spelled out in detail, it seems reasonable to assume that the NEGP is going to focus a great deal of its attention on *"early childhood assessments"* of school readiness. Clearly the "groups" are not happy with the current status of early childhood assessments, thus it would not be surprising if a ninth goal relating to early testing of all children emerges from their study. **The continued existence of the NEGP suggests that the list of six National Education Goals (under Bush) which became eight (under Clinton) may, over time, become even longer. Recall that *GOALS 2000* is only a "framework," and as such, invites addition and "filling in."**

The NEGP issues an annual report and ***Education Week*** (11/8/95) in an article entitled **"Goals Progress Report Shows Mixed Results"** states according to the latest report, "that objective [the goals which were to have been met by the year 2000] remain far out of reach." This is the fifth report put out by the NEGP; it tracks forty-three "indicators" of progress toward the goals. According to the *EW* article, "Progress was noted on seven points, a decline on seven others, and no meaningful difference was found for twelve. No comparable data is available to update the other seventeen statistics."

In summary, the NEGP is an appointed (not elected) body that has been given the "political plum" of this temporary appointment. In all likelihood, the yeoman's work is being done by the paid staff including the consultants they bring in, and the busy panel members will tend to accept the recommendations of these "subject experts" when they come together as a voting body. Despite the fact that the National Education Goals have been set and are now a part of ***P.L. 103-227***, and the real work of the panel should be already accomplished, **it looks as though this panel is taking on a life of its own and will become another self-perpetuating agency of the federal government.**

PART B—NATIONAL EDUCATION STANDARDS AND IMPROVEMENT COUNCIL

SEC. 211. PURPOSE.

It is the purpose of this part to establish a mechanism to—

(1) certify and periodically review voluntary national content standards and voluntary national student performance standards that define what all students should know and be able to do;

The term "national" rather than "federal" is a bit of semantic sleight of hand. Translation: Establish and put an official stamp of approval on the national/federal content standards (curriculum) and performance standards (benchmarks or reference points for making measurements, i.e., "How good is good enough?") that define *"what all students should know and be able to do."* This last phrase is **classic OBE-ese**. The *"be able to do"* is necessary in a system that will be based not on percentages or letter grades, but on "authentic assessments," "performances," "portfolios," and other novel ways of testing, consistent with OBE.

The *"national **content** standards"* are those prepared by private organizations (previously described in the introduction to the text of ***P.L.103-227,*** Sec. 3(4)). The *"national student **performance** standards,"* are described in ***Education Week*** (11/22/95). In her article, **"14-State Reform Project Releases Draft Standards,"** Karen Diegmueller described the **performance standards** prepared by the New Standards Project (NSP). She tells us that

> . . . a three-volume set of draft academic-performance standards . . . will be distributed in the coming weeks for review and comment. The draft standards and the samples of student work that accompany them mark another milestone for the **New Standards Project,** a group of researchers and policy specialists working **to define and identify just how well students meet high academic standards and to create a matching national examination system**. . . . New Standards leaders set out to produce performance standards and assessments for English-language arts, mathematics, science, and applied learning that students would have to meet by the end of the 4th, 8th, and 10th grades. . . . Numerous voluntary national content standards have been rolled out over the past nineteen months that describe what students should know and be able to do in individual academic disciplines. The New Standards Project's newly unveiled **performance standards, however, were designed to specify how students must demonstrate their knowledge and skills and at what level. In standards-setting parlance, it is known as "how good is good enough."** Each volume is by grade level . . . and contains the performance standards for the three disciplines, plus applied learning. In addition, student work samples illustrate specific performance tasks. The samples include commentary explaining how the student satisfied or did not satisfy the standard. Notes in the margin throughout the volumes refer readers to **international benchmarks for academic achievement** and other standards documents.

Though the ordering of presentation differs from the content standards, Elizabeth K. Stage of the NSP makes clear that "we've made a concerted effort to make sure that we're not creating another set of standards. . . . It's a matter of reordering the heading instead of changing the substance" (emphasis added). **(See chronology: 88, 101, and 107.)**

> *(2) certify State content standards and State student performance standards submitted by States on a voluntary basis, if such standards are comparable or higher in rigor and quality to the voluntary national content standards and voluntary national student performance standards certified by the National Education Standards and Improvement Council;*

Though the word ***"voluntary"*** is used three times, the intent is just the opposite when you realize that states not in compliance with the goals and objectives of *P.L.103-227* will no longer be eligible for monies under the *ESEA* and other legislation that's been tied to *GOALS 2000*. It's ***"voluntary"*** as long as a state doesn't care if it receives federal aid to education.

> *(3) certify and periodically review voluntary national opportunity-to-learn standards that describe the conditions of teaching and learning necessary for all students to have a fair opportunity to achieve the knowledge and skills described in the voluntary national content standards and the voluntary national student performance standards certified by the National Education Standards and Improvement Council;*

Set the O-T-L standards that are meshed with the curriculum and benchmarks. **(See glossary: O-T-L.)**

> *(4) certify opportunity-to-learn standards submitted by States on a voluntary basis, if such standards are comparable or higher in rigor and quality to the voluntary national opportunity-to-learn standards certified by the National Education Standards and Improvement Council; and*

See comments under (2) above.

(5) certify State assessments submitted by States or groups of States on a voluntary basis, if such assessments—

Because of the expense of creating new assessments, states will be permitted to form groups or consortia to work on tests together. This collaboration will have the effect of producing very similar tests from state to state.

(A) are aligned with and support State content standards certified by such Council; and

(B) are valid, reliable, and consistent with relevant, nationally recognized, professional and technical standards for assessment when used for their intended purposes.

In other words, they'll all pretty much follow the same formula. The NESIC will allow for individual or regional differences as long as all the basic requirements of *GOALS 2000* are met. **This promotes the fiction that these are not "top down" directives.**

Following the purpose are twelve pages on the workings of the National Education Standards and Improvement Council (NESIC). Sections covered are:

Establishment:

The NESIC is to be composed of nineteen members appointed by the President. Members are to come from both political parties, are to represent the country geographically and *"reflect the diversity of the United States with regard to race, ethnicity, gender, and disability characteristics,"* and represent a broad spectrum of interests, including professional educators, education experts, business and industry (including organized labor), the public (including representatives of advocacy, civil rights, and disability groups), parents, state and civic leaders—to name some, though not all of the suggested candidates.

Members have not been appointed and NESIC is not operational. The guess is (early 1996) that NESIC may never be activated. This good news, however, will do little, if anything, to slow the full enactment of *GOALS 2000*. And a differently composed Congress could always breathe life back into this council.

Duties:

The primary duties are to identify areas in which national content, performance, and O-T-L standards need to be developed, certify such standards when they are developed, forward them on to the NEGP for approval, and set up a process for periodically reviewing standards. They are also to certify state assessments for a period not to exceed five years. Criteria listed for standards [Sec. 213 (a)(2)(i)], are that they ***"are internationally competitive and comparable to the best in the world,"*** and that they are to be developed through *"an open and public process"* that *"provides for the input and involvement"* of many interested people, including teachers, parents, students, employers, postsecondary institutions, the public, and advocacy groups. With a lineup like that there is no way the process would not be politicized. Considerable space is given to the O-T-L standards (one of the most controversial aspects and one of the main reasons many Republicans wanted to do away with the council.) **O-T-L standards,** as spelled out in Section 213(c)(2) **will be very costly to implement. The seven areas that all schools will sooner or later have to be equal in are:**

> *(A) the quality and availability to all students of curricula, instructional materials, and technologies, including distance learning;*
>
> *(B) the capability of teachers to provide high-quality instruction to meet diverse learning needs in each content area to all students;*
>
> *(C) the extent to which teachers, principals, and administrators have ready and continuing access to professional development, including the best knowledge about teaching, learning, and school improvement;*
>
> *(D) the extent to which curriculum, instructional practices, and assessments are aligned to voluntary national content standards;*
>
> *(E) the extent to which school facilities provide a safe and secure environment for learning and instruction and have the requisite libraries, laboratories, and other resources necessary to provide an opportunity-to-learn;*

> *(F) the extent to which schools utilize policies, curricula, and instructional practices which ensure non-discrimination on the basis of gender; and*
>
> *(G) other factors that the Council deems appropriate to ensure that all students receive a fair opportunity to achieve the knowledge and skills described in the voluntary national content standards and the voluntary national student performance standards certified by the Council.*

To address the above, the council is charged with finding out what other countries are doing in these O-T-L areas—the international dimension of ***GOALS 2000*** again. They are also charged with certifying state standards in all three areas (content, performance, and O-T-L).

State assessments are covered in Section 213(5)(f). The main purposes of the assessments are listed: providing information about the progress of students toward the standards; improving classroom instruction and learning outcomes; exemplifying the kinds and levels of achievement that should be expected of all students, including the identification of state performance standards; measuring individual students, schools, districts, states, and the nation as a whole; and assisting education policymakers in making decisions about education programs.

The council will only certify state assessments if a state can demonstrate that all students have been prepared in the content areas being assessed; that assessments will not be used to make decisions regarding graduation, promotion, or retention (high stakes testing) until the year 1999; and that the state has submitted various information about the purposes and validity of the tests and that tests are aligned with the state content standards. States must further show tests are free of discrimination, include all students, and provide for the adaptations and accommodations necessary to permit the participation of all students with diverse learning needs.

There's so much going on in Section 213(5)(f), let's stop and unpack it before moving on. What does it mean for testing if a state has to show that **all** students have been prepared in **all** the required content areas and assessed with tests free from discrimination that are sufficiently adapted to accommodate students with diverse learning needs? (Remember this includes physically handicapped, children for whom English is not their first language, multicultural and gender considerations, students in special ed classes because of a variety of learning or behavior problems, etc.) To meet all the criteria given, **the test will have to be watered down, i.e. "deliberately dumbed-down," (DDD)** and, of course, show the proper amount of political correctness to satisfy all the diverse elements. **One of the fatal flaws of the *GOALS 2000* restructuring scheme is the underlying deception that "all" can learn to a high standard.** Because of differences in native ability, motivation, and many other factors, the only material that **all** children can learn is going to be the lowest common denominator variety (the triple-D curriculum). To say otherwise is to wishfully deny the obvious. **How can the United States hope to be internationally competitive with one standard—and that one set low to accommodate everyone?** This section also tells us that only states that have aligned their assessments with the content will be certified. This guarantees that, working backward from what is expected on the test, teachers will be obliged to **"teach to the test,"** or spend most of their classroom time on whatever will ensure passing scores. We are told here for the first time that the tests will be **"high stakes,"** (pass/fail, graduate/stay back) **in five years.** It is only natural that teachers will teach to these high stakes tests. After all, they, too, are going to be held accountable for test scores.

In the next section, **Performance of Duties,** the law spells out the various inputs and collaborations necessary for the council to do its work. The third point listed is:

> *(3) establish cooperative arrangements with the National Skill Standards Board to promote the coordination of the development of content and student performance standards under this title with the development of skill standards under title 5 of this Act;*

Because the current educational restructuring movement is labor-driven, skills "training" replaces "education"! In her report, ***Educational Restructuring,*** researcher Judy McLemore gives an interesting quote by Peter Shaw, of the National Association of Scholars. In his article, **"The Competitiveness Illusion—Does Our Country Need to be Literate in Order to be Competitive? If Not, Why Read?"** appearing in the January 18, 1993, ***National Review,*** Shaw says:

> **The technological society does not particularly depend on education. . . . Technological society turns out to work in the opposite way from that usually supposed: namely by actually requiring less rather than more education of its workers. This is because modern industry depends on reducing human error, which means reducing dependence on the individual worker's expertise and judgment. . . .**

That is why "training" skilled workers in areas government planners project they will be needed has far more value to the state's planned economy than broadly **"educating"** children in basic areas of knowledge that can then be applied anywhere the individual decides he wants to use them (the way your education was). **This is one of the basic paradigm shifts in *GOALS 2000*. (See chronology: 64, 66, 89, 91, 92, 96, 102, 107, 111, 112, and 128.)**

The council, like the NEG panel will issue an annual report, hold hearings, publish its proposed criteria in the ***Federal Register,*** and meet on a regular basis, with transcripts available to the public. The paid staff will consist of a director and staff hired and paid according to the same guidelines spelled out for the NEGP.

The final sections concern grants. The secretary of education is authorized to award opportunity-to-learn grants to consortia of individuals and organizations to develop O-T-L standards and to develop a listing of model programs. It is thought that consortia (with expenses shared) will encourage participation. The purpose of these standards and listings is to:

> *(A) provide all students with an opportunity to learn;*
>
> *(B) assess the capacity and performance of individual schools; and*
>
> *(C) develop appropriate actions to be taken in the event that the schools fail to achieve such standards.*

Regarding (C), does this look like litigation waiting to happen? Schools that don't measure up (or shape up) will be the target of equity lawsuits, giving the state justification for moving in and taking them over, as has happened in Paterson, Newark, and Jersey City, New Jersey.

The secretary is also authorized to make grants to state and local educational agencies or consortia to develop, field test, and evaluate state assessments. Such grants are required to:

> *(A) examine the validity and reliability of the State assessment for the particular purposes for which such assessment was developed;*
>
> *(B) ensure that the State assessment is consistent with relevant, nationally recognized professional and technical standards for assessments; and*
>
> *(C) devote special attention to how a State assessment treats all students, especially with regard to the race, gender, ethnicity, disability, and language proficiency of such students.*

The secretary is additionally authorized to make a grant to the National Academy of Sciences or the National Academy of Education to evaluate the work of the NEGP and the council.

PART C—LEADERSHIP IN EDUCATIONAL TECHNOLOGY

SEC. 231. PURPOSE.

It is the purpose of this part to promote achievement of the National Education Goals and—

(1) to provide leadership at the Federal level, through the Department of Education, by developing a national vision and strategy—

(A) to infuse technology and technology planning into all educational programs and training functions carried out within school systems at the State and local level;

Because of the widespread use of computers and other "high tech" equipment in business and industry, it has become inevitable and necessary to have more "hands-on" opportunities for students with technology. (A) begins, *"to infuse . . ."* and although the sense of this is clear, as used here, "infusion" is an interesting educational technique worthy of a closer look. **(See glossary: Infusion Model).**

> *(B) to coordinate educational technology activities among the related Federal and State departments or agencies, industry leaders, and interested educational and parental organizations;*

Will the *"interested educational and parental organizations"* include only the usual establishment organizations, or will grassroots parent groups be included?

> *(C) to establish working guidelines to ensure maximum interoperability nationwide and ease of access for the emerging technologies so that no school system will be excluded from the technological revolution; and*
>
> *(D) to ensure that Federal technology-related policies and programs facilitate the use of technology in education;*

Will there be waivers, tax breaks, and other dollar incentives to encourage facilitation? This will certainly be a growth industry as more and more technology is placed in the schools. California is primed to be one of the states leading the way. According to an article, **"Clinton Calls for National Education-Technology Effort,"** appearing in ***Education Week,*** September 27, 1995:

> Capping off a series of campaign-style appearances in California last week, President Clinton called for the formation of **public-private partnerships to ensure that every American classroom is connected to the Internet by 2000.** Saying it could serve as a model for the nation, the president announced a new private-sector project to link all of California schools to the information highway by the end of the current school year. . . . Under the plan announced last week,

an alliance of more than 50 information-technology companies has pledged that by the end of the current school year, all 12,000 public schools in California will have access to the Internet via modem or direct high speed connections. One-fifth of the schools will be wired into local networks as well. The school will also receive free access to America Online, a national commercial on-line service and AT&T has promised to provide voice-mail services. Among other companies participating in the partnership are Sun Microsystems Inc., Apple Computer Inc., Oracle Systems Corp., 3Com Corp., Silicon Graphics Inc., Applied Materials Inc., Tele-Communications Inc., and Cisco Systems Inc. No estimates of the project cost were available. (Emphasis added)

(2) to promote awareness of the potential of technology for improving teaching and learning;

(3) to support State and local efforts to increase the effective use of technology for education;

(4) to demonstrate ways in which technology can be used to improve teaching and learning, and to help ensure that all students have an equal opportunity to meet State education standards;

Availability and quality of technology will be used as one of the criteria of "equity" under O-T-L standards.

(5) to ensure the availability and dissemination of knowledge (drawn from research and experience) that can form the basis for sound State and local decisions about investment in, and effective uses of, educational technology;

(6) to promote high-quality professional development opportunities for teachers and administrators regarding the integration of technology into instruction and administration;

Let's not forget the expense of training teachers and other staff as technology comes of age in the classroom.

(7) to promote the effective uses of technology in existing Federal education programs, such as chapter 1 of title 1 of the Elementary and Secondary Education Act of 1965 and vocational education programs; and

(8) to monitor advancements in technology to encourage the development of effective educational uses of technology.

SEC. 232. FEDERAL LEADERSHIP.

This section calls for collaboration between the Department of Education, the Office of Science and Technology Policy, the National Science Foundation, the Department of Commerce, the Department of Energy, and National Aeronautics and Space Administration, *"and other appropriate Federal departments or agencies"* to formulate a national long-range technology plan.

The purposes of this plan include:

(A) how the Secretary will encourage the effective use of technology to provide all students the opportunity to achieve State content standards and State student performance standards, especially through programs administered by the Department of Education;

This asks: how can technology be used in curriculum, benchmarking, and O-T-L standards? Technology, of course, is a neutral tool. It's only a delivery system and becomes good or bad depending on what it's delivering. We learned that from our experience with television and are relearning it with the information superhighway. We need to be more concerned about the "content" of distance learning, auto-tutorial computer programs, and various other forms of technology in the classroom than with the use of the technology itself. Programs *"administered by the Department of Education"* is probably a reference to those "validated" for dissemination by the National Diffusion Network. **(See glossary: National Diffusion Network.)**

(B) joint activities in support of the overall national technology policy with other Federal departments or agencies, such as the Of-

fice of Science and Technology Policy, the National Endowment for the Humanities, the National Endowment for the Arts, the National Aeronautics and Space Administration, the National Science Foundation, and the Departments of Commerce, Energy, Health and Human Services, and Labor—

The national long-range technology plan called for in Section 232 is one of many ***GOALS 2000*** partnerships. **This sort of bureaucratic "central planning" has always been a hallmark of the socialist/communist states where nothing is left to chance, but usually doesn't function properly anyway.** Recall the Soviet "Five-Year Plans."

(i) to promote the use of technology in education, and training and lifelong learning, including plans for the educational uses of a national information infrastructure; and

Part of the *"national information infrastructure"* crucial to lifelong learning will be a national databank following the academic progress of all citizens from first entry (birth/social security number) through various levels of schooling and training (Certificates of Initial Mastery/Certificates of Advanced Mastery) through final entries (retirement entitlements/death). This is an example of a very dangerous use of technology that we should be enormously concerned about—the documenting and tracking of U.S. citizens cradle to grave. **(See chronology: 31, 44, 74, 115, 122, and 126; and glossary: Lifelong Learning and NCES.)**

(ii) to ensure that the policies and programs of such departments or agencies facilitate the use of technology for educational purposes, to the extent feasible;

(C) how the Secretary will work with educators, State and local educational agencies, and appropriate representatives of the private sector to facilitate the effective use of technology in education;

(D) how the Secretary will promote—

(i) higher achievement of all students through the integration of technology into the curriculum;

Will this prove to be the case? Will the enormous costs for bringing technology into the classroom pay off in *"higher achievement"* or just provide the government with more control over our lives?

> *(ii) increased access to the benefits of technology for teaching and learning for schools with a high concentration of children from low-income families.*

Technology appears to be an area where O-T-L standards will be strictly applied.

> *(iii) the use of technology to assist in the implementation of State systemic reform strategies;*

This is another area where the collection of data on students, teachers, schools, districts, and state to state comparisons will likely be used (and misused) in the name of "systemic reform."

> *(iv) the application of technological advances to use in education; and*

> *(v) increased opportunities for the professional development of teachers in the use of new technologies;*

> *(E) how the Secretary will determine, in consultation with appropriate individuals, organizations, industries, and agencies the feasibility and desirability of establishing guidelines to facilitate an easy exchange of data and effective use of technology in education;*

Another red flag item! The ***"easy exchange of data"*** between education and ***"appropriate individuals, organizations, industries, and agencies"*** will be accomplished by electronic access to a student's (and later worker's) data file, the "electronic portfolio." Without the extensive use of technology in the schools (in this case, computerized cumulative records), it would be impossible to track citizens in the way the federal government, acting as a Soviet-style Central Planning Committee, needs to do in order to plan, implement, budget for, and adjust in a continuous loop what it requires of its citizens. Without this control and tracking mechanism, the United States cannot be turned into a socialist state—a necessary transitional phase on the way to the one-world system. **(See chronology: 31, 44, 74, 115, 122, and 126; and glossary: PPBS, TQM, ISO 9000, and NCES.)**

> *(F) how the Secretary will utilize the outcome of the evaluation undertaken pursuant to section 908 of the Star Schools Program Assistance Act to promote the purposes of this part; and*

The Star Schools Program is a "distance learning" program funded by the DOE and administered by its Office of Educational Research and Improvement. **(See Title 9, Part F; and glossary: Distance Learning and Star Schools.)**

> *(G) the Secretary's long-range measurable goals and objectives relating to the purposes of this part.*

Section 216 calls for the creation of a new Office of Educational Technology (OET) within the Department of Education to carry out the functions and purposes spelled out in Part C above. A preexisting Office of Training Technology Transfer (established in 1988) is merged into the new OET (Sec. 236). The OET is to issue biennial reports to the public regarding: the uses of technology in elementary and secondary education throughout the United States upon which private businesses and federal, state, and local governments may rely for decisionmaking about the need for, and provision of, appropriate technologies in schools, by using, to the extent possible, existing information and resources.

> **PART D—AUTHORIZATION OF APPROPRIATIONS**
>
> **SEC. 241. AUTHORIZATION OF APPROPRIATIONS.**
>
> *(a) NATIONAL EDUCATION GOALS PANEL.—There are authorized to be appropriated $3,000,000 for fiscal year 1994, and such sums as may be necessary for each of the four succeeding fiscal years, to carry out part A of this title.*

(b) NATIONAL EDUCATION STANDARDS AND IMPROVEMENT COUNCIL.—*There are authorized to be appropriated $3,000,000 for fiscal year 1994, and such sums as may be necessary for each of the fiscal years 1995 through 1998, to carry out part B of this title.*

(c) OPPORTUNITY-TO-LEARN DEVELOPMENT GRANTS.—*There are authorized to be appropriated $2,000,000 for fiscal year 1994, and such sums as may be necessary for fiscal year 1995, to carry out section 219.*

(d) ASSESSMENT DEVELOPMENT AND EVALUATION GRANTS.—*There are authorized to be appropriated $5,000,000 for fiscal year 1994, and such sums as may be necessary for each of the 4 succeeding fiscal years, to carry out section 220.*

Count on *"such sums as may be necessary,"* being at least as much—and usually more—than originally specified. The total on this part of *GOALS 2000* alone is $13,000,000 **for the first year.**

Title 3— State and Local Education Systemic Improvement

A lengthy title, in which you will find the government calling for:

1. **Systemic changes** to the schools, so extensive and pervasive, they will **ultimately restructure all of society.**
2. States to draw up **Systemwide Improvement Plans (SIPs)** that have:
   - A. "coordinated access" of childcare, early childhood education, health care, nutrition, social services, and educational services for "all" students and families.
   - B. identified rules and regulations impeding coordination and other desired changes and that have made provision for waivers.
   - C. alignment with the *GOALS 2000* content, performance, O-T-L standards, and assessments.
   - D. effective mechanisms to get students into the work force, with an emphasis on vocational education and apprenticeships and that align with federal school-to-work programs.
   - E. a process for "improving" the state's system of teacher/administration preparation and licensure, as well as continuing professional development programs.
   - F. a major public and private mobilization effort involving broad-based community support, with an emphasis on parents' role and responsibilities.
3. Businesses to enter into **partnerships** with schools.

4. **Lifelong learning** (a radical, key element in *GOALS 2000*).
5. Grants for SIPs to promote the use of technology, with an emphasis on how this will enhance the sixth National Education Goal (Adult Literacy/Lifelong Learning).

TITLE 3— STATE AND LOCAL EDUCATION SYSTEMIC IMPROVEMENT

SEC. 301. FINDINGS

The Congress finds that—

(1) all students can learn and achieve to high standards and must realize their potential if the United States is to prosper;

There are two faulty assumptions here: 1) that ***"all"*** students can learn and achieve to ***"high standards."*** If that were so, children would not be tracked, placed in special ed classes, etc. Of course, all children should be encouraged to reach their full potential, whatever that is, but it obviously won't be the same for all children. 2) The second faulty assumption is that if this egalitarian dream isn't realized the U.S. will fail to prosper. In the first half of this century when students were given a solid foundation in the basic skills and core subjects (and little else), reaching one's full potential in a free market economy was theoretically available to everyone willing to work hard enough to overcome whatever obstacles of poverty, race, etc. stood in the way. It would be hard to argue that because some never reached their full potential that the United States as a whole has failed to prosper. The educrats and social planners behind ***GOALS 2000*** are not interested in individual potential. Statements about individuals are a smoke-screen to obscure the fact they are looking at our children collectively as "human capital" and little more than economic pawns to be moved around on the global chessboard.

(2) the reforms in education from 1977 through 1992 have achieved

some good results, but such reform efforts often have been limited to a few schools or to a single part of the educational system;

Presumably 1977 is mentioned because Jimmy Carter was President then and during his tenure, the Office of Education became elevated to a cabinet-level Department of Education (1979). Interestingly, in light of the "good results" cited above, during this fifteen-year period, in 1983, the government-sponsored report, ***A Nation at Risk,*** made the assertion that if a foreign power had done to our educational system what's been done, we might consider it an act of war. **(See chronology: 70 and 76.)**

(3) leadership must come from teachers, related services personnel, principals, and parents in individual schools, and from policymakers at the local, State, tribal, and national levels, in order for lasting improvements in student performance to occur;

A broad-based, bottom up consensus should have been obtained, so why was *GOALS 2000* rushed through the Congress with no public debate, let alone agreement? Implying that local input is sought and valued does not make it so. The federal government wants desperately for parents and other "locals" to get behind their *fait accompli* and make it work. **(See glossary: Community Action Toolkit.)**

(4) simultaneous top-down and bottom-up education reform is necessary to spur creative and innovative approaches by individual schools to help all students achieve internationally competitive standards;

There is no "bottom-up" in school restructuring. The federal government is handing down to every state the same framework they have determined will be ***"internationally competitive."*** Sure the states can individualize somewhat in how they fill in that framework, but only those states meeting the national education goals and standards will receive the official stamp of approval (federal money).

(5) strategies must be developed by communities and States to sup-

> *port the revitalization of all local public schools by fundamentally changing the entire system of public education through comprehensive, coherent, and coordinated improvement in order to increase student learning;*

Systemic change (*"changing the entire system"*) is **total change,** not piecemeal or cosmetic alterations—**every school a *GOALS 2000* school.** *"To increase student learning"*? That would be nice, but this is really about getting PPBS/TQM management strategies and lifelong learning in place, i.e., **restructuring the schools to restructure society. (See chronology: 32, 39, 45, 47, 52, 63, 72, 101, and 118; and glossary: PPBS, TQM, and ISO 9000.)**

> *(6) parents, teachers, and other local educators, and business, community, and tribal leaders must be involved in developing systemwide improvement strategies that reflect the needs of their individual communities;*

The reasoning goes: "People value what they feel ownership in." The only problem is the involvement will be the **controlled involvement** of facilitated planning committees, site-based management teams, and similar tightly reined groups. **(See chronology: 100; and glossary: Delphi Technique, Facilitator/Facilitation, and SBM.)**

> *(7) State and local education improvement efforts must incorporate strategies for providing all students and families with coordinated access to appropriate social services, health care, nutrition, and early childhood education, and child care to remove preventable barriers to learning and enhance school readiness for all students;*

"Coordinated access" is the marriage of schools, health care, and social workers. More and earlier intrusions into American homes.

> *(8) States and local educational agencies, working together, must immediately set about developing and implementing such systemwide improvement strategies if our Nation is to educate all children to*

meet their full potential and achieve the National Education Goals described in title 1;

"Immediately" is the operative word. For the first time since the passage of the ***ESEA,*** states will no longer receive the monies they have gotten accustomed to receiving over the past thirty years under ***ESEA*** until they show they are ***GOALS 2000*** states or hard at work attaining that status.

(9) State and local systemic improvement strategies must provide all students with effective mechanisms and appropriate paths to the work force as well as to higher education;

Since ***GOALS 2000*** is labor-driven, expect to see a major emphasis on vocational/technical education in this legislation. In Title 5 we'll see how this is to be accomplished.

(10) businesses should be encouraged—

(A) to enter into partnerships with schools;

This trend has been picking up steam since the 1980s. The November 8, 1995, issue of ***Education Week*** carried a notice of a $25,000,000 "Reinventing Education" initiative funded by IBM. The latest recipient of IBM's largesse ($2,000,000) is Broward County, Florida. The article states: "The Florida district will use the gift to create an integrated data system to keep track of student records, budgets, and other information. IBM will also help Broward officials use technologies such as 'data mining' to analyze large amounts of database information rapidly and efficiently."

(B) to provide information and guidance to schools based on the needs of area businesses for properly educated graduates in general and on the need for particular workplace skills that the schools may provide;

Proof that ***GOALS 2000*** is labor-driven exists in a number of U.S.

Labor Department reports, including one issued in 1991, whose title gives it away: ***What Work Requires of Schools: A SCANS Report for AMERICA 2000***. **(See chronology: 88, 92, 93, 96, 102, 107, 111, 112, 126, and 128.)**

> *(C) to provide necessary education and training materials and support; and*

A fairly recent trend is coaxing businesses into picking up some of the costs (*"support"*) for what were previously strictly tax-funded school expenses. The argument goes that since businesses will benefit from better turned-out graduates, they can't afford not to "invest" in the schools.

> *(D) to continue the lifelong learning process throughout the employment years of an individual;*

This law is addressing **you**! If a society is to be centrally planned and controlled, it will be necessary to keep close tabs on where everyone is and what their current state of employability (usefulness) is. Data on each individual from birth, through various levels of education and training (CIMs and CAMs), along with other records, is essential for tracking and planning. With the cross-referencing of data so easily accomplished by computers, it will be easy to maintain a cumulative record on everyone. This dossier would contain not only education and employment data, but also a full history of military service, criminal record, marriages, divorces, children, credit history, motor vehicle records, health records, insurance, **and anything else of potential interest to the government.** The health insurance plan, complete with "smart card" that was pushed so aggressively during the first part of Clinton's tenure was an obvious way to get this tracking system set up—**something desirable (health benefits) paired with something undesirable (tracking).**

Researcher Anita Hoge has written of tracking coming into Pennsylvania schools under expanded Medicaid coverage. She reports that through early screening and diagnosis, as well as by labeling students who do not meet state outcomes "disabled," states can tap into Medicaid funds under **special education.** Apparently income eligibility has been dropped and one needs only to be diagnosed as **"disabled"** to qualify. According to an article, **"The Medicaid Factor,"** appearing in ***Education Update*** of February 21, 1995, "Schools are now applying for partial hospitalization license under Medicaid in order to provide mental health wraparound services directly on school premises."

Another article, **"Millions from Medicaid Help Fund School Systems: Arcane Loophole Spurs Program's Cost,"** appearing in the January 2, 1996, ***Washington Times*** says critics claim Medicaid money has been a factor in **tripling the program's costs** over the last five years (from $51 billion in 1988 to $158 billion in 1995). According to Joyce Price, the author:

> Currently school systems with large enrollments of Medicaid eligible students are paid under a Medicaid program known as Early and Periodic Screening, Diagnosis and Treatment (EPSDT) services. ***The Omnibus Reconciliation Act of 1989*** **"opened the window for schools" to claim Medicaid reimbursement for special education services for Medicaid eligible children.** . . . Reimburseable services **include, but are not limited to,** vision, hearing, speech, and dental screening, nursing treatments, speech, occupational and physical therapy, social counseling and psychotherapy, and transportation. . . . Another source said the New York City public school system receives between $60 million and $70 million a year in Medicaid funds. . . . If people knew that $28 million [a year] in Medicaid funds have been used to support the Chicago public school system, I think they'd be very surprised and concerned, said Tom Randall, a Chicago writer who has investigated Medicaid funding in local schools. (Emphasis added)

A Chicago school administrator is quoted in the article as saying: "Special education has always been underfunded. . . . This money helps us maintain our current level of services."

So with or without a national health care plan, medical and social services are coming directly into the schools—and with them tracking—as educational records of students are combined with their health and social services records. **The government's preferred method is**

to pair something undesirable (tracking) with something desirable (free medical services or other "benefits"). ***GOALS 2000*** **is not just about our schools, it's the blueprint for restructuring American society. This bell is tolling for "all" of us. (See chronology: 31, 39, 44, 47, 52, 63, 68, 72, 74, 101, 115, 118, 122, and 126; and glossary: NCES.)**

> *(11) schools should provide information to businesses regarding how the business community can assist schools in meeting the purposes of this Act;*

> *(12) institutions of higher education should be encouraged to enter into partnerships with schools to provide information and guidance to schools on the skills and knowledge graduates need in order to enter and successfully complete postsecondary education, and schools should provide information and guidance to institutions of higher education on the skills, knowledge, and preservice training teachers need, and the types of professional development educators need in order to meet the purposes of this Act;*

Exchanges between high schools and colleges have gone on for years through professional associations that bridge both groups. A lack of communication is not the problem. The public schools have not been delivering a "product" of the same quality they once did and colleges have had to take up the slack by offering remedial courses to entering freshmen. What is really being said in (12) is that a whole new dialogue will have to ensue so that college schools of education will turn out *GOALS 2000*-trained teachers. Colleges will be obliged to retool their courses for a new breed of student accustomed to cooperative group learning, distance learning, high-tech presentations, OBE with portfolio assessments, and grades of A, B, or "not yet."

> *(13) the appropriate and innovative use of technology, including distance learning, can be very effective in helping to provide all students with the opportunity to learn and meet high standards;*

Technology as an important O-T-L criterion. *"Distance learning"* is anything that comes into the classroom from outside via whatever media. It could be as close as a taped session occurring down the hallway or as far away as a lesson from Russia coming via satellite. **(See chronology: 125; and glossary: Distance Learning and Star Schools.)**

> *(14) Federal funds should be targeted to support State and local initiatives, and to leverage State and local resources for designing and implementing systemwide education improvement plans;*

"Leverage" . . . "the action or effect of a lever (anything which brings influence to bear)" ***(NLWD).*** Leverage will be brought to bear on states through the 1994 reauthorization of the ***ESEA,*** and through grants to get the various parts of ***GOALS 2000*** up and running.

> *(15) all students are entitled to participate in a broad and challenging curriculum and to have access to resources sufficient to address other education needs; and*

O-T-L becomes an "entitlement"! Students have a right to *"challenging"* curriculum and to have *"other education needs"* met. Christian schools and homeschools would not provide students this entitlement.

> *(16) quality education management services are being utilized by local educational agencies and schools through contractual agreements among local educational agencies or schools and businesses providing quality education management services.*

One of the current controversial educational experiments is to have schools "managed" by private firms. Twelve schools in Baltimore were under such a contract with Education Alternatives, Inc. (EAI) from 1992 till late 1995 when the contract was terminated in a funding dispute. Hartford, Connecticut, another city using the same private firm, terminated its contract in January 1996. One obvious downside to privatizing the schools is that these management companies are not accountable in any direct way to parents as an elected board of education would be.

SEC. 303. AUTHORIZATION OF APPROPRIATIONS.

There are authorized to be appropriated $400,000,000 for the fiscal year 1994, and such sums as may be necessary for each of the fiscal years 1995 through 1998, to carry out this title.

A "Congressional Intent" paragraph makes it clear that this is all new money and does not replace or reduce any existing federal funding for education.

The next two sections deal with the allotment of funds (percentage formulas), etc., and with the application process for states. **The basic requirement is for states to show they are developing and implementing a systemic state restructuring plan (the SIP) that is in line with the *GOALS 2000* legislation.**

Section 306—State Improvement Plans—covers:

1. The development of the plan by a broad-based panel. You should be able to get information on your state's ***GOALS 2000*** panel by calling your state department of education. According to this section, public hearings will be held (at this point should have already been held) to solicit the opinions of parents and other interested members of the public. Reports of hearings and copies of state plans **should be** readily available to anyone wishing the information. Be persistent! Ask your elected representative to help you, if necessary.
2. Teaching, Learning, Standards (including O-T-L) and Assessments. Assessments are to:

(I) be aligned with such State's content standards;

(II) involve multiple measures of student performance;

(III) provide for—

(aa) the participation in such assessments of all students with diverse learning needs; and

(bb) the adaptations and accommodations necessary to permit such participation;

(IV) be consistent with relevant, nationally recognized professional and technical standards for such assessments;

(V) be capable of providing coherent information about student attainments relative to the State content standards; and

(VI) support effective curriculum and instruction.

The tests must be multiple measures of performance (OBE), adaptable to the entire range of students (DDD), consistent with the national standards that have been developed in each subject area, *"support"* the curriculum and instruction so that working backward from the assessments, teachers can teach to the tests, and they must provide the state with usable data (*"coherent information"*) so student's progress in attaining the state (*GOALS 2000*) standards can be tracked.

Since (I) through (VI) have to do with **"Assessments,"** let's take a closer look at assessments. Words are interesting, aren't they? We should always pay attention when we see a new word or phrase replacing other, more common terms and be aware (as we've tried to be here) that when words are used repeatedly in a document they have special significance. **"Assessment,"** used many times in ***GOALS 2000*** is just such a word. The first assumption is that it is just educational jargon for testing, but some researchers have suggested it's more than that. Here's how the ***NWLD*** defines ***"assess"***: "to fix the value or amount of, esp. for the purpose of taxation; to impose a charge for; to judge the value or worth of (other than in money)." The suggestion has been made that **an individual's worth (present and potential) to the state is being measured with each "assessment."** And won't the tracking system that accompanies the assessments be a very effective sorting mechanism, separating the sheep from the goats—the Alphas from the drones?

(1)(B) states that this process will include:

assessing the effectiveness and equity of the school finance program

> *of the State to identify disparities in the resources available to each local educational agency and school in such State and how such disparities affect the ability of the State educational agency and local educational agencies to develop and implement plans under this title;*

Here is the assurance that your state will soon be subjected (if it has not already been) to a "finance equity" scrutiny. When it is discovered that some districts spend more per pupil than others, the basis for prolonged wrangling in the courts to get everybody "leveled out" will have been established. **(See chronology: 98.)**

(1)(C) states there must be:

> *a process for developing, selecting, or recommending instructional materials, including gender equitable and multicultural materials, and technology to support and assist local educational agencies and schools to provide all students the opportunity to meet State content standards and State student performance standards;*

Textbook publishers and other curriculum vendors are doubtless retooling their products to ensure compliance with the ***GOALS 2000*** directives.

(E) says there must be:

> *a process for improving the State's system of teacher and school administrator preparation and licensure, and of continuing professional development programs, including the use of technology at both the State and local levels, so that all teachers, related services personnel, and administrators develop the subject matter and pedagogical expertise needed to prepare all students to meet State content standards and State student performance standards.*

A Carnegie-funded National Board for Professional Teaching Standards (NBPTS) has been busily at work on this for some years now. The new standards for licensure and continuing development are in place and need only be adopted formally by the states. The *"use of technology"* that will be a part of the new teacher training, etc. will include both "hands-on" training and subjecting teachers to "multiple measurements" (just like their OBE-assessed students). Candidates will assemble portfolios of their classroom activities over several months, may be videotaped presenting lessons, and will undergo exercises at an assessment center. **Certification does not come cheap.** In an article in ***Education Week*** (11/8/95), author Ann Bradley says:

> The board of directors of the private organization creating a voluntary nationwide system to certify accomplished teachers has raised the fee for candidates to $2,000. The decision last month by the National Board for Professional Teaching Standards was widely expected. . . . The organization's 63-member board **hopes states and districts will foot the bill for the $2,000 fee** which will cover the 1996–97 and 1997–98 school years. (Emphasis added.) **(See chronology: 49, 82, 87, and 113; and glossary: NASDTEC.)**

The short section on O-T-L standards tells us they are to be ***"voluntary"*** on the part of states, local educational agencies, and schools. This is litigation waiting to happen: ("opportunity-to-litigate"). We'll see how ***"voluntary"*** the standards are when the courts start ruling on them.

> *(f) Parental and Community Support and Involvement.—Each state improvement plan shall describe strategies for how the State educational agency will involve parents and other community representatives in planning, designing, and implementing the State improvement plan, including strategies such as—*
>
> *(1) focusing public and private community resources and public school resources on prevention and early intervention to address the needs of all students by identifying and removing unnecessary regulations and obstacles to coordination; and*

Waiving "unnecessary" regulations that would prevent the coordination of schools with health and social services. **(See chronology: 42, 55, 89, 103, and 104; and glossary: PAT.)**

> *(2) increasing the access of all students to social services, health care, nutrition, related services, and child care services, and locating such services in schools, cooperating service agencies, community-based centers, or other convenient sites designed to provide "one-stop shopping" for parents and students.*

Yes, ***"one-stop shopping"*** is **their** term for getting the school conveniently coordinated with all the services listed above under one roof (the school building, if possible, or close by, if not). This may be user-friendly, but it's definitely not family-friendly. **It's parental replacement by the state. (See chronology: 89, 103, and 104; and glossary: Lifelong Learning and Partnershipping.)** A short section called *"Promoting Bottom-up Reform"* lists two *"strategies"*:

> *(1) providing flexibility to individual schools and local educational agencies to enable such schools and agencies to adapt and integrate State content standards into courses of study appropriate for individual schools and communities; and*

Wherever this law reads ***"flexibility,"*** the translation is **"waivers."** Waivers for local adaptations to the curriculum will be tolerated within acceptable limits. Special interest groups would file lawsuits if *GOALS 2000* didn't allow for this. However, **waivers are only acceptable if they promote school restructuring.**

> *(2) facilitating the provision of waivers from State rules and regulations that impede the ability of local educational agencies or schools to carry out local improvement plans.*

Waivers to existing laws are a "legal" way to get around regulations that may be there for a very good reason. An example of this will be waivers necessary to get around existing child labor laws when large numbers of school children are released from school sites into the work force under the new school-to-work programs.

From the beginning *GOALS 2000* and its predecessor *AMERICA 2000* were touted as bottom-up reform plans. Yet, the vast majority of American parents (the bottom rung) aren't even aware there is such a thing as ***GOALS 2000.*** Most, however, are aware of changes taking place—of various "reforms" in their schools that preceded passage of this law. The restructuring effort, **usually brought in piecemeal, to avoid detection and widespread alarm,** has been underway for a long time. ***P.L.103-227*** is the official imprimatur and a large infusion of federal money to hasten and homogenize the process throughout the country.

> *(j)* Coordination with School-to-Work Programs.—*If a State has received Federal assistance for the purpose of planning for, expanding, or establishing a school-to-work program, then a State shall include in the State improvement plan a description of how such school-to-work program will be incorporated into the school reform efforts of the State. In particular, the State improvement plan shall include a description of how secondary schools will be modified in order to provide career guidance, the integration of academic and vocational education, and work-based learning, if such programs are proposed in the State's school-to-work plan.*

School-to-work is ***P.L.103-239,*** signed into law on May 4, 1994, and tied here directly to ***P.L.103-227.*** Like the ***ESEA,*** funding for school-to-work is tied to ***GOALS 2000.*** School-to-work establishes a formal partnership between the Department of Education and the Department of Labor through collaboration on an **OBE-based apprenticeship program ("work-based learning") culminating in Certificates of Mastery, referred to as "portable credentials."** There is grant money to link schools with the work force and to coordinate classroom lessons with worksite learning. This is another example of how **"voluntary"** language in ***GOALS 2000*** is, in actuality, **mandatory** when linked with other key pieces of legislation. When the impact of losing **other** federal money (in addition to the ***GOALS 2000*** funding) hits home, the four "hold out" states: Virginia, New Hampshire, Alabama, and Montana, may be forced to rethink their position. The "golden handcuffs" of federal aid to education are designed to work that way. Final sections deal with approval of State Improvement Plans. **(See also comments on *CAREERS* bill in the conclusion.)**

Section 307 covers the review of state applications by the secretary of education.

Section 308 covers state use of funds. Funding for the first year will go to developing and implementing improvement plans. For succeeding years, states shall:

> *(1) use at least 90 percent of such allotment to make subgrants—*
>
> *(A) in accordance with section 309(a), to local educational agencies for the implementation of the State improvement plan and of local improvement plans; and*
>
> *(B) in accordance with section 309(b), to improve educator preservice programs and for professional development activities that are consistent with the State improvement plan; and*
>
> *(2) use the remainder of such assistance for State activities designed to implement its State improvement plan, such as—*
>
> *(A) supporting the development or adoption of State content standards and State student performance standards, State opportunity-to-learn standards, and State assessments linked to such standards, including—*
>
> *(i) through consortia of States; or*
>
> *(ii) with the assistance of the National Education Standards and Improvement Council established under part B of title 2;*
>
> *(B) supporting the implementation of high-performance management and organizational strategies, such as site-based management, shared decisionmaking, or quality management principles, to promote effective implementation of such plan;*

Site-based management (SBM), also known as shared decisionmaking, can be a way to do an end-run around an elected and accountable school board. *"Quality management principles"* is a reference to Total Quality Management (TQM), a management strategy borrowed from the business world and currently enjoying popularity at the district and school level. **(See chronology: 32, 45, 98, 100, and 118; and glossary: PPBS, SBM, TQM, and ISO 9000.)**

> *(C) supporting the development and implementation, at the local educational agency and school building level, of improved human resource development systems for recruiting, selecting, mentoring, supporting, evaluating and rewarding educators;*

Remember when "human resources" were referred to simply as "employees" or "personnel"? These are now outmoded terms. Workers have become "human resources" or "human capital." Are people being treated in a more or less humane way under these new "human" labels? Omitted from (C) is "punishing" and "weeding out" educators. That is sure to be an activity carried on in these ***GOALS 2000*** *"human resource development systems,"* as many experienced teachers who know better will be making career changes or taking early retirements.

> *(D) providing special attention to the needs of minority, limited-English proficient, disabled, and female students, including instructional programs and activities that encourage such students in elementary and secondary schools to aspire to enter and complete postsecondary education or training;*

Encouragement is fine. Quotas based on political correctness and misguided charity are not. Throughout ***P.L. 103-227*** many groups are singled out for "special attention."

> *(E) supporting innovative and proven methods of enhancing a teacher's ability to identify student learning needs, and motivating students to develop higher order thinking skills, discipline, and creative resolution methods;*

Beware the words ***"innovative"*** and ***"creative"*** when linked with education. It's generally experimentation and usually involves the affective domain (feeling, believing, valuing). ***"Higher order thinking skills"*** **(HOTS)** can be taught in a variety of ways, but may be nothing more than a new name for the old discredited values clarification. ***"Proven methods"*** is anything, **good or bad,** which has been shown to work, such as the many affective programs "validated" by the National Diffusion Network. ***"Creative resolution methods,"*** probably refers to such classroom fads as "peer mediation" where, with the help of a "student facilitator," kids arbitrate their own disputes in student courts, etc. **(See chronology: 30, 34, 36, 50, and 71; and glossary: Higher Order Thinking Skills and National Diffusion Network.)**

> *(F) supporting the development, at the State or local level, of performance-based accountability and incentive systems for schools;*

"Performance-based" is another term for **outcome-based.** PB or PBE is not as identifiable to the public as OBE which has become a "hot-button" issue. Some states are using the term **"competency-based."** Many OBE programs have been brought in under other names. Back in the 1970s, OBE was called **"mastery learning,"** and also the more forthright and honest **"behavioral objectives."** As soon as an OBE program starts to get a bad smell, it's freshened with a new name. The educrats have been tirelessly inventive in throwing parents off the scent. *"Accountability and incentive systems"* is a nice way of saying a system of punishments and rewards. Section (F) calls for developing a state or local (district) level system of rewards and punishments for schools based on outcome-based education.

> *(G) outreach to and training for parents, tribal officials, organizations serving young children, classroom teachers, related services personnel, and other educators, and the public, related to education improvement;*

Public relations on the "benefits" of this *fait accompli,* along with the training to make it work.

> *(H) providing technical assistance and other services to increase the capacity of local educational agencies and schools to develop and implement systemic local improvement plans, implement new State assessments, and develop curricula consistent with the State content standards and State student performance standards;*

(I) promoting public magnet schools, public "charter schools," and other mechanisms for increasing choice among public schools, including information and referral programs which provide parents with information on available choices;

Many parents do not realize that **magnet schools were set up to promote integration not choice.** Their "distinctives" made them an attractive "choice" for some parents, but that was always a secondary purpose. Charter schools are public schools set up for a specific purpose or with a different "vision" from their regular counterparts and operated under a charter from the state department of education or local district. Because of the "charter," they are not subject to all the rules and regulations of regular public schools. Charter schools are, for the time being, the public school's answer to parents who clamor for "choice." Both magnet and charter schools are somewhat different from the norm, but that is all the "choice" the public schools are willing to concede (for now). Because of the perceived threat to the state monopoly on education, teachers' unions (who lead the charge in crying foul) have no interest in tuition tax credits, vouchers, or other "choice" plans which could be applied at private schools. Sooner or later, however, private schools will get federal money because it's the most efficient way to co-opt them, bring them under state authority and in line with state standards. **"Choice" proponents seem to forget that "who pays the piper calls the tune."** When you are able to get a tax credit or apply a voucher at the local Christian school (or apply the money toward your homeschool), you will have the illusion of "choice," and the state will have accomplished a bloodless coup, using only its golden handcuffs. **(See chronology: 72 and 75.)**

(J) supporting activities relating to the planning of, and evaluation of, projects under which local educational agencies or schools contract with private management organizations to reform a school;

The government, I suspect, is only interested in spending enough money on *"contracting with private management organizations to reform a school"* to see if this pays in the long run and on a large enough scale to replicate. So far the results with private management firms are spotty, as we've seen with Baltimore and Hartford. The teacher unions are very opposed to privatization and are fighting it aggressively. **Chris Whittle**, the entrepreneur who brought **Channel One** (TV news with commercials) into American classrooms, is one of the few still promoting privatization. Through his Edison Project, four state schools are privately managed. **Charter schools seem the clear winner in the "alternative" school debate and the wave of the foreseeable future.**

> *(K) supporting intergenerational mentoring programs;*

Grandmothers and grandfathers lending support and encouragement to children who lack good role models seems a fine idea. This should be done privately so we can be sure *"mentoring"* is limited to children who really need it and that seniors aren't coerced into "community service," or required by the government to keep records on their young charges.

> *(L) supporting the development, at the State or local level, of school-based programs that restore discipline and reduce violence in schools and communities, such as community mobilization programs; and*

"Community mobilization" is more "partnershipping." A phrase, attributed to an African folk saying, "It takes a whole village to raise a child," is heard a lot these days and is popular because it perfectly fits the socialist concept of the state/community as a parental replacement unit. Not surprisingly, it's also found in the title of Hillary Clinton's book, ***It Takes a Village and Other Lessons Children Teach Us.***

> *(M) collecting and analyzing data.*

There's a world of mischief in that short phrase. **(See chronology: 74, 115, and 122; and glossary: Lifelong Learning and NCES.)**

Section 309 deals with subgrants for local reform and professional development awarded by the state educational agencies (SEAs) to local educational agencies (LEAs). The requirements are essentially the same as for state grants, but are for projects at the district level. (D) and (F) of Section 309 are of interest because they show the emphasis on partnershipping, and social service concerns. Subgrants for local reform are to:

> *(D) describe a process of broad-based community participation in the development, implementation, and evaluation of the local improvement plan;*

This sounds like community-based PPBS. **(See chronology: 32, 42, 45, and 55; and glossary: PPBS and Partnerships.)**

> *(F) describe how the local educational agency will implement specific programs aimed at ensuring improvements in school readiness and the ability of students to learn effectively at all grade levels by identifying the most pressing needs facing students and their families with regard to social services, health care, nutrition, and child care, and entering into partnerships with public and private nonprofit agencies to increase the access of students and families to coordinated nonsectarian services in a school setting or at a nearby site;*

More PPBS with coordinated access to food, day care, social and health services in the new "one-stop shopping" school or other community hub. Government as nanny, a.k.a., **"parental replacement." (See chronology: 89, 91, 98, 103, and 104; and glossary: Parents as Teachers.)**

The subgrants for professional development give priority to LEAs or consortia serving a high percentage of disadvantaged students; forming partnerships with college educators to establish professional development sites; focusing on upgrading teachers' knowledge of content areas; or targeting development of teachers working with students with limited-English or those with disabilities.

Under (3), "Required Activities," we read that the subgrant is to be used for activities supporting—

> *(B) the development and implementation of new and improved forms of continuing and sustained professional development opportunities for teachers, principals, and other educators at the school or*

> *district level that equip educators with such expertise, and with other knowledge and skills necessary for leading and participating in continuous education improvement.*

Note ***"continuous education improvement."*** If we are to become "a nation of learners" and **lifelong** learners at that, educators must lead the way. ***"Continuous education"* is the term used for lifelong learning in Europe,** while "continuous improvement" is a term associated with Total Quality Management (TQM). *"Continuing and sustained"* in-servicing and other *"development opportunities"* will ensure that teachers climb on and never fall off the ***GOALS 2000*** bandwagon. (**See glossary: LL and TQM.**)

Section 310 deals with **availability of information and training.**

SEAs and LEAs are to make information about the national goals, standards, materials, and assessments, and training available to **private schools,** upon request. ("Won't you come into my parlor?" said the spider to the fly.) **Waivers** will be granted to SEAs or LEAs that are currently prohibited from giving this assistance to private schools.

In some states, homeschools are legally classified as private schools, so homeschoolers had better beware of getting drawn into this with the lure of free materials, training—or whatever. Cross-pollination between public and private schools already goes on in many states, in case you've ever wondered why your privately educated children are being exposed to some of the same ideas and materials their peers in public school are getting. Our family had the experience in a Christian high school of discovering that **every single textbook** our son was given was "on loan" from the local public school district. We had been assured they took no federal funds (which technically they didn't), but they saw nothing wrong with "saving money" this way.

Section 311 covers **waivers of statutory and regulatory requirements.** The secretary of education may grant to SEAs, LEAs, or individual schools, four-year waivers to any law or regulation that stands in the way of school reform efforts, subject to the stipulations spelled out in this section. Aside from doing a lot of paperwork, waivers should not be very hard to get. The waiver can then be extended beyond the four-year period if the secretary determines it has been effective in carrying out reform plans.

Subsection 311(2)(e) calls for a waiver program entitled the ***Education Flexibility Partnership Demonstration Act.*** **("Flexibility" is the euphemism for a waiver used throughout this law.)** This enables the secretary of education to grant up to six SEA waivers for a period of up to five years to set up demonstration programs. To date, Kansas, Massachusetts, Ohio, and Oregon have been selected as "Ed Flex" states. In return, the states will be held accountable for the performance of the students affected by the waivers. Waivers can be extended beyond the initial five years for demonstrations deemed **"effective."** The states get the legal green light to do what they otherwise could not; the federal government should get in return a few model programs that can be replicated. There's something for everyone. It's been called **"waivers for favors"** (and vice versa).

Section 312, **"Progress Reports,"** sets up annual reports for any SEA receiving funds under Title 3. The secretary of education is also to submit biennial reports to Congress on areas covered by Title 3. Section 312(3) states that reports on waiver grants will include:

> *(A) a listing of all State educational agencies, local educational agencies and schools seeking and receiving waivers;*
>
> *(B) a summary of the State and Federal statutory or regulatory requirements that have been waived, including the number of waivers sought and granted under each such statutory or regulatory requirement;*
>
> *(C) a summary of waivers that have been terminated, including a rationale for the terminations; and*
>
> *(D) recommendations to the Congress regarding changes in statutory or regulatory requirements, particularly those actions that should be taken to overcome Federal statutory or regulatory impediments to education reform.*

(D) above, is extremely interesting as it reveals an unstated intention of waivers. By having a period of experimentation with waivers, both states and the federal government will have a clearer idea of which laws they wish to change or do away with altogether—laws found to be ***"impediments to education reform."*** Hence waivers on a limited scale may be viewed as an intermediary stage to much broader changes in the law later. Such changes will be more readily accepted if introduced in this gradual and less obvious way.

Section 313, **"Technical and Other Assistance Regarding School Finance Equity,"** is an important section because it makes very clear the federal government's role in promoting finance equity. The secretary is authorized to make grants to and enter into contracts and cooperative agreements with SEAs and other public and private agencies, institutions, and organizations to provide technical assistance to state and LEAs to assist them in achieving ***"a greater degree of equity in the distribution of financial resources for education among local educational agencies in the State."***

Under "Activities," it is stated that a grant, contract, or cooperative agreement may support:

> *(A) the establishment and operation of a center or centers for the provision of technical assistance to State and local educational agencies;*
>
> *(B) the convening of conferences on equalization of resources within local educational agencies, within States, and among States; and*
>
> *(C) obtaining advice from experts in the field of school finance equalization.*

Further, each SEA or LEA **receiving funds under the *ESEA*** is to provide ***"such data and information on school finance as the Secretary may require to carry out this section."*** (Yet another example of **ESEA** money tied to ***GOALS 2000.***) The secretary is also authorized to develop directly or through grants, etc., models and materials useful to states in planning and implementing revisions of state school finance systems and to disseminate these.

We knew it was no "coincidence" that state after state has been undergoing finance equity scrutiny and court challenges. Section 313 is proof of the federal government's interest in encouraging financial "leveling." **(See chronology: 98; and glossary: O-T-L.)**

Section 314, **"National Leadership,"** provides for technical assistance to SEAs and LEAs to gather data, conduct research on, and evaluate systemic improvement plans; disseminate findings of outstanding examples of such plans through existing systems within the DOE, including publications, electronic and telecommunications media, and conferences; support national demonstration projects that unite SEAs, LEAs, colleges, government, business and labor in collaborative arrangements; support model projects to integrate multiple content standards; and provide grants to tribal (American Indian) divisions of education in support of school reform.

Section 315, **"Assistance to the Outlying Areas and to the Secretary of the Interior,"** details how the various parts of Title 3 are to be carried out in schools serving American Indians and operated by the Bureau of Indian Affairs (under the Department of the Interior). The purposes of Title 3 are to be also applied to Department of Defense schools (schools overseas for children of servicemen/women). **No one getting federal money is left out.**

Section 316 states in one sentence that state standards or assessments *"shall not be required to be certified by the Council"* (*"Council"* being NESIC). **See Title 2—Part B.**

Section 317, **"State Planning for Improving Student Achievement through Integration of Technology into the Curriculum,"** authorizes the secretary to award grants for systemic statewide plans to increase the use of state-of-the-art technologies that enhance elementary and secondary student learning and staff development in support of the NEG and content standards. Such plans shall have as their objectives:

> *(1) the promotion of higher student achievement through the use of technology in education;*

"Higher student achievement" may or may not prove to be a reality with the increased use of technology. Higher costs we can bank on.

> *(2) the participation of all schools and school districts in the State,*

> *especially those schools and districts with a high percentage or number of disadvantaged students;*

Does this mean funds go first to the *"disadvantaged"*?

> *(3) the development and implementation of a cost-effective, high-speed, statewide, interoperable, wide-area-communication educational technology support system for elementary and secondary schools within the State, particularly for such schools in rural areas; and*

State-of-the-art computers, satellite dishes, etc. in elementary and high schools (with preference given to rural areas). Though not named, this sounds like the Star Schools Program. **(See glossary: Star Schools Program.)**

> *(4) the promotion of shared usage of equipment, facilities, and other technology resources by adult learners during afterschool hours.*

Making this expensive technology available after school to adults is a way to defray criticism about the costs, but more importantly, a way to ensure a nation of "lifelong learners," as the schools become community hubs/work force centers for training and retraining workers.

There are fifteen plan requirements for the integration of technology into the curriculum. Those worth a closer look state that, at a minimum, each systemic statewide plan shall:

> *(2) be developed in collaboration with the Governor, representatives of the State legislature, the State board of education, institutions of higher education, appropriate State agencies, local educational agencies, public and private telecommunication entities, parents, public and school libraries, students, adult literacy providers, and leaders in the field of technology, through a process of statewide grassroots outreach to local educational agencies and schools in the State;*

Legislators will be needed to draft new laws. Colleges will need to align what they are doing now with what they will have to do for students who are more technologically than print-oriented. Interlibrary loan programs will likely be expanded to include elementary and secondary schools. Adult literacy providers will have to ensure the setup is user-friendly for dropouts and other adult clients. **Restructuring society to accommodate LL is an extensive undertaking.**

> *(3) identify and describe the requirements for introducing state-of-the-art technologies into the classroom and school library in order to enhance educational curricula, including the installation and ongoing maintenance of basic connections, hardware and the necessary support materials;*

Card catalogs in school libraries will be computerized as they have already been in most public libraries. This, of course, is no guarantee that students will check out or read more books. It only makes the access to books and other materials a different process. The telecommunications giants and spinoff companies will be providing much of the know-how, material, installation, and servicing for this changeover—and can be expected to profit handsomely.

> *(8) establish a funding estimate (including a statement of likely funding sources) and a schedule for the development and implementation of such plan;*

The original *AMERICA 2000* proposal (1991), upon which this law is based, assured us that the restructuring of the schools was not going to cost any more than we were currently spending. How quickly that line was abandoned! *"Likely funding sources,"* apart from the obvious beleaguered taxpayer, will include the business community, especially the telecommunications industry that is going to play a major, lucrative role in the technological transformation of classrooms. Once the equipment is in, schools will be seeing "billable" time to run it.

> *(10) describe how the State educational agency and local educational agencies in the State will coordinate and cooperate with business and industry, and with public and private telecommunications entities;*

See comment on (8) above.

> *(11) describe how the State educational agency will promote the purchase of equipment by local educational agencies that, when placed in schools, will meet the highest possible level of interoperability and open system design;*

It wouldn't make sense to have districts buying equipment incompatible with that in neighboring districts, nor would it make sense to buy what can't be easily upgraded in the world of rapidly changing high-tech equipment.

> *(13) describe how the State educational agency will apply the uses of technology to meet the needs of children from low-income families;*

In what way are the academic *"needs"* of these children different? This sounds like quotas and set-asides and (taking into account [15] below,) more intrusion into families.

> *(15) describe how the State educational agency will facilitate collaboration between State literacy resource centers, local educational agencies, and adult and family literacy providers, to ensure that technology can be used by adult and family literacy providers during afterschool hours.*

This is how technology will promote the sixth goal (adult literacy and lifelong learning). The new high-tech schools (and computerized public libraries) are to be the lifelong learning/relearning centers. Note the use of the term *"family literacy providers,"* as distinct from *"adult literacy."* Is ***"family literacy"*** another term for **"parent education,"** a.k.a the **PAT program? (See Title 4. See also glossary: Lifelong Learning, PAT, and Partnerships.)**

$5,000,000 is authorized to be appropriated for FY-94 to carry out this section.

> **SEC. 318. PROHIBITION ON FEDERAL MANDATES, DIRECTION, AND CONTROL.**

> *Nothing in this Act shall be construed to authorize an officer or*

employee of the Federal Government to mandate, direct, or control a State, local educational agency, or school's curriculum, program of instruction, or allocation of State or local resources or mandate a State or any subdivision thereof to spend any funds or incur any costs not paid for under this Act.

This classic edu-speak says that only those areas funded under ***GOALS 2000*** are subject to mandate, direct(ion), or control by the federal government.

SEC. 319. STATE AND LOCAL GOVERNMENT CONTROL OF EDUCATION.

(a) FINDINGS.—The Congress finds as follows:

(1) Congress is interested in promoting State and local government reform efforts in education.

*(2) In **Public Law 96-88** the Congress found that education is fundamental to the development of individual citizens and the progress of the Nation.*

*(3) In **Public Law 96-88** the Congress found that in our Federal system the responsibility for education is reserved respectively to the States and the local school systems and other instrumentalities of the States.*

P.L.96-88 signed October 17, 1979, established the Department of Education. (3) above essentially restates what the Tenth Amendment to the U.S. Constitution said over two hundred years ago. If Congress took the Constitution (or their own "findings" in ***P.L.96-88***) seriously, there would have been no Department of Education set up in 1979 and no ***GOALS 2000*** legislation in 1994. Both laws, though declaring otherwise, usurped individual and states' rights.

*(4) In **Public Law 96-88** the Congress declared the purpose of the Department of Education was to supplement and complement the efforts of States, the local school systems, and other instrumentali-*

ties of the States, the private sector, public and private educational institutions, public and private non-profit educational research institutions, community based organizations, parents, and schools to improve the quality of education.

The intent of the U.S. Department of Education to *"supplement and complement"* the states, etc., becomes in ***GOALS 2000,*** if stated candidly, to **"supplant and commandeer."**

(5) With the establishment of the Department of Education, Congress intended to protect the rights of State and local governments and public and private educational institutions in the areas of educational policies and administration of programs and to strengthen and improve the control of such governments and institutions over their own educational programs and policies.

Predictably, it didn't work out that way.

(6) ***Public Law 96-88*** *specified that the establishment of the Department of Education shall not increase the authority of the Federal Government over education or diminish the responsibility for education which is reserved to the States and local school systems and other instrumentalities of the States.*

The educrats and lawyers who wrote ***GOALS 2000*** understood the clear intent of the Tenth Amendment—that education is an area reserved to the states or "the people." This acknowledgment makes the law even more reprehensible. They knew it wasn't their domain but laid claim to it anyway.

(7) ***Public Law 96-88*** *specified that no provision of a program administered by the Secretary or by any other officer of the Department of Health, Education, and Welfare shall be construed to authorize the Secretary or any such officer to exercise any direction, supervision or control over the curriculum, program of instruction, administration, or personnel of any educational institution, school, or school system, over any accrediting agency or association or over*

> *the selection or content of library resources, textbooks, or other instructional materials by any educational institution or school system.*

At the time ***P.L.96-88*** was signed (1979), education was under the old Department of Health, Education, and Welfare (DHEW). Now we have two cabinet-level departments: Health and Human Services, and a separate Department of Education, both enhanced in authority, size, and annual budgets. Few would argue that public education has improved during the fifteen-year cabinet-level tenure of the DOE. The abusive and illegal expansion of influence and authority over our education system by this agency of the federal government, culminating in the power grab known as ***GOALS 2000***, should sound the call for the **immediate and total abolition of the U.S. Department of Education.**

> *(b)* REAFFIRMATION.—*The Congress agrees and reaffirms that the responsibility for control of education is reserved to the States and local school systems and other instrumentalities of the States and that no action shall be taken under the provisions of this Act by the Federal Government which would, directly or indirectly, impose standards or requirements of any kind through the promulgation of rules, regulations, provision of financial assistance and otherwise, which would reduce, modify, or undercut State and local responsibility for control of education.*

Hidden agendas, subterfuge, and disinformation have characterized ***AMERICA 2000/GOALS 2000*** from the beginning. Sections 318 and 319 are blatant examples of the deceitful reassurances that no doubt encouraged many states to sign onto ***GOALS 2000*** and line up for the promised federal subsidies.

Title 4—
Parental Assistance

In which you will be introduced to an **entry point of "lifelong learning"** through a national program, designed for children from birth through five years. Here you will also learn the applied meaning of the popular saying: "It takes a whole village to raise a child," as you discover the government wants parents to become "partners" with the school—and a variety of health and social service agencies—and to undergo "parent education" to get their young children prepared for "educational achievement." In some states the program is called **Parents as Teachers (PAT)**. Names vary; the concept does not. Parents are relegated to "caretaker" status in various "partnershipping" schemes.

TITLE 4— PARENTAL ASSISTANCE

SEC. 401. PARENTAL INFORMATION AND RESOURCE CENTERS

(a) PURPOSE.—The purpose of this title is—

(1) to increase parents' knowledge of and confidence in child-rearing activities, such as teaching and nurturing their young children;

Title 4 enables the first National Education Goal—"School Readiness." See Title 1, Section 102(1).

(2) to strengthen partnerships between parents and professionals in meeting the educational needs of children aged birth through 5 and the working relationship between home and school;

"Partnerships" are the key concept and few parents are aware of the legal, contractual nature of partnerships. If you voluntarily enter into a partnership with social workers (referred to under PAT as ***"parent educators"***), the school, or others professing expertise in child-rearing, you have, whether you intended to or not, given up authority over your home and children. You've said, in effect, "You do your share and I'll do my share—but **I acknowledge that bringing up this child is a shared responsibility."** Notice that the intent is to begin with "birth." Parents will be recruited in prenatal programs or in hospitals before they bring their babies home. Parents participating in birth through five programs are being prepped to next enter into "partnerships" with schools. **(See chronology: 42, 55, 66, 89, 91, 103, and 104; and glossary: Partnerships.)**

(3) to enhance the developmental progress of children assisted under this title; and

That's the hook to be stuck in the jaw of many unsuspecting parents. Of course parents (especially anxious first-time parents) want to be sure their children are developing normally—and to do what they can to enhance that progress.

(4) to fund at least 1 parental information and resource center in each State before September 30, 1998.

Title 4 is about getting the PAT model (*"parental information and resource center"*) into every state by this target date.

The secretary is authorized to award grants to nonprofit organizations or consortia of nonprofits with LEAs to set up parent training centers. These are to serve both urban and rural areas. At least fifty percent of the funds are to go to areas with high concentrations of low-income families *"in order to serve parents who are severely educationally or economically disadvantaged."* Centers are to network with clearinghouses, parent centers serving children with disabilities, other organizations and agencies, parents of school-aged children, and established national, state, and local parent groups. Part of the funds are to be used to *"establish, expand, or operate Parents as Teachers programs or Home Instruction for Preschool Youngsters programs."* HIPPY, based on a program developed in Israel (where many children are raised communally in *kibbutzes*), is very similar to PAT but serves children ages three through five. **(See glossary: PAT.)**

SEC. 403. USES OF FUNDS.

Grant funds received under this title may be used—

(1) for parent training, information, and support programs that assist parents to—

(A) better understand their children's educational needs;

These *"needs"* are not defined by the parents, but by government "experts." This is **parental replacement masquerading as assistance.**

> *(B) provide followup support for their children's educational achievement;*

What happens to parents who don't want the *"followup support"* i.e., choose not to go along with the suggestions of social or health care workers who have evaluated their children? Increasingly, parents are being charged with neglect and abuse and are having their children taken from their homes when they find themselves at odds with the system.

> *(C) communicate more effectively with teachers, counselors, administrators, and other professional educators and support staff;*

These days you **could** use a "parental advocate" advising and coaching you when you go into school with a problem, but I'd advise you **not** to take one paid by the state.

> *(D) participate in the design and provision of assistance to students who are not making adequate educational progress;*

They sound like advocates, but will they advocate anything that is not part of the system's closed loop? And in the case of a real dispute, whose side would they take? **Remember who pays them.**

> *(E) obtain information about the range of options, programs, services, and resources available at the national, State, and local levels to assist parents described in subparagraphs (A) and (B) of section 401(b);*

> *(F) seek technical assistance regarding compliance with the requirements of this title and of other Federal programs relevant to achieving the National Education Goals;*

PAT is to be coordinated with goals and programs other than "school readiness."

(G) participate in State and local decisionmaking;

(H) train other parents; and

Once parents have been serviced (remediated) they can become parent-trainers themselves. It's sort of like peer counseling in the schools.

(I) plan, implement, and fund activities that coordinate the education of their children with other Federal programs that serve their children or their families; and

Partnershipping education with a broad range of social services.

(2) to include State or local educational personnel where such participation will further the activities assisted under the grant.

SEC. 404. TECHNICAL ASSISTANCE.

The Secretary shall provide technical assistance, by grant or contract, for the establishment, development, and coordination of parent training, information and support programs and parental information and resource centers.

It might be argued that some parents need and desire *"support programs"* as well as information and resources about child-rearing. Some may even wish *"training."* But let's not forget that all these services and materials will be from a strictly secular/humanist perspective. Government training programs and centers will often be at odds with biblical instructions on bringing up children. For Christian parents to whom this matters, such centers and programs will counsel and indoctrinate in an anti-biblical worldview.

SEC. 405. DEFINITIONS.

For purposes of this title—

(1) the term "parent education" includes parent support activities,

the provision of resource materials on child development, parent-child learning activities and child rearing issues, private and group educational guidance, individual and group learning experiences for the parent and child, and other activities that enable the parent to improve learning in the home;

Note that some of the training is private (in the parents' home) and some is in groups (with other parents). **What parents are not told is that the social worker who comes into their home does a written "evaluation" on each visit.** This is how data is collected for the programs and how referrals to other services and agencies are made for children determined to be "at risk." "At risk" for what? **"At risk" of possible later failure in school** because the social worker checked off an item on a list of very subjective "indicators." For programs like PAT to self-perpetuate, workers will have to show lots of need for the program and its spinoff services. No need/low need equals no funding/ reduced funding. Every effort will be made to ensure that doesn't happen. **(See glossary: Parents as Teachers.)**

(2) the term "Parents as Teachers program" means a voluntary early childhood parent education program that—

(A) is designed to provide all parents of children from birth through age 5 with the information and support such parents need to give their child a solid foundation for school success;

Note the use of the phrase ***"all*** parents of children from birth through age 5." Certain populations have been targeted for the launching of PAT, but ***"all"*** means, sooner or later, ***"all"*** parents. Also note the assumption that parents ***"need"*** information and support to give their child a solid foundation for school success. This ***"need"*** is the justification for the program that provides a convenient point of entry into lifelong learning as called for by UNESCO. **(See chronology: 39, 47, 52, 63, 68, 72, and 101.)**

(B) is based on the Missouri Parents as Teachers model with the philosophy that parents are their child's first and most influential teachers;

But clearly those behind this program don't feel that parents are the "**best**" teachers. ***"Influential,"*** yes, but possibly in the "**wrong way.**" The Missouri PAT program began in 1981 and was already being replicated in some forty states before passage of ***GOALS 2000.*** PAT had been introduced as a stand-alone bill during the Bush administration, but was so controversial and received so much vocal opposition (in large part from alert homeschooling parents) that it was beaten back several times. PAT probably could not have passed as a stand-alone where it would have been debated (and at least some of its more egregious aspects exposed) on the floor of the House and Senate. That's why it was "piggybacked" onto the fast-track ***GOALS 2000*** legislation. **I am certain that few who voted for this law read through its 155 pages.** Because the federal government is offering funding over a three-year period to start up (or beef up) PAT programs, those states not already participating almost certainly will pick up the option now.

(C) provides—

> *(i) regularly scheduled personal visits with families by certified parent educators;*

The recommended number is not less than eight home visits a year. Who are these ***"certified parent educators"***? What are the eligibility requirements and what sort of training do they receive for certification?

> *(ii) regularly scheduled developmental screenings; and*

This will be appealing to parents who might not be able to afford expensive screenings, but **what happens when parents don't agree with a followup treatment** recommended after screening? They have just put their child "**at risk.**"

> *(iii) linkage with other resources within the community in order to provide services that parents may want and need, except that such services are beyond the scope of the Parents as Teachers program;*

The seamless cloth where home, health care, school, social services, and employment are woven together so well you cannot distinguish the individual threads or tell where one ends and the other begins.

> *(3) the term "Home Instruction for Preschool Youngsters program" means a voluntary early-learning program for parents with one or more children between the ages of 3 through 5, that—*

The provisions spelled out under (3) for HIPPY are virtually identical to those for PAT.

> SEC. 406. REPORTS.
>
> *Each organization receiving a grant under this title shall submit to the Secretary, on an annual basis, information concerning the parental information and resource centers assisted under this title, including—*
>
> *(1) the number of parents, including the number of minority and limited-English-proficient parents, who receive information and training;*
>
> *(2) the types and modes of training, information, and support provided under this title;*
>
> *(3) the number of Parents as Teachers programs and Home Instruction for Preschool Youngsters programs which have been assisted under this title; and*
>
> *(4) the strategies used to reach and serve parents of minority and limited-English-proficient children, parents with limited literacy skills, and other parents in need of the services provided under this title.*

The emphasis seems to be on **minority** and **limited-English-proficiency parents** (and elsewhere in Title 4 on families who are **economically or educationally disadvantaged** or those with **disabled** children). Those five are **currently** the priority **"at risk"** (of later school failure) categories. Recall that **"disabled" is now broadly interpreted** under special education and qualifies a student for Medicaid funding and a wide array of health and social services.

SEC. 407. GENERAL PROVISION.

Notwithstanding any other provision of this title—

(1) no person, including a parent who educates a child at home, public school parent, or private school parent, shall be required to participate in any program of parent education or developmental screening pursuant to the provisions of this title;

PAT begins as entirely **"voluntary,"** but as with the likely expansion of **"at-risk"** populations, once the programs are in place and have gained acceptance, I'm sure the voluntary will become increasingly mandatory. Who's to say that being a Christian homeschooling family will not become a high priority **"at risk"** category? With this program, we can see clearly the importance and urgency of settling once and for all the question: **Who owns the children? (See chronology: 42, 55, 66, 91, 103, and 104.)**

(2) no program assisted under this title shall take any action that infringes in any manner on the right of a parent to direct the education of their children; and

What about the fact that "parent educators" can turn parents in to the authorities for practices not directly related to education, e.g., health issues, discipline, and others, which social workers decide put children **"at risk." (See the twelve classification codes [risk factors] in the PAT glossary entry.)**

SEC. 408. AUTHORIZATION OF APPROPRIATIONS.

There are authorized to be appropriated such sums as may be necessary for each of the fiscal years 1995 through 1998 to carry out this title.

Since no dollar amount is specified, it will be at the discretion of the DOE. This is a high priority item in *GOALS 2000* and one especially dear to the heart of Hillary Clinton who served on the board of trustees of HIPPY USA and promoted the program in Arkansas.

Title 5—
National Skill
Standards Board

In which you will learn of the creation of a new federal entity, the National Skill Standards Board (NSBB). This board exists to:

1. identify "occupational clusters" (work-related groups).
2. identify and maintain a catalog of skill standards used by industry in the United States **and internationally.**
3. develop a common nomenclature for the skill standards.
4. based on 1–3 above, develop national skill standards and encourage their adoption and widespread use.
5. develop assessments (tests) of the national skill standards and encourage their adoption.
6. based on 1–5 above, develop certifications of attainment, also referred to in *GOALS 2000* as "portable credentials" and encourage their use. These have recently appeared in some of our states as **"Certificates of Mastery,"** and earlier in communist countries simply as "work cards."
7. serve as a clearinghouse of information on skill standards.

Standards are to:

1. be outcome-based.
2. facilitate linkages with job training programs, vocational-technical education, and the recently passed school-to-work legislation.
3. increase opportunities for women and minorities, especially

in "nontraditional" employment.

4. be consistent with federal civil rights laws (no waivers here)!

TITLE 5—
NATIONAL SKILL STANDARDS BOARD

SEC. 502. PURPOSE.

It is the purpose of this title to establish a National Skill Standards Board to serve as a catalyst in stimulating the development and adoption of a voluntary national system of skill standards and of assessment and certification of attainment of skill standards—

A federal board to develop skill standards and skill certificates for American workers! A ***"skill standard"*** is defined in Section 508(4) as—*"a standard that specifies the level of knowledge and competence required to successfully perform work-related functions within an occupational cluster,"* . . . to develop tests for each cluster (work-related groups), and certificates (work cards) for those meeting set standards. If this sounds like something that would be more at home in a communist or socialist state, you're absolutely right. **These are universal skill standards being developed for a global economy/global work force. Another paradigm shift. (See chronology: 66, 88, 92, 93, 96, 102, 107, 111, 112, 126, and 128.)**

(2) that will result in increased productivity, economic growth, and American economic competitiveness; and

Empty promises like those heard before passage of NAFTA and GATT.

(3) that can be used, consistent with civil rights laws—

Notice as we move through Title 5 how compliance with civil rights laws is stressed.

(A) by the Nation, to ensure the development of a high skills, high quality, high performance workforce, including the most skilled front-line workforce in the world;

With one international standard our workers will be no better—and no worse—than those anywhere else in the world. **All workers will be trained to their "need to know" level and no further. This is true international "leveling."**

(B) by industries, as a vehicle for informing training providers and prospective employees of skills necessary for employment;

What Work Requires of Schools.
See chronology: 102.

(C) by employers, to assist in evaluating the skill levels of prospective employees and to assist in the training of current employees;

(D) by labor organizations, to enhance the employment security of workers by providing portable credentials and skills;

Certificates of Initial Mastery (CIMs) and **Certificates of Advanced Mastery (CAMs)**, known in other parts of the world as **work cards**, will determine ***"employment security"*** (entry into and advancement in a given field). ***"Portable credentials"*** is a euphemism for the work card **(CIM and CAM)**.

(E) by workers, to—

(i) obtain certifications of their skills to protect against dislocation;

This is both a thinly veiled threat (no protection without a CIM/CAM)—and a hint that **dislocation/relocation is the lot of the "brave new worker."**

(ii) pursue career advancement; and

(iii) enhance their ability to reenter the workforce.

Once this system is in place, no one will enter, reenter, or advance without the proper CIM/CAM. **These work cards will be issued only for those "occupational clusters" where the government needs workers. Other areas will be frozen. Workers will be trained and employed in areas based on the government's needs; that will control the economy. Work cards will be granted based not only on one's skills, but on political reliability (attitudes, values, and beliefs) and that will effectively control the individual.** Under socialism, the state owns industry outright, controlling all aspects, including the training of workers. Under fascism, ownership remains private, but the state effectively controls commerce through its directives and regulations. Which form of government is this micromanagement of our economy moving us into? Whether socialism, fascism, or some hybrid, the term currently preferred by the one-worlders is **"democracy"** or **"constitutional democracy"**—and it would appear that virtually everyone, from satellites of the former Soviet Union to the United States, now qualifies for this desirable status and label. **See Title 6, Section 601(6)(iii) and (I).**

(F) by students and entry level workers, to determine the skill levels and competencies needed to be obtained in order to compete effectively for high wage jobs;

Certificates of Initial Mastery—CIM.

(G) by training providers and educators, to determine appropriate training services to offer;

Training will be offered in those *"appropriate"* areas where the government says there is need.

(H) by government, to evaluate whether publicly funded training assists participants to meet skill standards where such standards exist and thereby protect the integrity of public expenditures;

The government will be the final judge as to whether the training meets its skill standards. **Federal funding = federal control. Always.**

> *(I) to facilitate the transition to high performance work organizations;*

Government-approved training + CIM = entrance level job. Bottom line: farewell freedom.

> *(J) to increase opportunities for minorities and women, including removing barriers to the entry of women into nontraditional employment; and*

Will this mean quotas and the lowering of physical strength standards as witnessed in the military?

> *(K) to facilitate linkages between other components of the national strategy to enhance workforce skills, including school-to-work transition, secondary and postsecondary vocational-technical education, and job training programs.*

Partnerships between Title 5 and a wide variety of high school and college job training programs including apprenticeships and the recently passed *School-to-Work Opportunities Act.* **(See chronology: 112 and 128.)**

SEC. 503. ESTABLISHMENT OF NATIONAL BOARD.

This section calls for the appointment of a National Skill Standards Board (National Board). It's to be composed of twenty-eight members: the secretaries of labor, education, and commerce; chairperson of the NESIC; eight representatives of business; eight representatives of organized labor; two *"neutral, qualified human resource professionals"*; and six members representing educational institutions (including vo-tech), state and local governments, and nongovernmental organizations (NGOs) *"with a demonstrated history of successfully protecting the rights of racial, ethnic, or religious minorities, women, individuals with disabilities, or older persons."* They are to represent a broad cross-section of occupations and industries, be geographically representative of the United States, and reflect racial, ethnic, and gender diversity. Appointment, with some exceptions, is for four years.

Paid positions will include an executive director appointed by the chairperson of the National Board, paid at a rate not to exceed level V of the executive schedule ($108,200). The executive director may appoint and compensate *"such additional staff as may be necessary to enable the Board to perform its duties."* Salary for these individuals is subject to the same cap as for the executive director.

The National Board may use (with consent) the research, equipment, services, and facilities of any agency or instrumentality of the United States. The National Board may also assign, on a reimbursable basis, personnel of any federal agency to assist them in carrying out their mission.

Anyone serving on the National Board may not have a financial interest in any testing or certification system developed or endorsed under Title 5 for three years after leaving the board.

The National Board is to cease existence on September 30, 1999. This, of course, remains to be seen. **(See Section 509.)**

SEC. 504. FUNCTIONS OF THE NATIONAL BOARD.

(a) IDENTIFICATION OF OCCUPATIONAL CLUSTERS.—

(1) IN GENERAL.—Subject to paragraph (2), the National Board shall identify broad clusters of major occupations that involve 1 or more than 1 industry in the United States and that share characteristics that are appropriate for the development of common skill standards.

(2) PROCEDURES FOR IDENTIFICATION.—Prior to identifying broad clusters of major occupations under paragraph (1), the National Board shall engage in extensive public consultation, including solicitation of public comment on proposed clusters through publication in the Federal Register.

(b) ESTABLISHMENT OF VOLUNTARY PARTNERSHIPS TO DEVELOP STANDARDS.—

(1) IN GENERAL.—For each of the occupational clusters identified pursuant to subsection (a), the National Board shall encourage and facilitate the establishment of voluntary partnerships to develop a skill standards system in accordance with subsection (d).

(2) REPRESENTATIVES.—Such voluntary partnerships shall include the full and balanced participation of—

(A)(i) representatives of business (including representatives of large employers and representatives of small employers) who have expertise in the area of workforce skill requirements, and who are recommended by national business organizations or trade associations representing employers in the occupation or industry for which a standard is being developed; and

(B) employee representatives who have expertise in the area of workforce skill requirements and who shall be—

This section calls for representatives who are involved in the occupation or industry for which a standard is being developed and are either recommended by national labor organizations or are nonmanagerial employees with significant experience in a particular cluster area; representatives of: educational institutions; community-based organizations; state and local agencies with administrative control or direction over education, vo-tech education, or employment and training; other policy development organizations with expertise in work force skill requirements; independent, qualified experts in their fields; NGOs *"with a demonstrated history of successfully protecting the rights of racial, ethnic, or religious minorities, women, individuals with disabilities, or older persons;"* and individuals with expertise in measurement and assessment, *"including relevant experience in designing unbiased assessments and performance-based assessments."*

These requirements ensure that the tests will **not be unbiased** but will bow to the prevailing political winds and **will be outcome-based** (*"performance-based"*). Another seamless web of partnershipping and political correctness. Title 5 makes clear that ***GOALS 2000*** is labor-driven. The needs of a centrally-planned economy, *a la* the former Soviet Union, will determine what is required, what is taught to support those requirements, and who will be the recipient of the government's largesse. **Title 5 of *P.L.103-227* is the blueprint for our economic enslavement.**

> *(c) Research, Dissemination, and Coordination.*

The first four items the National Board is charged with are:

> *(1) conduct workforce research relating to skill standards (including research relating to use of skill standards in compliance with civil rights laws) and make such research available to the public, including the voluntary partnerships described in subsection (b);*
>
> *(2) identify and maintain a catalog of skill standards used by other countries and by States and leading firms and industries in the United States;*

We must know what other countries are doing since the concealed agenda is to have an **international** set of skill standards,

> *(3) serve as a clearinghouse to facilitate the sharing of information on the development of skill standards and other relevant information among representatives of occupations and industries identified pursuant to subsection (a), the voluntary partnerships described in subsection (b), and among education and training providers through such mechanisms as the Capacity Building and Information and Dissemination Network established under section 453(b) of the Job Training Partnership Act (29 U.S.C. 1733(b)) and the Educational Resources Information Center Clearinghouses;*
>
> *(4) develop a common nomenclature relating to skill standards;*

Henceforth every occupation cluster and skill will have a government-approved name. That's a first step in standardization, and standardization is a first step in internationalization.

(5) encourage the development and adoption of curricula and training materials, for attaining the skill standards developed pursuant to subsection (d), that provide for structured work experiences and related study programs leading to progressive levels of professional and technical certification and postsecondary education;

Encourage curricula and training materials that tie the apprenticeship programs *("structured work experiences and related study programs")* to the CIMs and CAMs *("progressive levels of professional and technical certification")*.

(6) provide appropriate technical assistance to voluntary partnerships involved in the development of standards and systems described in subsection (b); and

(7) facilitate coordination among voluntary partnerships that meet the requirements of subsection (b) to promote the development of a coherent national system of voluntary skill standards.

Sure, the *"partnerships"* are voluntary (for now) and so are the *"skill standards,"* but this is, after all, a *"national system,"* intended for use in all states. It will be easy to make "partnerships" mandatory for employers who wish to participate in programs getting federal funds. Where will the CIMs and CAMs leave the homeschooled or Christian-schooled student who doesn't care to participate in government training programs? **Certificates of Mastery necessary to go on to higher education, enter the work force or the military, look like the "choke point" to force everyone into this brave new world of government-approved training, skill standards, and work cards.** It's almost like saying to parents, "Do what you want with your children's education, but if they're not equipped to enter and compete in the 'real world,' (don't have a CIM/CAM) don't blame us."

(d) ENDORSEMENT OF SKILL STANDARDS SYSTEMS.—

(1) DEVELOPMENT OF ENDORSEMENT CRITERIA.—(A) The National Board, after extensive public consultation, shall develop objective criteria for endorsing skill standards systems relating to the occupa-

tional clusters identified pursuant to subsection (a). Such criteria shall, at a minimum, include the components of a skill standards system described in subparagraph (B). The endorsement criteria shall be published in the Federal Register, and updated as appropriate.

(B) The skill standards systems endorsed pursuant to paragraph (1) shall have one or more of the following components:

(i) Voluntary skill standards, which at a minimum—

(I) take into account relevant standards used in other countries and relevant international standards;

Notice that this is mentioned first. The program is launched as "national" skill standards, but is intended to be ***"international"*** from day one.

(II) meet or exceed the highest applicable standards used in the United States, including apprenticeship standards registered under the Act of August 16, 1937 (commonly known as the "National Apprenticeship Act," 50 Stat. 664, chapter 663, 29 U.S.C. 50 et seq.);

(III) take into account content and performance standards certified pursuant to title 2;

Skill standards will be aligned with ***GOALS 2000*** content and performance standards under Title 2 and both are **outcome-based. (See Title 2, Sections 211 and 213.)**

(IV) take into account the requirements of high performance work organizations;

What Work Requires of Schools—
and what the NWO requires of workers.

(V) are in a form that allows for regular updating to take into

account advances in technology or other developments within the occupational cluster;

If the National Board is disbanding in 1999 (per Section 503), who will do this *"regular updating"*?

(VI) are formulated in such a manner that promotes the portability of credentials and facilitates worker mobility within an occupational cluster or industry and among industries; and

The work card euphemistically referred to as a portable credential will make it easy for workers to move around (the globe) within occupational clusters and industries. Since many industries are already multinational and many more will be in the wake of NAFTA and GATT, isn't it logical for the work card to be benchmarked to one universal standard to make it truly "portable"? This explains the emphasis seen throughout Title 5 on being in step with what other industrialized countries are doing. **(See (I) above).**

(VII) are not discriminatory with respect to race, color, gender, age, religion, ethnicity, disability, or national origin, consistent with Federal civil rights laws.

(ii) A voluntary system of assessment and certification of the attainment of skill standards developed pursuant to subparagraph (A), which at a minimum—

(I) has been developed after taking into account relevant methods of such assessment and certification used in other countries;

You can't merge if your standards don't mesh.

(II) utilizes a variety of evaluation techniques, including, where appropriate, oral and written evaluations, portfolio assessments, and performance tests; and

This is another way of saying the skill standards will be **outcome-**

based without using that forbidden term. The emphasis on a variety of *"evaluating techniques"* is typical of outcome-based education where a dim view is taken of traditional pencil and paper tests based on recall of facts.

> *(III) includes methods for establishing that the assessment and certification system is not discriminatory with respect to race, color, gender, age, religion, ethnicity, disability, or national origin, consistent with Federal civil rights laws.*

Curious how Title 5 is so solicitous of the federal civil rights laws, while in Title 3, Section 311 (and elsewhere) in **GOALS 2000**, states are told it's perfectly all right to ignore (get waivers to) other existing laws and regulations **if they stand in the way of restructuring.**

The last three points under this heading deal with developing a means for using and disseminating skill standards, assessments, and certification systems; evaluation of these three; and periodically revising and updating the systems to ***"take into account changes in standards in other countries."***

(g) Financial Assistance, covers contracts, cooperative agreements, and grants for the development of skill standards systems.

Section 505, Deadlines, states that by December 31, 1995, the National Board is to have identified the occupational clusters for a substantial portion of the work force and is to have promoted the development of an initial set of skill standards for these clusters.

Section 506, Reports—the National Board is to prepare and submit annually (1994–1999) to the President and Congress a report on the activities conducted under this title.

> **SEC. 507. AUTHORIZATION OF APPROPRIATIONS.**
>
> *(a)* IN GENERAL.—*There are authorized to be appropriated to carry out this title $15,000,000 for fiscal year 1994 and such sums as may be necessary for each of fiscal years 1995 through 1999.*

Section 504(g)(3)(A) specifies that not more than twenty percent of the funds appropriated can be used by the National Board for the costs of administration (staff, space, equipment, supplies, conducting meetings, travel, or per diem). That leaves **$12,000,000** in the first year for contracts, agreements, and grants. **This is the largest appropriation given to any title under *GOALS 2000*.**

Section 509, **Sunset Provision**, says that although this title is repealed on September 30, 1999, Congress should review the accomplishments of the National Board prior to that date to determine whether to *"extend the authorities provided under this title for a period beyond such date."* So **don't count on the National Skills Standards Board riding off into the "sunset" in 1999.**

Title 6—
International Education Program

In which you will see. . . . that our State Department is to be actively involved in a series of educational exchange programs with foreign countries in three curricular areas: civics, government and economics.

Grants will be awarded for comparative studies of the curriculum, methodology, and organizational structure (with emphasis on the length of the school day and year) of other countries. Grants will also be awarded to compare international achievements, with the eventual (though unstated) aim being the universal standardization of education.

We are to export our ideas in civics, government and economics to the former Soviet-bloc countries. Oddly, we are also to **import** programs for our students which draw upon the experiences of these collectivist countries referred to in Title 6 as **"emerging constitutional democracies."** The United States is also **(mistakenly)** referred to throughout as a **"constitutional democracy"** (highlighted where quoted in Title 6 for emphasis).

Research is called for to determine "knowledge, skills, and traits of character essential for the preservation of constitutional democracy," i.e., what needs to be done to get students from where they are to where the internationalists want them to be.

Seminars, school, and home visits are encouraged.

The DOE is authorized to assist foreign countries in establishing and maintaining a data base (or other effective methods) to improve delivery systems, structure, and organization.

Model curricular frameworks in civics, government, and economics are called for (and have for the most part already been prepared).

TITLE 6— INTERNATIONAL EDUCATION PROGRAM

SEC. 601. INTERNATIONAL EDUCATION PROGRAM.

(a) PROGRAM ESTABLISHED.—The Secretary, with the concurrence of the Director of the United States Information Agency and with the foreign policy guidance of the Secretary of State, shall carry out an International Education Program in accordance with this section that shall provide for—

The U.S. Information Agency is the federal agency that runs Voice of America broadcasts and handles overseas public relations. ***"Foreign policy guidance of the Secretary of State"***? Are you surprised that the State Department is involved in educational restructuring? For many it's bad enough to learn that our public schools are being commandeered and nationalized by the U.S. Department of Education. It's even more alarming to realize that ***GOALS 2000*** is actually part of a much larger, **international** strategy intended to merge us into the coming one-world economy/one-world government. **(See chronology: 1, 5, 6, 10–12, 13, 15–20, 26, 28, 40, 41, 47, 52, 55, 56, 60, 63–68, 73, 77, 81, 84, 85, 93, 95, 101, 108, 109, 114, 119, and 126; and glossary: Lifelong Learning and UNESCO.)**

(1) the study of international education programs and delivery systems; and

"Programs," as used here means curriculum (content). A *"delivery system"* is a methodology for presenting curriculum. OBE is an example of a delivery system.

(2) an international education exchange program.

There have been many international exchange programs over the years. One of the strangest was the U.S./Soviet exchange signed in 1985 when the Cold War was a political reality and Ronald Reagan was referring to the Soviet Union as an "evil empire." Why would we be getting involved in international exchanges if the intent was not to get the content, standards, and assessments of the world's schools as closely synchronized as possible? The coming global society will need a universal school system, with all parts meshing. **(See chronology: 81 and 93; and glossary: U.S./Soviet Agreements.)**

> *(b)* Assessment and Information.—*The Secretary shall award grants for the study, evaluation, and analysis of education systems in other nations, particularly Great Britain, France, Germany and Japan. Such studies shall focus upon a comparative analysis of curriculum, methodology, and organizational structure, including the length of the school year and school day. In addition, the studies shall provide an analysis of successful strategies employed by other nations to improve student achievement, with a specific focus upon application to schooling and the National Education Goals.*

Concerning *"the length of the school year and school day,"* the federal government has already done a major study of this subject with the interesting title, ***Prisoners of Time***. Its thesis is that compared to other countries, **our children are not spending enough hours in school** and this somehow makes them "prisoners of time." This study, and others yet to be commissioned, will, no doubt, lead to **lengthening both the school day and the school year so that the U.S. will be more closely aligned with other nations.** Great Britain, France, Germany, and Japan, mentioned above, are not the only countries with whom we will be looking at and entering into exchanges, agreements, and partnerships. The central planners are casting a wide net that's meant to eventually cover the entire globe. **(See chronology: 91.)**

> *(c)* International Education Exchange.—

> *(1)* Requirements.—

> *(A)* In general.—*The Secretary in consultation with the Director*

> *of the United States Information Agency, shall carry out a program to be known as the International Education Exchange Program. Under such program the Secretary shall award grants to or enter into contracts with organizations with demonstrated effectiveness or expertise in international achievement comparisons, in order to—*

"International achievement comparisons" is the key here. If you're going to have a one-world economy and government, it's very important to know how member nations compare, so the system can be fine-tuned. **You can't merge if you can't mesh. (See glossary: NCES.)**

> *(i) make available to educators from eligible countries exemplary curriculum and teacher training programs in civics and government education and economic education developed in the United States;*

Section 601(6) defines an *"eligible"* country as *"a Central European country, an Eastern European country, Lithuania, Latvia, Estonia, Georgia, the Commonwealth of Independent States, and any country that formerly was a republic of the Soviet Union whose political independence is recognized in the United States."* This sounds like more of the help we are currently giving former Soviet Union satellites to enable them to restructure their governments and get on their feet economically. **Why should foreign aid be a part of our national education program?**

> *(ii) assist eligible countries in the adaptation and implementation of such programs or joint research concerning such programs;*

> *(iii) create and implement educational programs for United States students which draw upon the experiences of emerging **constitutional democracies**;*

Exporting our form of government—**if such help has been sought**—should be our total interest in these *"emerging constitutional democracies."* The hidden agenda behind all this cross-pollination between our **constitutional republic** and the *"constitutional democracies,"* i.e., social democrats, socialists, communists, and other collectivist systems (whatever they are calling themselves) is to **promote "tolerance," and blur the lines between what we are doing and what they're doing, so that soon we can meet in the middle, reach consensus, and enter into a new blended system.** Students of philosophy and political science will recognize this as the **Hegelian dialectic.**

> *(iv) provide a means for the exchange of ideas and experiences in civics and government education and economic education among political, educational, and private sector leaders of participating eligible countries; and*

Economics and the private sector are never far from the center of *GOALS 2000.* If the eventual aim is to blend and merge the world's economies, the private sector is a key element and must be involved in educational exchanges.

> *(v) provide support for—*
>
> *(I) research and evaluation to determine the effects of educational programs on students' development of the knowledge, skills, and traits of character essential for the preservation and improvement of* ***constitutional democracy****; and*

Is it possible that the writers of ***GOALS 2000*** or the attorneys who carefully look these laws over before final passage do not know that we live in a constitutional **republic** (not a democracy) and that preserving our republic is what Americans should be concerned about? Since that doesn't seem very likely, I suggest the intent is for the United States to be subtly shifted into a system of ***"constitutional democracy."*** This will be the triumph of the **Hegelian dialectic** where **thesis** (our form of government) and **antithesis** (communism/socialism) meet and merge in a mushy middle (**synthesis**), which they call throughout Title 6 a ***"constitutional democracy."*** The internationalization of education will require ongoing evaluation and fine-tuning of students' ***"knowledge, skills, and traits of character"*** to produce ideal workers for the NWO. This relates to the communist notion of **social evolu-**

tion, where **change is the norm and whatever works is right.** Under this model, the *"knowledge"* will be the dumbed-down, politically correct curriculum; the *"skills"* only those useful for workers in a one-world economy; and the *"traits of character,"* the attitudes, values, and beliefs necessary to embrace globalism and that prove to be politically reliable. **(See John Dewey's thoughts on "socialization" and "democracy" in the Whole Language glossary entry.)**

> *(II) effective participation in and the preservation and improvement of an efficient market economy.*

Note they don't say "free market" economy because a **managed global economy** is the intent. Throughout *GOALS 2000*, the writers have used terms that closely resemble ideas patriotic Americans identify with, but by making small, subtle, semantic changes (often eliminating or substituting just one **key word)** the entire meaning changes. **Social engineering requires and begins with verbal engineering.**

In the next section (B), Program Administration, the secretary and director of the U.S. Information Agency are jointly responsible for setting up an oversight committee to determine specifications for requests for proposals, the eligibility and review criteria for proposals, and the review process for proposals, for grants and contracts under Title 6. The money spent on authorized projects is to be divided equally between civics/government education and economic education. The DOE and USIA are authorized to contract with independent nonprofit educational organizations to carry out programs. Such organizations shall—

> *(i) be experienced in—*
>
> *(I) the development and national implementation of curricular programs in civics and government education and economic education for students from grades kindergarten through 12 in local, intermediate, and State educational agencies, in schools funded by the Bureau, and in private schools throughout the Nation with the cooperation and assistance of national professional educational organizations, colleges and universities, and private sector organizations;*

(II) the development and implementation of cooperative university and school-based inservice training programs for teachers of grades kindergarten through grade 12 using scholars from such relevant disciplines as political science, political philosophy, history, law and economics;

(III) the development of model curricular frameworks in civics and government education and economic education;

This is an example of how much that's in *GOALS 2000* preceded the law itself. *"Model curricular frameworks,"* i.e. "standards" for civics were done by the Center for Civic Education **(with DOE and foundation funding)** and economics is being developed (privately) by the National Council on Economic Education and should be ready by summer 1996.

(IV) the administration of international seminars on the goals and objectives of civics and government education or economic education in ***constitutional democracies*** *(including the sharing of curricular materials) for educational leaders, teacher trainers, scholars in related disciplines, and educational policymakers; and*

(V) the evaluation of civics and government education or economic education programs;

(3) ACTIVITIES.—The international education program described in this subsection shall—

(A) provide eligible countries with—

(i) seminars on the basic principles of United States ***constitutional democracy*** *and economics, including seminars on the major governmental and economic institutions and systems in the United States, and visits to such institutions;*

(ii) visits to school systems, institutions of higher learning, and nonprofit organizations conducting exemplary programs in civics

and government education and economic education in the United States;

(iii) home stays in United States communities;

You have, no doubt, noticed in your local media glowing accounts of exchange visits by teachers and students to and from foreign countries. Visits between the former Soviet Union and the U.S. have become especially popular. While exchanges are nothing new, in the past these programs were privately funded and, therefore, less common and less publicized. Such visits should remain at the option (and expense) of the individuals involved which would greatly reduce their incidence and influence.

(iv) translations and adaptations regarding United States civics and government education and economic education curricular programs for students and teachers, and in the case of training programs for teachers translations and adaptations into forms useful in schools in eligible countries, and joint research projects in such areas;

(v) translation of basic documents of United States constitutional government for use in eligible countries, such as The Federalist Papers, selected writings of Presidents Adams and Jefferson and the Anti-Federalists, and more recent works on political theory, constitutional law and economics; and

Basic historical documents, such as those listed sound fine, but I'd like to see a list of the *"more recent works"* that will be selected for export.

(vi) research and evaluation assistance to determine—

(I) the effects of educational programs on students' development of the knowledge, skills and traits of character essential for the preservation and improvement of ***constitutional democracy****; and*

"Character education" is one of the hot new classroom fads. Don't be misled by this latest renaming of attitudes, values, and beliefs training! The only basis for developing *"traits of character"* will be those humanist/secular principles deemed common to all cultures and offensive to no one, especially the NWO. **(See chronology: 7, 8, 14, 23–25, 34, 36, 50, 54, 56, 57, 66, 86, 120, and 121.)**

(II) effective participation in and the preservation and improvement of an efficient market economy;

See earlier comment on verbal engineering and semantic deception.

(B) provide United States participants with—

(i) seminars on the histories, economics, and government of eligible countries;

(ii) visits to school systems, institutions of higher learning, and organizations conducting exemplary programs in civics and government education and economic education located in eligible countries;

Those familiar with the military may see parallels between educational exchanges and the many cross-training programs going on between the United States and foreign countries. Globalism is the driving force behind both.

(iii) home stays in eligible countries;

(iv) assistance from educators and scholars in eligible countries in the development of curricular materials on the history, government and economics of such countries that are useful in United States classrooms;

Any country formerly under the Soviet Union whose political independence is recognized in the United States, is *"eligible."* How likely is it they will give us anything ***"useful"*** for our classrooms?

(v) opportunities to provide on-site demonstrations of United States curricula and pedagogy for educational leaders in eligible countries; and

(vi) research and evaluation assistance to determine—

(I) the effects of educational programs on students' development of the knowledge, skills and traits of character essential for the preservation and improvement of ***constitutional democracy****; and*

(II) effective participation in and improvement of an efficient market economy; and

(C) assist participants from eligible countries and the United States in participating in international conferences on civics and government education and economic education for educational leaders, teacher trainers, scholars in related disciplines and educational policymakers.

(4) Participants.—The primary participants in the international education program assisted under this subsection shall be leading educators in the areas of civics and government education and economic education, including curriculum and teacher training specialists, scholars in relevant disciplines, and educational policymakers, from the United States and eligible countries.

(5) Personnel and technical experts.—The Secretary is authorized to provide Department of Education personnel and technical experts to assist eligible countries to establish and implement a database or other effective methods to improve educational delivery systems, structure and organization.

The database is needed to facilitate OBE (the content delivery system) and to give countries which have been slow in getting computerized the capability to track their students' progress toward international standards and goals. Doubtless, the NCES will be involved in this assistance. **(See glossary: NCES.)**

(d) AUTHORIZATION OF APPROPRIATIONS.—

(1) ASSESSMENT AND INFORMATION.—*There are authorized to be appropriated $1,000,000 for fiscal year 1995, and such sums as may be necessary for each of the fiscal years 1996 through 1999, to carry out subsection (b).*

(2) INTERNATIONAL EDUCATION EXCHANGE.—*There are authorized to be appropriated $10,000,000 for fiscal year 1995, and such sums as may be necessary for each of the fiscal years 1996 through 1999, to carry out subsection (c).*

Title 7— Safe Schools

In which you will see. . . .

- law enforcement agencies becoming a partner in the "it takes a whole village . . ." concept.
- grants to be awarded to local educational agencies (LEAs) to enable the Sixth National Education Goal (Adult Literacy/ Lifelong Learning).
- fifty percent of this money is to be spent on a "national model city" project in Washington, D.C.
- most of the remainder will go as grants to LEAs for crime reduction/prevention. Preference will be given to:

    1. LEAs with high need/anticipated high use.
    2. LEAs that have formed partnerships with community-based organizations and/or law enforcement agencies.

To be eligible for funds, recipients must do a PPBS (Planning, Programming, Budgeting System) for their community/problem.

Title 7 places a heavy emphasis on ***partnershipping** between parents, schools, law enforcement, businesses, local government, the media, health, social service, "and other appropriate agencies and organizations."*

Additionally, the secretary of education may use funds to conduct R&D, for data collection, training and technical assistance, dissemination of successful project strategies, and public awareness activities, including grants for video projects dealing with conflict resolution and "responsible decisionmaking."

TITLE 7— SAFE SCHOOLS

(a) SHORT TITLE.—This title may be cited as the "Safe Schools Act of 1994".

This was a stand-alone bill, H.R. 2455, one of several rolled into the omnibus ***GOALS 2000*** legislation.

(b) STATEMENT OF PURPOSE.—It is the purpose of this title to help local school systems achieve Goal Six of the National Education Goals, which provides that by the year 2000, every school in America will be free of drugs and violence and will offer a disciplined environment conducive to learning, by ensuring that all schools are safe and free of violence.

Section 702, Safe Schools Program Authorized, states that grants to eligible LEAs for projects and activities designed to achieve the sixth NEG will not exceed two fiscal years duration or $3,000,000. Grants are to be awarded to eligible rural, as well as urban areas. Fifty percent of the money is to be spent for a *"national model city"* project to be conducted in the District of Columbia.

SEC. 703. ELIGIBLE APPLICANTS.

(a) IN GENERAL.—To be eligible to receive a grant under this title, a local educational agency shall demonstrate in the application submitted pursuant to section 704(a) that such agency—

(1) serves an area in which there is a high rate of —

(A) homicides committed by persons between the ages of 5 to 18, inclusive;

Five years old? This would have to include accidental shootings by small children playing with loaded guns. These should not be lumped in with intentional killings by older youth such as teen gang members. The purpose of such padded statistics may be to make a "worst case scenario" for the restriction of private gun ownership.

(B) referrals of youth to juvenile court;

(C) youth under the supervision of the courts;

(D) expulsions and suspensions of students from school;

(E) referrals of youth, for disciplinary reasons, to alternative schools; or

(F) victimization of youth by violence, crime, or other forms of abuse; and

"Victimization" is always a loaded concept, subject to the shifting sands of politically correct interpretation. In the context of the list above, the sense may seem clear, but who can say how ***"violence"*** and especially ***"other forms of abuse"*** will be interpreted? Violence could include corporal punishment in the home, i.e., **spanking**. "Victims" could be students of various racial, ethnic, and religious groups, or homosexuals subjected to verbal or other abuse (hate crimes).

(2) has serious school crime, violence, and discipline problems, as indicated by other appropriate data.

(b) PRIORITY.—In awarding grants under this title, the Secretary shall give priority to a local educational agency that submits an application that assures a strong local commitment to the projects or activities assisted under this title, such as—

(1) the formation of partnerships among the local educational agency, a community-based organization, a nonprofit organization with a demonstrated commitment to or expertise in developing education programs or providing educational services to students or the public, a local law enforcement agency, or any combination thereof; and

More partnerships. Title 7 partnerships, however, involve **law enforcement** agencies.

(2) a high level of youth participation in such projects or activities.

This will include experimental programs of student-led conflict resolution such as peer mediation, peer counseling, and student courts.

SEC. 704. APPLICATIONS AND PLANS.

This section lays out thirteen requirements for grant recipients. They must do an assessment of the current crime problem in their community (as well as) school, and show how the grant project will help to reduce crime and violence in both places; show they have a written policy covering school safety, student discipline, and the handling of violent or disruptive acts; describe educational materials to be developed in a non-English language, if applicable; how activities using Title 7 money will be coordinated with *"any systemic education improvement plan"* receiving other federal money; their plan to establish school-level advisory committees to assist in designing and assessing the school's programs, policies, and practices addressing violence and discipline problems. Committees are to include faculty, parents, staff, and students; a description of how the grantee will inform parents of the extent of crime and violence in their children's schools and maximize the participation of parents in violence prevention activities; a description of how the grantee will coordinate the school's crime and violence prevention efforts with activities carried out under the ***Drug-Free Schools and Communities Act of 1986,*** as well as with education (apparently other than the school itself), law enforcement, judicial, health, and social service programs under the ***Juvenile Justice and De-***

linquency Prevention Act of 1974, *"and other appropriate agencies and organizations serving the community"*; have a plan for collecting baseline and future data to monitor violence and discipline problems and measure progress in achieving the purpose of Title 7; assure that applicants will cooperate with the secretary in gathering statistics and other data needed to determine the effectiveness of projects; and any *"such other information as the Secretary may require."* In order to receive funds for a second year, the grantee must submit a comprehensive, long-term school safety plan for reducing and preventing school violence and discipline problems. This plan must include a description of how the school has coordinated its efforts with education, law-enforcement, judicial, health, social service, and other appropriate agencies and organizations serving the community.

This is a classic, community-based PPBS. The preset agenda here is to demonstrate a clear need (problem) and then set up a plan for increased community partnershipping and collaborations (solution). "It takes a whole village to raise a child." Parents are **partners**, but in a lopsided arrangement, top-heavy with government bureaucracy. **(See chronology: 32, 45, and 55; and glossary: Partnerships and PPBS.)**

Sec. 705. Use of Funds.

(a) In General.—A local educational agency shall use grant funds received under this title for one or more of the following activities:

(1) Identifying and assessing school violence and discipline problems, including coordinating needs assessment activities with education, law enforcement, judicial, health, social service, and other appropriate agencies and organizations, juvenile justice programs, and gang prevention activities.

(2) Conducting school safety reviews or violence prevention reviews of programs, policies, practices, and facilities to determine what changes are needed to reduce or prevent violence and promote safety and discipline.

(3) Planning for comprehensive, long-term strategies for address-

ing and preventing school violence and discipline problems through the involvement and coordination of school programs with other education, law enforcement, judicial, health, social service, and other appropriate agencies and organizations.

(4) Training school personnel in programs of demonstrated effectiveness in addressing violence, including violence prevention, conflict resolution, anger management, peer mediation, and identification of high-risk youth.

Where is the evidence of ***"demonstrated effectiveness"*** for these programs? Don't they all fall into the **"experimental"** category? How much time out of the "academic day" will they take up? **No wonder educrats want to lengthen the school day and year!** And how much coercion and loss of freedom will be required to maintain them? We will look back on these programs five years from now and see another expensive but failed attempt to curb school discipline problems. And the educrats will, as they always do, claim the programs failed for lack of sufficient funding.

(5) Activities which involve parents in efforts to promote school safety and prevent school violence.

What sort of *"activities"*? Are they thinking of **contracts** between the parents and the school? If students get into trouble and it can be shown that parents have not lived up to their part of the agreement, will parents be held liable along with their children? Virginia has instituted a mandatory "parental-responsibility contract," which parents are required to sign and return—or face a $50 fine. According to a **"News Roundup"** notice in ***Education Week*** (9/27/95), Virginia is facing a court challenge on this.

(6) Community education programs, including video- and technology-based projects, informing parents, businesses, local government, the media and other appropriate entities about—

(A) the local educational agency's plan to promote school safety

and reduce and prevent school violence and discipline problems; and

(B) the need for community support.

If it takes a whole village to raise a child and everyone is to assume some share of the responsibility, won't citizens be encouraged to watch one another and report any lapses in "**responsible behavior**" to the authorities? **Doesn't this lay the groundwork for "block surveillance cadres,"** ***a la*** **China and the former Soviet Union?**

(7) Coordination of school-based activities designed to promote school safety and reduce or prevent school violence and discipline problems with related efforts of education, law enforcement, judicial, health, social service, and other appropriate agencies and organizations and juvenile justice programs.

Notice how many of the grant activities involve setting up **partnerships**. While it can be argued that better coordination of programs will (or should) reduce costs and red tape, they all tend toward a system where the **parent becomes merely a junior partner in a corporation where senior partners (representatives of the government) have the majority vote.**

(8) Developing the implementing violence prevention activities and materials, including—

(A) conflict resolution and social skills development for students, teachers, aides, other school personnel, and parents;

Parents will be encouraged to use the same humanistic/secular psychology conflict resolution and social skills models the schools have adopted. This will conflict with the biblically-based values of Christian parents.

(B) disciplinary alternatives to expulsion and suspension of students who exhibit violent or antisocial behavior;

The term *"antisocial behavior"* is problematic because it can mean anything the government decides is "against society," e.g., a belief in absolutes, being intolerant, refusal to take part in certain school activities, etc. One of the *"disciplinary alternatives"* being seriously considered for dealing with "**violent or antisocial**" children is to remove them from their homes and place them in "**protective custody.**" We need to be very aware that ideas that seem like a possible—even reasonable—answer to the most intractable discipline problems, can be turned on Christians and other "politically incorrect" citizens.

> *(C) student-led activities such as peer mediation, peer counseling, and student courts; or*

Every one of these is experimental and potentially very dangerous. The flawed assumption behind these programs is that with a few hours of "leader training," students will have enough maturity and wisdom to counsel other students (including some with very serious problems) and have enough sound, impartial judgment to settle disputes.

> *(D) alternative after-school programs that provide safe havens for students, which may include cultural, recreational, educational and instructional activities, and mentoring and community service programs.*

What is left for parents to do but pick up their children, feed them dinner (perhaps that will be taken care of at the "after-school program," too), tuck them into bed, and get them up in time for another "school day"? **These babysitting services are a *de facto* way to lengthen the school day and gain additional access to children.** Funneling students from the after-school programs into *"community service programs"* allows the government to utilize valuable "human resources" that would otherwise be unavailable to them. **Sadly, however, many working parents will probably not see a hidden agenda, and will be thrilled at the convenience of on-site, after-school care (and the other services) provided at minimal or no additional cost.**

> *(9) Educating students and parents regarding the dangers of guns*

and other weapons and the consequences of their use.

Here's a modest albeit politically incorrect proposal: Let the gun owners' associations that have produced excellent materials on gun safety (that I'll bet would be glad to **"partnership"** with the schools) provide gun safety materials and speakers. Since this seems a very unlikely scenario, this part of ***GOALS 2000*** may be used to lobby tirelessly for the **weakening of Second Amendment rights and more restrictions on private gun ownership**, with the eventual aim of outlawing private gun ownership entirely. (If and) when that happens, the only armed citizens will be the military **"peacekeepers"** and civilians who could care less if their guns have been obtained legally, including the violent, criminal element from which such laws were supposed to protect us. An interesting contrast to the direction we're heading is peaceful, law-abiding **Switzerland where adults are required to own and be trained in the proper handling and use of firearms.**

(10) Developing and implementing innovative curricula to prevent violence in schools and training staff how to stop disruptive or violent behavior if such behavior occurs.

One of the reasons entering the teaching field is not the attractive career option it once was, is that this is now part of the job description.

(11) Supporting "safe zones of passage" for students between home and school through such measures as Drug- and Weapon-Free School Zones, enhanced law enforcement, and neighborhood patrols.

This is either wishful thinking like those ubiquitous signs announcing a **"Drug Free School Zone,"** or will be carried out by extremely Draconian measures that infringe on First and Second Amendment rights, turning neighborhoods into block surveillance and reporting units.

(12) Counseling programs for victims and witnesses of school violence and crime.

How about "compensation" by perpetrators to their victims? That might be far more effective than the humanistic/psychological counseling schools will be offering.

> *(13) Acquiring and installing metal detectors and hiring security personnel.*

Why would any parent send their children to spend time daily in a DMZ that's been heavily fortified "just in case" someone gets in armed? Isn't it time to look at a totally different alternative to state schools when it has reached the point of your child's physical safety? This was brought home to us when we entered our son in a Christian high school and the person doing the interview told us he was surprised that we didn't ask about safety. Apparently, these days **most parents ask.** Our son had been homeschooled for the six preceding years and during that time we never even thought about safety. That's as it should be and is a **normal** state of affairs. Being concerned about your child's physical safety in the place you send him five times a week for six or so hours a day is **abnormal** and shouldn't be tolerated as though it's "just the way things are nowadays." **Any place that cannot promise the absolute enforcement of a drug and violence free environment is not deserving of your child—period.**

> *(14) Reimbursing law enforcement authorities for their personnel who participate in school violence prevention activities.*

Paying consultants and off-duty police officers to enforce law and order will be an additional tax burden for schools.

> *(15) Evaluating projects and activities assisted under this title.*

> *(16) The cost of administering projects or activities assisted under this title.*

> *(17) Other projects or activities that meet the purpose of this title.*

That wonderful catchall category, **"other."**

Under "**(b) Limitations**," we learn that only five percent of funds may be used for (11), (13), and (14) above, and only if funding for these is not available from other federal sources and that only five percent may be spent for administration. An LEA may not use Title 7 grant funds for construction.

Sec. 706. National Activities.

(a) National Activities.—

(1) In general.—To carry out the purpose of this title, the Secretary—

(A) is authorized to use funds reserved under section 702(b)(2) to—

(i) conduct national leadership activities such as research, program development and evaluation, data collection, public awareness activities, training and technical assistance, dissemination (through appropriate research entities assisted by the Department of Education) of information on successful projects, activities, and strategies developed pursuant to this title;

The emphasis on research, development, and public awareness indicates how much of this is **experimental**. Dissemination of projects, etc., deemed successful will be made available nationwide through the National Diffusion Network (NDN) and other dissemination channels of the DOE. **(See glossary: ERIC and NDN.)**

(ii) provide grants to noncommercial telecommunications entities for the production and distribution of national video-based projects that provide young people with models for conflict resolution and responsible decisionmaking; and

"Noncommercial"? Will the Public Broadcasting System (PBS) be the recipient of a share of this grant money? They're certainly set up to do national distribution.

(iii) conduct peer review of applications under this title; and

Who are the "peers"?

(B) shall develop a written safe schools model so that all schools can develop models that enable all students to participate regardless of any language barrier.

(2) Special rule.—The Secretary may carry out the activities described in paragraph (1) directly, through interagency agreements, or through grants, contracts or cooperative agreements.

(b) National Model City.—The Secretary shall designate the District of Columbia as a national model city and shall provide funds made available pursuant to section 702(b)(2) in each fiscal year to a local educational agency serving the District of Columbia in an amount sufficient to enable such agency to carry out a comprehensive program to address school and youth violence.

It's fitting, I suppose, that the city with the nation's highest crime rate is chosen to be a "model city" under Title 7.

Section 707, National Cooperative Education Statistics System, makes two changes in the statistics provisions of the ***General Education Provisions Act (GEPA)***.

Section 708, Reports, calls for each LEA receiving funds under Title 7 to submit a report by March 1, 1995, to the secretary. The secretary, in turn, is to submit to Congress a detailed report on grant awards by October 1, 1995.

Sec. 709. Coordination of Federal Assistance.

The Secretary, as a member of the Coordinating Council on Juvenile Justice and Delinquency Prevention of the Department of Justice, shall coordinate the programs and activities carried out under this title with the programs and activities carried out by the departments and offices represented within the Council that provide assistance under other Federal law for purposes that are determined by

> *the Secretary to be similar to the purpose of this title, in order to avoid redundancy and coordinate Federal assistance, research, and programs for youth violence prevention.*

This is a tacit admission that some of what's proposed under this title is already ongoing with funding by other federal agencies. In this portion of *GOALS 2000,* we see the Department of Education **laying claim to a new area (crime and violence prevention), utilizing partnershipping, to reach into the community and individual homes.**

Title 8—
Minority-Focused Civics Education

In which you will see . . .

in the name of "diversity," "multiculturalism," and political correctness, a misguided attempt to be sensitive to everyone.

that because minority (not defined) and Native American students are perceived to learn differently and to have special needs (also not defined), American history, civics, and government must be presented to them in a different way than to non-minority students.

that to accomplish this, special accredited summer seminars for teachers and other staff are to be conducted.

that grants are to be awarded to develop and implement such seminars.

that teachers attending minority-focused seminars are to bring back the ideas learned and materials obtained to share with their colleagues.

TITLE 8—
MINORITY-FOCUSED CIVICS EDUCATION

SEC. 802. PURPOSES.

It is the purpose of this title—

(1) to encourage improved instruction for minorities and Native Americans in American government and civics through a national program of accredited summer teacher training and staff development seminars or institutes followed by academic year inservice training programs conducted on college and university campuses or other appropriate sites, for—

(A) social studies and other teachers responsible for American history, government, and civics classes; and

(B) other educators who work with minority and Native American youth; and

Why should *"improved instruction"* be limited to or even targeted specifically for certain groups of students? This sounds like reverse discrimination. (A) indicates that all teachers, K–12, will have to undergo these *"seminars, institutes, and inservice training programs"* as "social studies" begins in the first years of school.

(2) through such improved instruction to improve minority and Native American student knowledge and understanding of the American system of government.

When the schools functioned as a "melting pot," it was thought that the sooner various groups were blended into the general "American" stew, the better. Singling out certain groups and belaboring their distinctives can only promote feelings of separateness for those singled out. For the rest, this "instruction" will heighten differences that might not have been noticed if time had not been spent dwelling on them. Whatever the intention of multicultural/diversity education, it does not seem likely it will bring children from various groups closer together. The place for children to learn about their cultural, racial, or national heritage is not in the classroom, but in their own homes and communities.

Section 803, Grants Authorized; Authorization of Appropriations, empowers the secretary to make grants over a wide geographic area to *"eligible entities"* for the development and implementation of seminars in American government and civics for elementary and secondary school teachers and other educators who work with minority and Native American students. To carry out Title 8, $5,000,000 is authorized for fiscal 1995, and *"such sums as may be necessary,"* for fiscal years 1996–1998.

Section 804, Definitions, says:

> *(1) the term "eligible entity" means a State educational agency, an institution of higher education or a State higher education agency, or a public or private nonprofit organization, with experience in coordinating or conducting teacher training seminars in American government and civics education, or a consortium thereof;*
>
> *(2) the term "State higher education agency" means the officer or agency primarily responsible for the State supervision of higher education.*

Grants for this minority-focused, multicultural/diversity training will go to the State Department of Education, colleges and universities (state and private), and to organizations already experienced in running these seminars.

> *SEC. 805. APPLICATIONS.*
>
> *(a) APPLICATION REQUIRED.—Each eligible entity desiring a grant*

under this title shall submit an application to the Secretary, at such time, in such manner and containing or accompanied by such information as the Secretary may reasonably require.

(b) CONTENTS OF APPLICATION.—*Each application submitted pursuant to subsection (a) shall—*

(1) define the learning objectives and course content of each seminar to be held and describe the manner in which seminar participants shall receive substantive academic instruction in the principles, institutions and processes of American government;

Too bad the requirements don't end with this single statement.

(2) provide assurances that educators successfully participating in each seminar will quality for either graduate credit or professional development or advanced credit according to the criteria established by a State or local educational agency;

Career advancement is the **"carrot."** Teachers are not going to be voluntarily lining up to take these seminars. The **"stick"** is that teachers who fail to take the seminars won't be at the top of the list for various "perks" or may find themselves substandard in professional development at the time of their annual evaluations. Title 8 is one place in ***P.L.103-227*** where we are not assured that this is all just **"voluntary."**

(3) describe the manner in which seminar participants shall receive exposure to a broad array of individuals who are actively involved in the political process, including political party representatives drawn equally from the major political parties, as well as representatives of other organizations involved in the political process;

More partnershipping as elected (and appointed) officials are drawn into this effort. *"Other organizations involved in the political process"* should include Christian groups. Do you think they will be included, or just the PC?

> *(4) provide assurances that the seminars will be conducted on a nonpartisan basis;*
>
> *(5) describe the manner in which the seminars will address the role of minorities or Native Americans in the American political process, including such topics as—*
>
> *(A) the history and current political state of minorities or Native Americans;*
>
> *(B) recent research on minority or Native American political socialization patterns and cognitive learning styles; and*
>
> *(C) studies of political participation patterns of minorities or Native Americans;*
>
> *(6) describe the pedagogical elements for teachers that will enable teachers to develop effective strategies and lesson plans for teaching minorities or Native American students at the elementary and secondary school levels;*

These imply that minorities learn differently (*"cognitive learning styles"*), and are inherently so different that teachers need special teaching strategies (*"pedagogical elements"*) to teach these students. Minorities may just find all this **patronizing, if not downright insulting.** This PC smokescreen of sensitivity to everyone's unique differences and needs will only serve to further polarize and politicize our classrooms. **The Balkanization of our nation is the result we can expect if these ideas are fully implemented.**

> *(7) identify the eligible entities which will conduct the seminars for which assistance is sought;*
>
> *(8) in the case that the eligible entity is an institution of higher education, describe the plans for collaborating with national organizations in American government and civics education;*

Like other national standards, those for civics have already been developed by the Center for Civic Education. Colleges running these seminars will be expected to align course content with those standards.

> *(9) provide assurances that during the academic year educators participating in the summer seminars will provide inservice training programs based upon what such educators have learned and the curricular materials such educators have developed or acquired for their peers in their school systems with the approval and support of their school administrators; and*

Those attending the summer seminars are expected, in turn, to train their colleagues and share the minority-focused/diversity materials with them. This will keep down the costs of dispersing this new material throughout the schools.

> *(10) describe the activities or services for which assistance is sought, including activities and services such as—*
>
> *(A) development of seminar curricula;*
>
> *(B) development and distribution of instructional materials;*
>
> *(C) scholarships for participating teachers; and*
>
> *(D) program assessment and evaluation*
>
> *(c) Priority.—The Secretary, in approving applications for assistance under this title, shall give priority to applications which demonstrate that—*
>
> *(1) the applicant will serve teachers who teach in schools with a large number or concentration of economically disadvantaged students;*
>
> *(2) the applicant has demonstrated national experience in con-*

ducting or coordinating accredited summer seminars in American government or civics education for elementary and secondary school teachers;

(3) the applicant will coordinate or conduct seminars on a national or multistate basis through a collaboration with an institution of higher education, State higher education agency or a public or private nonprofit organization, with experience in coordinating or conducting teacher training programs in American government and civics education;

(4) the applicant will coordinate or conduct seminars designed for more than one minority student population and for Native Americans; and

(5) the applicant will coordinate or conduct seminars that offer a combination of academic instruction in American government, exposure to the practical workings of the political system, and training in appropriate pedagogical techniques for working with minority and Native American students.

Prior to the 1930s, American history, government, and civics were core subjects, were taught individually, and were taught very rigorously. In the 1930s, these three subjects were devalued and watered down by being rolled together into a **new subject area** called **"social studies."** Getting back to a clear focus on government, civics, and nonrevisionist American history seems a good idea. However, **using the study of American government to work in all the hidden agendas of multiculturalism, diversity, and other politically correct themes is a fraud, divisive, essentially un-American (if you accept the role of the public schools as assimilation not separation), and a total waste of the academic day and taxpayer dollars. (See chronology: 4, 15, 19, 20, 60, and 64; and glossary: Infusion Model.)**

Title 9— Educational Research and Improvement

In which you will see . . .

not just a "routine reauthorization" of the Office of Educational Research and Improvement (OERI), an office already existing within the DOE, but a naked power grab as OERI enlarges its empire by adding:

1. **A board**, the National Educational Research Policy and Priorities Board, charged with determining priorities for OERI, reviewing and approving standards for R&D and dissemination efforts, and making recommendations about appointments, e.g., directors for five new institutes.
2. **An office**, the Office of Reform Assistance and Dissemination (ORAD), charged with coordinating the existing dissemination outlets within the DOE, coordinating with other federal agencies, active outreach to identify promising programs and facilitating their dissemination into classrooms.
3. **Five institutes** (directorates). The duties of these are too numerous to list here; their names are suggestive of their mission:
   A. **National Institute on Student Achievement Curriculum and Assessment**
   B. **National Institute on the Education of At-Risk Students**
   C. **National Institute on Early Childhood Development and Education**
   D. **National Institute on Educational Governance, Finance,**

Policy-making, and Management

E. **National Institute on Postsecondary Education, Libraries and Lifelong Learning**

4. **A library**, the National Library of Education, to absorb the DOE's existing research library, reference section, and information branch, and to offer expanded services, including an electronic network linking the educational resources of major libraries, schools, and educational centers across the U.S.
5. **A new assistant secretary** position, necessitated by "partnershipping" to coordinate educational activities with outside agencies.

Evidence that OERI plans to use its data collecting authority to help enforce O-T-L, race, gender, equity, "at-risk," and other agendas.

TITLE 9— EDUCATIONAL RESEARCH AND IMPROVEMENT

Title 9 is by far the largest section of this 155-page law, taking up fifty-three pages or **almost one-third** of it. Therefore, it's the longest chapter in this book. **Title 9 should never have been included in *GOALS 2000*.** It started out as a stand-alone **reauthorization for the already existing and very influential Office of Educational Research and Improvement, OERI,** (referred to in Title 9 as ***"the Office"***).

Early in 1993 reauthorization for OERI was introduced into the House as H.R.856 and into the Senate as S.286. It was clear from a reading of these two bills that this was **anything but a routine reauthorization** and that OERI was planning an enormous grab of new turf. OERI has always been one of the most, if not the most, **controversial** office within the DOE. Because they are involved with **"educational research,"** most of the psychologically-based programs that have been so objectionable to parents over the years originated in, and were disseminated by OERI. Clearly these fifty-three pages, packed with empire-expansion and a tremendous increase in funding, **should have received very close scrutiny.** If that had happened, this reauthorization might have been pared down to something approaching a funding of existing programs. However, instead of going over S.286/H.R.856 with a fine-toothed comb which would certainly have alarmed the fiscal conservatives in Congress, S.286, like other stand-alone bills we've seen in earlier titles, was strategically rolled into S.1150, the Senate version of ***GOALS 2000***. Once there, it was not subjected to the close examination it might have been given as a stand-alone. And once attached to ***GOALS 2000***, it was virtually assured of passage as part of a high priority, fast track piece of legislation. **Our loss.**

Expansion of the OERI empire under Title 9 includes a **new board, an office, five directorates, a national library of education, and a position for a new assistant secretary.** Because of its length, I will selectively highlight the contents of Title 9.

Section 902 is a justification for why **more** educational research, development, dissemination, and replication is needed. Under Section 902(1)(c) are the following ***"priorities:"***

> *(7) A National Educational Research Policy and Priorities Board should be established to work collaboratively with the Assistant Secretary to forge a national consensus with respect to a long-term agenda for educational research, development, dissemination, and the activities of the Office.*

This board is established by Section 921.

> *(8) Existing research and development entities should adopt expanded, proactive roles and new institutions should be created to promote knowledge development necessary to accelerate the application of research findings to high priority areas.*

These institutes are established by Section 931.

> *(9) Greater use should be made of existing technologies in efforts to improve the educational system of the United States, including efforts to disseminate research findings.*

A national dissemination system called the **Office of Reform Assistance and Dissemination (ORAD)** is established by Section 941.

> *(10) Minority educational researchers are inadequately represented throughout the Department of Education, but particularly in the Office. The Office therefore should assume a leadership position in the recruitment, retention, and promotion of qualified minority educational researchers.*

Quota hiring.

(11) The coordination of the mission of the Office with that of other components of the Department of Education is critical. The Office should improve the coordination of the educational research, development, and dissemination function with those of other Federal agencies.

Under Part A, General Provisions Regarding the Office of Educational Research and Improvement, they list the following *"authorized activities":*

(i) conduct and support education-related research activities, including basic and applied research, development, planning, surveys, assessments, evaluations, investigations, experiments, and demonstrations of national significance;

Note the broad scope of these *"authorized activities."* Since they are in charge of these areas, they will determine what has ***"national significance."*** OERI is now charged to work collaboratively with its new board and with the **National Education Goals Panel. (See Title 2.)**

(ii) disseminate the findings of education research, and provide technical assistance to apply such information to specific problems at school sites;

This is done primarily through the National Diffusion Network (NDN) and the ten Regional Education Laboratories (RELs). **(See glossary: NDN and RELs.)**

(iii) collect, analyze, and disseminate data related to education, and to library and information services;

Done through a variety of entities, including the Educational Resources Information Center (ERIC). **(See glossary: ERIC.)**

(iv) promote the use of knowledge gained from research and statistical findings in schools, other educational institutions, and communities;

Done through **all** their dissemination outlets, including NDN, ERIC, and the RELs.

> *(v) provide training in education research; and*
>
> *(vi) promote the coordination of education research and research support within the Federal Government, and otherwise assist and foster such research.*

These six are the ***"authorized activities"*** of OERI.

Section 912 continues with a discussion of a Research Priorities Plan, standards for the conduct and evaluation of research, and publication and promulgation of standards. Additional responsibilities of the assistant secretary include the following:

> *(4) shall ensure that all statistics and other data collected and reported by the Office shall be collected, cross-tabulated, analyzed, and reported by sex within race or ethnicity and socioeconomic status whenever feasible (and when such data collection or analysis is not feasible, ensure that the relevant report or document includes an explanation as to why such data collection or analysis is not feasible);*

OERI's vehicle for the collection, analysis, and distribution of such data is the **National Center for Education Statistics (NCES).** Data on students cross-tabulated by ***"race, ethnicity, socioeconomic status and sex is to be collected."*** What on earth do they need that information for? The answer appears below: **(See glossary: NCES.)**

> *(6) is authorized to offer information and technical assistance to State and local educational agencies, school boards, and schools, including schools funded by the Bureau, to ensure that no student is—*
>
> *(A) denied access to the same rigorous, **challenging** curriculum that such student's peers are offered; or*

I have highlighted "challenging" each time it's used in Title 9.

> *(B) grouped or otherwise labeled in such a way that may impede such student's achievement.*

Data will be used to enforce race, gender, and equity funding agendas.

Section 912 (l), Definitions, defines the following terms used in Title 9:

> *(1) ASSISTANT SECRETARY.—The term "Assistant Secretary" means the Assistant Secretary for Educational Research and Improvement established by section 202 of the Department of Education Organization Act.*
>
> *(2) AT-RISK STUDENT.—The term "at risk student" means a student who, because of limited English proficiency, poverty, race, geographic location, or economic disadvantage, faces a greater risk of low educational achievement or reduced academic expectations.*
>
> *(3) BOARD.—The term "Board" means the National Educational Research Policy and Priorities Board.*
>
> *(4) DEVELOPMENT.—The term "development"—*
>
> *(A) means the systematic use, adaptation, and transformation of knowledge and understanding gained from research to create alternatives, policies, products, methods, practices, or materials which can contribute to the improvement of educational practice; and*
>
> *(B) includes the design and development of prototypes and the testing of such prototypes for the purposes of establishing their feasibility, reliability, and cost-effectiveness.*

Unfortunately, the testing of *"prototypes"* to establish the *"feasibility, reliability, and cost-effectiveness"* of OERI's *"alternatives, policies, products, methods, practices, or materials"* will not be on some new gadget produced in a factory, but on the "human resources," known as our children.

> *(5) Dissemination.—The term "dissemination" means the communication and transfer, through the provision of technical assistance and other means, of the results of research and proven practice in forms that are understandable, easily accessible and usable or adaptable for use in the improvement of educational practice by teachers, administrators, librarians, other practitioners, researchers, policymakers, and the public.*
>
> *(6) Educational research.—The term "educational research" includes basic and applied research, inquiry with the purpose of applying tested knowledge gained to specific educational settings and problems, development, planning, surveys, assessments, evaluations, investigations, experiments, and demonstrations in the field of education and other fields relating to education.*

Most of the experimental, psychologically-based programs designed to change attitudes, values, and beliefs have come through this "educational research." **(See chronology: 37, 58, 74, and 100.)**

> *(7) Field-initiated research.—The term "field-initiated research" means education research in which topics and methods of study are generated by investigators, including teachers and other practitioners, not by the source of funding.*
>
> *(8) National education dissemination system.—The term "national education dissemination system" means the activities carried out by the Office of Reform Assistance and Dissemination established by section 941.*
>
> *(9) Office.—The term "Office," unless otherwise specified, means the Office of Educational Research and Improvement established in section 209 of the Department of Education Organization Act.*
>
> *(10) National research institute.—The term "national research institute" means an institute established in section 931.*

> *(11) TECHNICAL ASSISTANCE.—The term "technical assistance" means assistance in identifying, selecting, or designing solutions based on research to address educational problems, planning, and design that leads to adapting research knowledge to school practice, training to implement such solutions, and other assistance necessary to encourage adoption or application of research.*

Under Authorization of Appropriations, the following sums are appropriated: $68,000,000 for FY-95 for the National Institutes; $30,000,000 each to the National Institute on Student Achievement, Curriculum, and Assessment and the National Institute on the Education of At-Risk Students for FY-96 and *"such sums as may be necessary"* (SSAN) for each for fiscal years 1997–99; $10,000,000 is authorized for FY-96 and SSAN for FY-1997–99 and $15,000,000 each for the National Institute on Early Childhood Development and Education, and for the National Institute on Postsecondary Education, Libraries, and Lifelong Learning, for FY-96 and SSAN for FY-97–99.

Specific appropriations under (2), National Education Dissemination System, are as follows: $23,000,000 for FY-95 and SSAN for FY-96–99 for various dissemination efforts under Section 941; $8,000,000 during any fiscal year for ERIC; $41,000,000 for FY-95 and SSAN for FY-96–99 for the regional labs; $20,000,000 for FY-95 and SSAN for FY-96–99 for the teacher research dissemination demonstration program, and for the GOALS 2000 Community Partnerships programs; $30,000,000, for FY-95, $50,000,000 for FY-96, and SSAN for FY-97–99. For the National Educational Research Policy and Priorities Board and the Research Priorities Plan, $1,000,000, or two percent of the total given to the National Institutes and the National Education Dissemination System (whichever is less) during any fiscal year.

Ninety-five percent of the monies listed above are to be spent on grants, cooperative agreements, or contracts. No money is to be awarded for FY-96 or beyond if the National Educational Research Policy and Priorities Board has not been appointed in accordance with section 921.

The only specific grant authorized is one not to exceed $5,000,000 as follows:

to a public or private institution, agency or organization for a period not to exceed 5 years for the purpose of conducting a State-by-State poll to determine the perceptions of recent graduates of secondary schools, their instructors in institutions of higher education, parents of recent such graduates, and employers of recent such graduates on how well schools have prepared students for further education or employment.

Your tax dollars at work.

Section 913 **establishes a new position within DOE, the assistant secretary for educational research and improvement. This is a presidential appointment.**

PART B—NATIONAL EDUCATIONAL RESEARCH POLICY AND PRIORITIES BOARD

Section 921, Establishment Within Office of Educational Research and Improvement, sets up **"the Board"** to: work with the assistant secretary to determine priorities to guide OERI; to review and approve the Research Priorities Plan, and standards for the conduct and evaluation of research, development, and dissemination under OERI. Additional duties include: making recommendations to the assistant secretary concerning qualified people to be directors of the five institutes; making recommendations to the President as to qualified people for the assistant director's position; reviewing and commenting upon proposed contracts, etc., made under the institutes; advising Congress on OERI's efforts; recommending ways to strengthen partnerships among researchers, educational practitioners, librarians, policymakers, and program offices; soliciting advice from a broad segment of the educational field, particularly teachers, on research and dissemination needs; recommending "missions" for the national research centers; recommending how to translate research findings into workable models for use in policy and practice across different settings, as well as methods of dissemination; and recommending incentives to draw talented young people into the field of educational research, including scholars from disadvantaged and minority groups.

The board may establish a standing subcommittee for each of the institutes and for the Office of Reform Assistance and Dissemination.

The board is empowered to appoint a director and additional staff. It will consist of fifteen members with experience in educational research and development and is to be *"broadly representative of the diversity of the United States."* The secretary will appoint these fifteen, of whom:

> *(1) five shall be appointed from among researchers in the field of education who have been nominated by the National Academy of Sciences;*

The involvement of NAS is interesting. Why five individuals with national standing in the sciences?

> *(2) five shall be outstanding school-based professional educators; and*

> *(3) five shall be individuals who are knowledgeable about the educational needs of the United States and may include parents with experience in promoting parental involvement in education, Chief State School Officers, local educational agency superintendents, principals, members of State or local boards of education or Bureau-funded school boards, and individuals from business and industry with experience in promoting private sector involvement in education.*

Notice that the parents sought are those with a certain type of experience useful to the objectives of the board. The business/industry representatives will likewise be those who have a proven track record in fund raising and other partnershipping efforts with schools.

> *(i) Nominations for Board Membership.—Prior to appointing any member of the Board, the Secretary shall actively solicit and give due consideration to recommendations from organizations such as the National Education Association, the American Federation of Teachers, the National Parent-Teachers Association, the American Library Association, the American Association of School Adminis-*

trators, the National Association of State Boards of Education, the National Indian School Board Association, the Association of Community Tribal Schools, the National Indian Education Association, and other education-related organizations and interested members of the public.

With the exception of the Native American organizations, **the usual cast of educational establishment "clubs."**

(j) Ex Officio Members.—The ex officio, nonvoting members of the Board shall include the Assistant Secretary and may also include—

(1) the Director of Research for the Department of Defense;

(2) the Director of Research for the Department of Labor;

(3) the Director of the National Science Foundation;

(4) the Director of the National Institutes of Health;

(5) the chair of the National Endowment for the Arts;

(6) the chair of the National Endowment for the Humanities;

(7) the Librarian of Congress; and

(8) the Director of the Office of Indian Education Programs of the Department of the Interior.

This wide range of government agencies shows the extent of areas to be overlapped with education. The usual term of office for board members will be six years. The board will select a chair from among its members to serve for a renewable term of two years. No one can serve for more than twelve consecutive years. The secretary is not to remove board members before their terms are up. The board is to have its first meeting not later than May 15, 1995, and is to meet quarterly, thereafter. Meetings are "open," subject to the ***Sunshine Act (5 U.S.C. 552b).***

PART C—NATIONAL RESEARCH INSTITUTES

Five institutes are established, each to be headed by a director appointed by and reporting to the assistant secretary. Each institute is to either directly or through grants, contracts, and cooperative agreements with institutions of higher education, the regional educational labs, public and private organizations, institutions, agencies, and individuals or consortia: conduct research and development (R&D); fund dissertations; award fellowships for graduate study in educational research "by qualified African-American, Hispanic, American Indian, and Alaska Native, and other individuals from groups which have been traditionally under-represented in the field of educational research"; award fellowships in the DOE for scholars, researchers, policymakers, education practitioners, librarians, and statisticians engaged in the use, collection, and dissemination of information about education and educational research. The institutes are to maintain a balance between applied and basic research; expand the role of field-initiated research and set aside twenty to twenty-five percent of their funds through FY-99 for this purpose; provide for long term R&D on *"core issues and concerns"* (not identified) conducted by university-based centers by setting aside not less than one-third of their funding for such R&D centers; support research leading to policy formation by state legislatures, state and local boards of education and other policy and governing bodies to assist them in developing effective policies to promote student achievement and school improvement; promote research related to the core content areas; plan and coordinate syntheses of research on student performance *"preschool to postsecondary"*; conduct "sustained R&D on improving the educational achievement of poor and minority individuals as an integral part of its work"; and coordinate the institute's activities with those of the RELs (federal labs), and other educational service organizations in designing the institute's research "agenda" and projects in order to be increasingly responsive to the needs of teachers and to bring research findings directly into schools.

Requirements for financial assistance (grants, etc.) are spelled out. The following is part of this section:

(5) Historically underutilized researchers and institutions.—The

> *Assistant Secretary shall establish and maintain initiatives and programs to increase the participation in the activities of each Institute of groups of researchers and institutions that have been historically underutilized in Federal educational research activities, including—*
>
> *(A) researchers who are women, African-American, Hispanic, American Indian and Alaska Native, or other ethnic minorities;*
>
> *(B) promising young or new researchers in the field, such as postdoctoral students and recently appointed assistant or associate professors;*
>
> *(C) Historically Black Colleges and Universities, Tribally Controlled Community Colleges, and other institutions of higher education with large numbers of minority students;*
>
> *(D) institutions of higher education located in rural areas; and*
>
> *(E) institutions and researchers located in States and regions of the United States which have historically received the least Federal support for educational research and development.*

The awarding of quota-oriented grants will result in an emphasis on multicultural and other politically correct R&D projects which will, in turn, affect policy decisions and classroom practice.

The assistant secretary is authorized to utilize the services of *"experts or consultants with scientific or professional qualifications in the disciplines relevant to the purposes of such Institute,"* and (with consent) *"the services, equipment, personnel, information, and facilities of other Federal, State, or local public agencies, with or without reimbursement."*

The next twelve pages of ***P.L.103-227*** are taken up with specifics for the five new institutes. The first institute is the National Institute on Student Achievement, Curriculum and Assessment (NISACA). Notice how well the provisions for this institute align with Title 2 (dealing with standards and assessments). The findings (formal justification for what is being done) are worth including here:

(1) FINDINGS.—The Congress finds as follows:

(A) The current achievement levels of students in the United States are far below those that might indicate competency in ***challenging*** *subject matter in core content areas.*

See earlier comments on the use of the word **"challenging,"** in Title 1, Goal 4 (B)(ii). **(See also chronology: 30.)**

(B) During the last 20 years, relatively little changed in how students were taught. Despite much research suggesting better alternatives, classrooms continue to be dominated by textbooks, teacher lectures, short-answer activity sheets, and unequal patterns of student attention.

It's very important to understand educrats feel classrooms *"dominated by textbooks and teacher lectures,"* in other words, **the traditional American classroom,** is a big part of the problem. "Fill-in-the-blank" activity sheets can certainly be overused, but are hardly to blame for the sorry state of American education. What is meant by *"unequal patterns of student attention,"* and how does the government mean to address this inequality? Isn't this a classic teacher's dilemma? Every student finds some subjects more interesting than others; some students learn better one way than another. Some children are just brighter than others and grasp material more quickly. Student attention can be "equalized" in a number of ways including: 1) making the basic (required) material easier for the slower students—or for everyone; 2) offering "horizontal" (more of the same) or enrichment activities for the brighter students; 3) offering material in a variety of ways to appeal to different "learning styles"; and 4) having individualized education plans (IEPs) that wed each student to the appropriate mix of difficulty and manner of presentation. An understanding of this makes clear how important the computer is going to be in the future in addressing all of these concerns.

(C) Despite progress in narrowing the gaps, the differences in performance between Caucasian students and their minority counter-

> *parts remain unacceptably large. While progress has been made in reducing the gender gap in mathematics, such gap still remains at higher levels of problem solving. Too little progress has been made in reducing gender performance gaps favoring males in science and females in writing.*

Will science be "dumbed down" for girls, and writing for boys so that everyone can be equal?

The stated purpose of the NISACA is to improve and integrate student achievement in core content areas:

> *(A) identify, develop, and evaluate innovative and exemplary methods to improve student knowledge at all levels in the core content areas, such as—*
>
> *(i) student learning and assessment in various subject matters;*
>
> *(ii) the effects of organizational patterns on the delivery of instruction, including issues of grouping and tracking, ungraded classrooms, and on the effects of various pedagogies, including the issues of technology in education;*

Since numerous experiments have already been conducted with tracking and untracking, ungraded classrooms, and every sort of teaching methodology, the big underresearched area is technology **(especially use of the computer to directly deliver curriculum)**. The enormous infusion of money through ***GOALS 2000*** and its Siamese twin, the ***ESEA*** reauthorization, will bring the long-dreamed-of technological classroom much closer to reality.

> *(iii) standards for what students should know and be able to do, particularly standards of desired performance set to internationally competitive levels;*

Recall that ***"what students should know and be able to do"*** is a classic OBE phrase. In other words, **research on OBE aligned with international standards.**

(iv) methods to improve the process of reading, the craft of writing, the growth of reasoning skills, and the development of information-finding skills;

Reading accurately, word for word, to understand the author's meaning is a precise skill, **not** a *"process."* It becomes a process when **whole language,** the current classroom craze, is used. In whole language the "process" involves looking for approximate meaning in contextual and other "clues," otherwise known as **"guessing."** In this technological era, **"information-finding"** is becoming more valued than the acquisition of a personal skill like reading with accuracy. Another example of the value attached to "information finding" would be placing more importance on knowing how to use a hand-held calculator than on memorizing the addition/subtraction facts or the multiplication tables. Certainly knowing how to use the computer to access the information superhighway is increasingly important; but basic **"hard skills"** (those you still have in the event of a power outage) need to be mastered **before** relying on technology. **(See chronology: 2, 22, and 83; and glossary: Whole Language.)**

(v) enabling students to develop higher order thinking skills;

HOTS is a current incarnation of values clarification/values restructuring. **(See chronology: 7, 8, 25, 30, 34, 36, 50 54, 71, 86, 89, 120, and 121; and glossary: HOTS.)**

(vi) methods to teach effectively all students in mixed-ability classrooms;

After a long struggle to have "special ed" classrooms, the current fad is to, once again, put everyone back together. They're calling it **"inclusion."** Teachers are expected somehow to cope and effectively teach **all** students. Doesn't the very fact that the educrats swing wildly back and forth between one idea and then its opposite, suggest they don't know what they're doing? Laboratory rats aren't the only ones being experimented on.

(vii) curriculum, instruction, and assessment, in vocational education and school-to-work transition;

Assistance for Title 5

(viii) the impact and effectiveness of Federal, State, and local efforts to provide gender-fair educational opportunities to elementary and secondary students;

(ix) programs, policies, and approaches which promote gender equity in elementary and secondary education;

You might assume this means practices that discriminate against girls, but who knows what will end up here. Radical feminists (and others with their own agenda) define "**gender**" to include: homosexuals, lesbians, and transsexuals, as well as males and females. We got a brief look at where this verbal engineering would take us at the September 1995 United Nations Fourth World Conference on Women in Beijing. If you don't think UN conferences, publications, and spinoff activities through their many agencies bear bitter fruit, go back and reread the **chronology** starting with our entry into the UN in 1945.

Subsections (x)–(xv) cover: improving the working conditions of teachers; curriculum development; teacher training methods; activities to reduce and prevent violence; use of technology; and *"other topics relevant to the mission of the institute."*

(B) conduct basic and applied research in the areas of human learning, cognition, and performance, including research and development on the education contexts which promote excellence in learning and instruction, and motivational issues related to learning;

R&D on rewards and punishments *("motivational issues")* related to learning.

(C) identify, develop, and evaluate programs designed to enhance academic achievement and narrow racial and gender performance gaps in a variety of subject areas, including research and develop-

> *ment on methods of involving parents in their children's education and ways to involve business, industry and other community partners in promoting excellence in schools; and*

R&D for racial and gender equity. R&D to make parents (and others in the community) **partners with the schools.**

The next page-long section deals with assessments and enables Title 2, especially section 220.

> *(D) include a comprehensive, coordinated program of research and development in the area of assessment which—*
>
> *(i) addresses issues such as—*
>
> *(I) the validity, reliability, generalizability, costs, relative merits, and most appropriate uses of various approaches and methods of assessing student learning and achievement;*
>
> *(II) methods and approaches to assessing student opportunities to learn (including the quality of instruction and the availability of resources necessary to support learning) and evaluating the quality of school environment;*

Remember "opportunity-to-learn"? *(II)* is the **R&D for O-T-L. (See glossary: O-T-L.)**

> *(III) the impact of high-stakes uses of assessment on student performance and motivation, narrowing of curriculum, teaching practices, and test integrity.*

Whenever you see ***"motivation,"*** think **"rewards and punishments,"** as indeed, it is linked here with ***"high-stakes uses of assessments."*** Any **"high stakes"** test is one where there is a considerable **penalty for failure**, e.g, you don't advance to the next grade; you don't score high enough to get into a good college; you don't graduate; you don't get your Certificate of Initial Mastery, etc.

> *(IV) the impact of various methods of assessment on children of*

different races, ethnicities, gender, socioeconomic status, and English language proficiencies, and children with other special needs;

(V) standards of performance, quality, and validity for various methods of assessment and the means by which such standards should be developed;

(VI) current and emerging testing practices of State and local education agencies within the United States, as well as other nations;

Tie-in with Title 2—(National Standards and Assessments) and Title 6—(International Education Program) to get assessments aligned internationally.

(VII) the diverse effects, both intended and unintended, of assessments as actually used in the schools, including effects on curriculum and instruction, effects of equity in the allocation of resources and opportunities, effects on equity of outcomes, effects on other procedures and standards for judging students and practitioners and possible inflation of test scores;

More fodder for O-T-L suits. Standards for judging *"practitioners,"* (presumably classroom teachers).

(VIII) identifying and evaluating how students with limited-English proficiency and students with disabilities are included and accommodated in the various assessment programs of State and local education agencies;

More O-T-L

(IX) the feasibility and validity of comparing or equating the results of different assessments;

(X) test security, accountability, validity, reliability, and objectivity.

(XI) relevant teacher training and instruction in giving a test, scor-

ing a test, and in the use of test results to improve student achievement;

(See chronology: 37, 43, 49, 59, 82, 87, and 113; and glossary: NASDTEC.)

(XII) developing, identifying, or evaluating new educational assessments, including performance-based and portfolio assessments which demonstrate skill and a command of knowledge; and

R&D on OBE

(XIII) other topics relevant to the purposes of the Institute; and

(ii) may reflect recommendations made by the National Education Goals Panel.

(See Title 2, Part A, Section 201 for the role of NEGP.)

The next section (nearly four pages) deals with the second institute:

(E) National Institute on the Education of At-Risk Students.—

The findings section lays out its rationale for creating this institute. Such factors as poor student performance in the inner city; disparity between reading scores of Caucasians, African Americans, and Hispanics; the underserved status of rural schools; large numbers of limited-English proficiency students; large concentrations of poor students in urban and rural areas; high dropout, illiteracy, and poverty rates of Indian and Alaska native populations and their unaddressed needs are all listed as proof of the need for creation of the National Institute on the Education of At-Risk Students (NIEARS). Finally, it is contended that underutilized minority scholars, institutions, and groups need to be mobilized in the effort *"to develop a new generation of programs, models, practices, and schools capable of responding to the urgent needs of students who are educationally at-risk."*

(2) Purpose.—It shall be the purpose of the Institute on the Education of At-Risk Students to carry out a coordinated and comprehensive program of research and development to provide nonpartisan, research-based leadership to the United States as it seeks to improve educational opportunities for at-risk students. Such program shall—

(A) undertake research necessary to provide a sound basis from which to identify, develop, evaluate, and assist others to replicate and adapt interventions, programs, and models which promote greater achievement and educational success by at-risk students, such as—

"Interventions" is a social services term for stepping into a private area, like the home, for the alleged purpose of "rescuing" someone from a bad situation. The term has become widely used in situations where medical, psychological, or social service help is deemed necessary. An example of an "intervention" that most people are familiar with is when family members conspire to have an alcoholic or drug abusing relative put into a residential substance abuse program. **Interventions applied to "at-risk" children will usually be directed at the student's family situation, forcing the family to do certain things the state requires, or even removing the child from the home.**

(i) methods of instruction and educational practices (including community services) which improve the achievement and retention of at-risk students;

Partnershipping of the school with health, employment, and social services by making these **attractive** (free), **convenient** (on-site at school or nearby), and by **relieving parents of the responsibility** of even having to think about providing these services on their own. If making them attractive and convenient doesn't work, **they can always be made mandatory and tied to school attendance (like vaccinations are now).**

(ii) the quality of educational opportunities afforded at-risk students, particularly the quality of educational opportunities afforded

> *such students in highly concentrated urban areas and sparsely populated rural areas;*

O-T-L research to prove that inequities exist and must be addressed.

> *(iii) methods for overcoming the barriers to learning that may impede student achievement;*

> *(v) methods to improve the quality of the education of American Indian and Alaska Native students . . .*

This is spelled out in five points and calls for the establishment of tribal departments of education; R&D on culturally appropriate curriculum; research on recruiting and training of local teachers from these communities, including waivers of requirements, referred to here as *"flexibility in the criteria for certification of such teachers"*; research to improve educational achievement, increase graduation rates, reduce dropout rates, and performance of limited-English students from these two groups on standardized achievement tests.

> *(vi) means by which parents and community resources and institutions (including cultural institutions) can be utilized to support and improve the achievement of at-risk students;*

Research in this area will lend support to parts of Title 4 (Parental Assistance), Title 7 (Safe Schools), and Title 8 (Minority-Focused Civics Education).

> *(vii) the training of teachers and other educational professionals and paraprofessionals to work more effectively with at-risk students;*

Greater attention will, doubtless, result in more diagnoses of *"**at-risk**"* and more recommendations for **interventions**. The teacher as social worker. **(See chronology: 42, 55, 66, 91, 103, and 104.)**

> *(viii) the most effective uses of technology in the education of at-risk students;*

Where reading scores are low, there will be experimentation to see if putting students on computers programmed for low literacy levels brings improvement in other areas. Whatever short-term gains this might produce, there is no substitute for good reading ability.

> *(ix) programs designed to promote gender equity in schools that serve at-risk students;*

Given the new definitions of "gender," if **"homophobia"** is recognized as a gender equity issue, then students identified as anything other than heterosexual will be classified as **"at risk."** Students identified as **"homophobic"** will also need social services (sensitivity/diversity training) to overcome the influences that have made them this way.

> *(x) improving the ability of classroom teachers and schools to assist new and diverse populations of students in successfully assimilating into the classroom environment;*

"Diverse" is the key word here. The trend back from separate classrooms into "inclusion" means newly arrived and other limited-English students, physically handicapped students, children with behavior problems, children with learning disabilities, average students, and very bright students will all be grouped together in one classroom—the only common denominator being their approximate age and grade.

> *(xi) methods of assessing the achievement of students which are sensitive to cultural differences, provide multiple methods of assessing student learning, support student acquisition of higher order capabilities, and enable identification of the effects of inequalities in the resources available to support the learning of children throughout the United States; and*

Won't there have to be separate tests for various groups? And if so, can this do anything other than Balkanize our nation? We know with OBE there will be *"multiple methods of assessing,"* not just pen and paper tests. This also calls for research to support **HOTS** *("higher order capabilities")* and to enable the **O-T-L** agenda *("effects of inequalities in the resources available")*.

(B) maximize the participation of those schools and institutions of higher education that serve the greatest number of at-risk students in inner city and rural areas, and on Indian reservations, including model collaborative programs between schools and school systems, institutions of higher education, cultural institutions, and community organizations.

As the NIEARS is launched, its focus will be the inner city, the rural poor, and Native Americans. **It is usually the populations least able to effectively resist government experimentation and manipulation that get the first and heaviest dose of it.** Recall that the **ESEA** which brought the federal government into our classrooms thirty years ago was sold as a "War on Poverty" program and was only gradually expanded through its five-year reauthorizations to include everyone. **(See chronology: 33, 43, and 129.)**

(F) National Institute on Early Childhood Development and Education.—

(1) Findings.—The Congress finds as follows:

(A) Despite efforts to expand and improve preschool programs, many children still reach school age unprepared to benefit from formal education programs.

(B) Early intervention for disadvantaged children from birth to age five has been shown to be a highly cost-effective strategy for reducing later expenditures on a wide variety of health, developmental, and educational problems that often interfere with learning. Long-term studies of the benefits of preschool education have a demonstrated return on investment ranging from three to six dollars for every one dollar spent.

There are also studies showing that after about second grade, gains made from programs such as Head Start largely disappear.

(C) The Federal Government should play a central role in provid-

> *ing research-based information on early childhood education models which enhance children's development and ultimately their success in school.*

Why? To facilitate entry into the lifelong learning loop. (See chronology: 39, 47, 52, 63, and 68; and glossary: Lifelong Learning.)

Purposes for creating the National Institute on Early Childhood Development and Education (NIECDE) are identified as comprehensive R&D to identify, develop, evaluate, and assist others to replicate methods and approaches to improve early childhood education, such as—

> *(A) social and educational development of infants, toddlers, and preschool children;*

Recall that the PAT program begins at birth. Research generated by the NIECDE will support PAT, HIPPY, Success by Six, and all the other programs aimed at infants, toddlers, and children up to five years old. **(See glossary: PAT.)**

> *(B) the role of parents and the community in promoting the successful social and educational development of children from birth to age five;*

More PAT enablement.

> *(C) topics relating to children's readiness to learn, such as prenatal care, nutrition, and health services;*

When programs are extended down into prenatal clinics, "client families" can be identified even before birth. **(See chronology: 91.)**

> *(D) family literacy and parental involvement in student learning;*

Support for Goal 6, Adult Literacy and Lifelong Learning; and Goal 8, Parental Participation.

> *(E) methods for integrating learning in settings other than the classroom, particularly within families and communities;*

Goal 6, Adult Literacy and Lifelong Learning.

> *(F) practices and approaches which sustain the benefits of effective preschool and child care programs;*

Perhaps this is a tacit admission that some of those early gains "wear off."

> *(G) effective learning methods and curriculum for early childhood learning, including access to current materials in libraries;*

Since materials in public libraries are already accessible, could they be referring to **school libraries?** This seems likely as one of the ideas that greatly enables partnershipping is to make the school a **"community hub"** of one-stop shopping for all educational, medical, social services, and job-related needs.

> *(H) the importance of family literacy and parental involvement in student learning;*

NEG 6, Adult Literacy and Lifelong Learning, and NEG 8, Parental Participation (again).

> *(I) effective teaching and learning methods, and curriculum;*

> *(J) instruction that considers the cultural environment of children;*

Preschool multiculturalism.

> *(K) access to current materials in libraries;*

Why is this repeated? Access is already easy and free through local public libraries, bookmobiles, interlibrary loans, etc. Will social workers bring library materials into homes and require parents to use them as part of the home/school contract?

> *(L) the impact that outside influences have on learning, including television, and drug and alcohol abuse;*

This has been thoroughly studied—and just as thoroughly ignored.

(M) the structure and environment of early childhood education and child care settings which lead to improved social and educational development;

Any environment is to be preferred to a child's home—unless "enriched" by government programs.

(N) training and preparation of teachers and other professional and paraprofessional preschool and child care workers;

Lots of money to train, retrain, and certify teachers and their assistants.

(O) the use of technology, including methods to help parents instruct their children; and

Videos to train parents? Making parents computer literate? Electronic teaching/learning modalities will be increasingly important as print media is de-emphasized.

(P) other topics relevant to the purpose of the Institute.

That wonderful catchall "**other**."

(G) NATIONAL INSTITUTE ON EDUCATIONAL GOVERNANCE, FINANCE, POLICY-MAKING, AND MANAGEMENT.—

(1) FINDINGS.—The Congress finds as follows:

(A) Many elementary and secondary schools in the United States—

(i) are structured according to models that are ineffective and rely on notions of management and governance that may be outdated or insufficient for the challenges of the next century; and

This is a direct challenge to the existing **local control model**, i.e., **an elected board of education,** the time-tested model that has kept control as close to the hands of parents as possible. **(See chronology: 100; and glossary: SBM, TQM, and ISO-9000.)**

> *(ii) are unsuccessful in equipping all students with the knowledge and skills needed to succeed as citizens and in the working world.*

The fact that many schools are unsuccessful has less to do with governance, finance, policy-making, and management than with a variety of other factors including: the student's own desire to learn; parental expectations and follow-through with students at home; orderly and disciplined classrooms; choice of curriculum materials; skill and dedication of individual teachers; and a day so crowded with nonacademic distractions that there is not enough time to cover the basics properly.

> *(B) New approaches are needed in the governance and management of elementary and secondary education within the United States at the State, local, school building and classroom level.*

I hope everyone from superintendent to classroom teacher can see the pink slip in this *"new approaches"* envelope. That's **your** job they're talking about.

> *(C) Not enough is known about the effects of various systems of school governance and management on student achievement to provide sound guidance to policymakers as such policymakers pursue school restructuring and reform.*

Never mind that *"not enough is known."* With the creation of this institute (and your tax dollars) experimentation can proceed on novel ways to change policy, finance, governance, and management.

> *(D) A concentrated Federal effort is needed to support research, development, demonstration, and evaluation of approaches to school governance, finance and management which promise to improve*

> *education equity and excellence throughout the United States.*

Since the NIEGFPM is one of the mechanisms to achieve school equity, there will be "improvement" in that area, but if there is no improvement in academic *"excellence,"* and/or parents are unhappy at their loss of local control, **there will be no going back to the "old way" once the local control model has been thoroughly dismantled.**

The purposes of the NIEGFPM are listed as R&D *"to improve student achievement through school restructuring and reform"* by identifying, developing, and evaluating approaches such as—

> *(A) open enrollment programs, public school choice, magnet schools and other systems through which parents may select the public schools and educational programs in which their children are enrolled;*

It won't matter which public school your child attends once the standardized curriculum and testing are in place. Differences will be very superficial and hardly worth having your child bussed across town or county to a new building or the promise of a "new" program.

> *(B) innovative school design, including lengthening the school day and the school year, reducing class size and building professional development into the weekly school schedule and, as appropriate, conducting such further research as may be recommended or suggested by the report issued by the National Education Commission on Time and Learning pursuant to section 102 of the* ***Education Council Act of 1991 (20 U.S.C. 1221–1 note)****;*

The report issued by this commission is entitled ***Prisoners of Time***, and makes the case for lengthening the school day and school year. (See Title 6, Section 601(2)(b).) Teacher unions will like having part of the school week set aside for teacher training (*"professional development"*). *"Further research"* on the use of time by the NIEGFPM will result in "proving" that time spent in school must be totally "restructured." After all, **if time spent on learning is a variable, as the proponents of OBE claim, then no doubt we've had wrong assumptions about the length of the school day and school year as well.**

> *(C) effective approaches to organizing learning;*

This could be **anything**!

> *(D) effective ways of grouping students for learning so that a student is not labeled or stigmatized in ways that may impede such student's achievement;*

All ability levels together—the "inclusive" classroom that we're going back to.

> *(E) effective approaches to organizing, structuring, and financing vocational education;*

> *(F) the provision of financial and other rewards and incentives to schools and educators based on performance to improve student achievement;*

"Achievement" will be based on *"performance"* (assessments); so teachers will soon learn to teach to the test in order to get the financial rewards that come with improved student scores. Principals *("schools")* will hold their teachers accountable for the school's overall scores and ranking, so there's an unspoken penalty system for teachers whose students fall below the norm.

> *(G) the use of regulatory flexibility on the State or school district level to promote innovation and school restructuring;*

More waivers to bypass existing regulations. **Waivers are okay if they promote *"restructuring."* Not okay if they don't.**

> *(H) policy decisions at all levels and the impact of such decisions on school achievement and other student outcomes;*

R&D in this area will, no doubt, include site-based management and other experiments in shifting the power around.

> *(I) the effective use of dollars for classroom construction;*

> *(J) expanding the role of teachers in policymaking and administration at the school and school district-wide level;*

Union activists will play a key role in this.

> *(K) disparity in school financing among States, school districts, schools, and schools funded by the Bureau;*

This research will be used to "level the playing field," i.e., the Robin Hood plan for school financing.

> *(L) the use of technology in areas such as assisting in school-based management or ameliorating the effects of disparity in school financing among States, school districts, and schools funded by the Bureau;*

Putting the data collected by NIEGFPM and other research conducted under the auspices of OERI into cross-referenced data banks so that it will be highly available to those challenging O-T-L standards and school finance equity. **(See glossary: NCES.)**

> *(M) the involvement of parents and families in the management and governance of schools and the education of their children;*

A junior partner is still subordinate to the senior.

> *(N) effective approaches to increasing the representation of women and minorities among leadership and management positions in education;*

Has this been much of a problem for the last twenty years?

> *(O) approaches to systemic reforms involving the coordination of multiple policies of each level of government to promote higher levels of student achievement;*

Translation: Ways to coordinate reform policies emanating from different agencies that might conflict with each other in order to achieve "the agenda."

(P) approaches to coordinated services for children;

Best ways to marry school, medical, employment, and social services delivery.

(Q) teacher certification at the State and tribal levels;

(R) school-based management, shared decisionmaking and other innovative school structures, and State and local reforms and educational policies, which show promise for improving student achievement;

This is not about *"improving student achievement."* It's about squeezing parents and elected officials who are accountable to parents out of the picture and usurping local control. **(See chronology: 100; and glossary: SBM, TQM, and ISO-9000.)**

(S) policies related to school-to-work transitions and preparing non-college-bound students; and

There are certainly going to be new legal considerations with children out in the work force. Protections under the child labor laws, for example, will have to be waived. **Schools will seek ways to limit their liability if students are injured while traveling to work or on the job, etc.**

(T) other topics relevant to the mission of the Institute.

The stated mission is *"school restructuring and reform."*

(H) National Institute on Postsecondary Education, Libraries, and Lifelong Learning.—

(1) Findings.—The Congress finds as follows:

(A) The American system of postsecondary education is foremost in

> *the world in such system's achievement of both academic excellence and equity in access, but maintaining that preeminence requires renewed efforts to strengthen the quality of postsecondary education. Disappointing student performance on achievement tests and licensure examinations, declining rates of postsecondary education persistence and completion among minorities, and other troubling trends in the quality of postsecondary education should be addressed by the United States as part of its overall drive to improve American education.*

If our college and university system is the best in the world, will it remain that way long once the federal government starts meddling as it has for the past thirty years in our elementary and secondary schools?

> *(B) The need to improve our economic productivity of the United States to meet the competitive challenges of a new, international economy, coupled with high levels of mobility in the United States labor market and demographic changes in the workforce, now demands more and higher quality programs of learning and training in the American workplace.*

For all of this century, we have been a major player and in many areas "the major player" in the *"international economy."* A mobile work force within a nation is a plus, not a cause for alarm or some new government corrective. The *"demographic changes"* referred to here are **global** in nature, and are occurring because of the planned shifting of jobs through NAFTA, GATT, the WTO and other treaties and arrangements that relocate our factories and industries outside the U.S. For workers who may find themselves following jobs to foreign countries, a new type of training will, indeed, be required.

NEA Today (Oct. 1995) reports that Mary Futrell, president of Education International, told delegates at EI's First World Conference: "What's uniting educators is the multifaceted economic, political, and social revolution that's transforming how the world works. In today's new 'internationalized' global environment, boundaries between countries count for less and less." Expanding on that theme, Fred van Leeuwen, general secretary of EI, said: "What counts for more and more are huge multinational corporations that routinely move plants and jobs from country to country, searching for the lowest tax rates and the cheapest labor." Before leaving the conference in Zimbabwe, conferees approved resolutions to: "1) Protect human and trade union rights around the world; 2) Reject continuing moves to privatize education; and 3) Promote reforms that help make schools effective tools for achieving social and economic progress." **(See chronology: 66, 88, 92, 96, 102, 111, 112, 119–126, and 128.)**

> *(C) The more than 1,000,000 men and women incarcerated in the prisons and jails in the United States are among the most severely educationally disadvantaged in the United States, with high rates of functional illiteracy and extremely low levels of educational attainment. Since an estimated 90 percent of these individuals are expected to be released by the end of the decade, the United States must act to assure that our correctional system has the means to equip these Americans with the knowledge and skills they will need to participate productively in our society.*

Isn't this an area that should be left to the correctional system?

> *(D) The development of a "Nation of Students" capable of and committed to the pursuit of formal and informal lifelong learning and literacy is essential to sustain both national and individual economic success and to provide a nurturing environment in which all children and youth can learn and achieve. Historically the most effective community resource for lifelong learning, the public library system of the United States, should expand and restructure its delivery of services to take full advantage of the potential of new information technologies to meet the needs of learning communities.*

The concept of ***"lifelong learning"*** is one of the most outrageous **paradigm shifts** in *GOALS 2000* and proves that **school restructuring is really thinly disguised social engineering to restructure all of society**. Human resources are simply too valuable to the New World Order to be trained for ten or eleven years and then released to do as they please; ". . . *national and individual economic success*" cannot just be left to chance. Is there anyone wanting information or further education and training that doesn't currently have access to one or more of the following: bookstores, libraries, adult education programs conducted in high schools and junior colleges, colleges and universities, or to correspondence courses and other programs geared to the needs of busy adults? (D) above seems to suggest that public libraries will be utilized, through technology, to reach into homes that may not even want their services. The phrase "*to provide a nurturing environment in which all children and youth can learn and achieve,*" supports the first and eighth NEGs (School Readiness and Parental Participation).

> *(2) Purpose.—The purpose of the National Institute on Postsecondary Education, Libraries, and Lifelong Learning is to promote greater coordination of Federal research and development on issues related to adult learning and to carry out a program of research and development in adult learning to provide nonpartisan, research-based leadership to the United States as it seeks to improve libraries, postsecondary education, literacy, and lifelong learning throughout the United States. Such program—*

R&D by NIPELLL (an unintentionally appropriate acronym) to improve adult learning and the partnershipping of everyone currently involved in the delivery of adult education services. You don't get weaned from this one.

> *(A) shall only support research and development in those areas of postsecondary education, libraries, literacy, and lifelong learning which are not being addressed by other entities within the Federal Government;*

> *(B) may include basic and applied research, development, replication, and evaluation activities in areas such as—*

> *(i) methods of assessing and evaluating individual, program, and institutional performance;*

> *(ii) the uses and applications of new technologies to improve pro-*

gram effectiveness and enhance student learning;

Though they aren't *"new,"* computers will be the predominant technology.

(iii) the most effective training methods for adults to upgrade education and vocational skills;

Will this "upgraded" education include demonstrating the same attitudes, values, and beliefs in which school students are being indoctrinated? Political "reliability" is something the NWO planners will want to see some evidence of when handing out work cards.

(iv) opportunities for adults to continue their education beyond higher education and graduate school, in the context of lifelong learning and information-finding skills;

Anyone smart enough and/or persistent enough to have made it through college or graduate school doesn't need the government to provide *"opportunities"* to continue their education. Of course, we thought our degrees were "terminal" and not *"in the context of lifelong learning. . . ."*

(v) adult literacy and effective methods, including technology, to eliminate illiteracy;

The same method that works best for children, **intensive phonics** (not gimmicks or technology), works best for adults.

(vi) preparing students for a lifetime of work, the ability to adapt through retraining to the changing needs of the work force and the ability to learn new tasks;

Since the planners themselves don't know with certainty what *"needs of the work force"* will be in the future, what's paramount is to train workers who are **tolerant, work well in groups, adapt readily to change, and are amenable to training in new technologies/areas of**

employment as they evolve. (See chronology: 38, 92, and 102.)

> *(viii) institutional and classroom policies and practices at the postsecondary level necessary to improve matriculation, persistence, achievement and graduation by students who are economically disadvantaged, ethnic and racial minorities, women, older, working, and who have children;*

Providing incentives—maybe quotas—for some groups.

> *(ix) instructional practices and programs which are effective in correctional settings;*

In what ways will these programs differ from other adult literacy and education programs?

> *(x) new models of service delivery for public library systems which expand opportunities for lifelong learning;*

This could be anything from computer linkups between the public library and homes to expanded bookmobile service. **Public libraries are emphasized as an important link in the LL chain.**

> *(xi) effective programs and approaches which promote greater access to and success by minorities in postsecondary programs which prepare such minorities for scientific, technical, teaching, and health career fields;*
>
> *(xii) effective teaching for the preparation and continuing education of teachers;*
>
> *(xiii) the development and evaluation of curricular materials for the initial and continuing education of teachers and teacher educators;*
>
> *(xiv) the role of Historically Black Colleges and Universities, Tribally Controlled Indian Community Colleges, women's colleges, and*

other special mission institutions in providing access, excellence, and equal opportunity in higher education;

(xv) methods for evaluating the quality of education at different types of institutions of higher education at all levels and the roles and responsibilities of regional and national accrediting agencies;

Bad news for colleges, as the intrusion of the federal government there will have the same effect it has had on our elementary and secondary schools since 1965 and passage of the **ESEA. (See chronology: 33 and 129.)**

(xvi) methods for evaluating the productivity of different types of institutions of higher education;

(xvii) financial barriers to postsecondary educational opportunity, including—

Listed here are: the role of federal programs in mitigating barriers; the impact of rising costs of education; and the extent of student reliance on student loans.

(xviii) opportunities for adults to continue their education beyond higher education and graduate school, in the context of lifelong learning and information-finding skills;

"Lifelong learning" for those who are already college educated can mean anything the government decides. It may mean that even those who are currently well educated and qualified in their fields will have to return to school to obtain Certificates of Mastery (work cards). This could be tied in with ISO 9000. *"Information-finding skills"* can only refer to computer access and literacy as it's increasingly true that you can get anything you want (and plenty you **don't** want, too!) on the information superhighway. **(See glossary: ISO 9000.)**

(xix) preparing students for a lifetime of work, the ability to adapt through retraining to the changing needs of the work force

and the ability to learn new tasks; and

I highlighted this because it is (for *GOALS 2000*) uncharacteristically candid. **Adaptability to change from entry-level job until retirement is the key point** ***("the ability to adapt through retraining to the changing needs of the work force")***. This is the lot of the twenty-first century "brave new worker": **limited access to career choices, government-controlled training and certification, and even then, no job security**—only the grim prospect of adapting (perhaps many times over the course of one's working years) to the needs of the NWO global economy. **The only surety, insecurity—the only constant, change.**

(xx) other topics relevant to the mission of the Institute.

(3) Involvement of Certain Agencies and Organizations, lists five offices within the DOE for coordination of R&D and the following outside agencies and organizations for partnershipping:

(B) the National Institute for Literacy;

(C) the National Board for Professional Teaching Standards;

(See chronology: 82, 87, and 113.)

(D) the Employment and Training Administration of the Department of Labor;

(E) the Administration for Children and Families within the Department of Health and Human Services;

(F) the National Institutes of Health;

(G) the National Endowment for the Humanities;

(H) the National Endowment for the Arts;

(I) the Bureau of Prisons of the Department of Justice;

(J) the Department of Commerce;

(K) the Department of Defense; and

(L) the Office of Indian Education Programs of the Department of the Interior.

(4) Additional Responsibilities, states that the activities of the National Center on Literacy are to be coordinated with those of the National Institute for Literacy.

(i) Coordination and Research Synthesis, charges the assistant secretary with promoting the coordination of R&D activities among the five new institutes, as well as work done by the **National Center for Education Statistics,** any other offices of the DOE, or other federal agencies or departments **(See glossary: NCES.)**

(j) Dates for Establishment of Institutes calls for the five institutes to be established on October 1, 1995, and this has been done; all five were up and running (with staffs averaging ten to fifteen people) by that date.

PART D—NATIONAL EDUCATION DISSEMINATION SYSTEM

The findings section establishes that to improve American education, achieve the NEGs, and *"provide for greater educational equity,"* teachers and parents must have access to the *"best information and methods available."*

(2) Purpose.—The purpose of this section is to—

(A) create a national system of dissemination, development, and educational improvement in order to create, adapt, identify, validate, and disseminate to educators, parents, and policymakers those educational programs that have potential or have been shown to improve educational opportunities for all students; and

A number of such "systems" already exist, e.g, ERIC with sixteen specialized clearinghouses, the NDN with a facilitator in each state, the ten RELs, twenty-three university-based R&D centers, and ten regional consortia of the Eisenhower National Program for Mathematics and Science Education. That a program has been "**validated**" is **not** an assurance of merit; it's simply been tested and found to achieve the desired/intended result—which may well be its ability to change a student's values. **(See glossary: ERIC, NDN, and RELs.)**

> *(B) empower and increase the capacity of teachers to participate in the research and development process.*

Most experienced, dedicated teachers do their own research (evaluate what their classes need), development (put together materials and programs tailored to meet these needs), and validation (try them out for effectiveness). This is also done on a school-wide or district-wide level which helps to assure the materials and programs are appropriate for the children who will actually use them. Teachers don't require "empowerment" by the DOE to do R&D. Empowerment is a term used frequently by change agents when the hidden agenda is not to help or "empower" an individual or group, but to bring about a desired change.

> *(3) Definition of educational program.—For the purposes of this section, the term "educational program" includes educational policies, research findings, practices, and products.*

> *(b) Establishment of Office.—*

> *(1) In general.—There is established within the Office an Office of Reform Assistance and Dissemination (hereafter in this section referred to as the "Dissemination Office") through which the Secretary shall carry out all functions and activities described in this section. Such office shall be headed by a Director who shall be appointed by the Assistant Secretary and have demonstrated expertise and experience in dissemination, including promoting the effective use of research in the classroom.*

The **Office of Reform Assistance (ORAD)** is a new entity within OERI, seen as necessary to coordinate all of OERI's expanded activities.

(2) Certain duties.—The Dissemination Office shall—

(A) disseminate relevant and useful research, information, products, and publications developed through or supported by the Department of Education to schools, educators, parents, and policymakers throughout the United States;

It is through such dissemination by the various arms of OERI that the Department of Education has for many years in a quasi-legal manner (skirting the Tenth Amendment prohibition on federal involvement in matters left to the states and to individuals) placed "federal" curriculum in the schools.

(B) operate a depository for all Department of Education publications and products and make available for reproduction such publications and products;

Who will have access to these materials? Will parents and the general public? Will they be reproduced for cost plus S&H, or will this be a profit venture for ORAD?

(C) provide technical and financial assistance to individuals and organizations in the process of developing promising educational programs but who might not, without such assistance, be able to complete necessary development and assessment activities;

The **carrot** is the "financial assistance." The **stick** is that whatever is developed will be under the scrutiny and control of ORAD. Federal money **always** comes with strings.

(D) coordinate the dissemination efforts of the Office, the regional educational laboratories, the research institutes, the National Diffusion Network, and the Educational Resources Information Center Clearinghouses;

Since all of these except the institutes were already in operation, the creation of ORAD is really necessitated by the creation of the five new institutes.

> *(E) provide training and technical assistance regarding the implementation and adoption of exemplary and promising programs by interested entities;*

If a program is politically incorrect or otherwise out of favor it will not be included in this process. For example, there are "exemplary" intensive phonics programs and sexual abstinence programs far more "promising" than the whole language and values clarification/you choose programs currently in vogue. Will these ever see a penny of ***GOALS 2000*** money, or be field-tested for validation so they can be widely disseminated?

> *(F) carry out a program of research on models for successful knowledge dissemination, and utilization, and strategies for reaching education policymakers, practitioners, and others interested in education;*

How to sell the programs to education policymakers and others in key positions to ensure they are implemented.

> *(G) develop the capacity to connect schools and teachers seeking information with the relevant regional educational laboratories assisted under subsection (h), the National Diffusion Network, and Institutes assisted under this section, and the Educational Resources Information Center Clearinghouses; and*

All but the institutes have existed for years and any teacher interested in their offerings can easily access them.

> *(H) provide a biennial report to the Secretary regarding the types of information, products, and services that teachers, schools, and school districts have requested and have determined to be most useful, and describe future plans to adapt Department of Education products and services to address the needs of the users of such information,*

products, and services.

(3) ADDITIONAL DUTIES.—The Dissemination Office shall carry out a process for the identification of educational programs that work, dissemination through electronic networking and new technologies and the functions and activities performed by the following;

(A) The Educational Resources Information Center Clearinghouses.

(B) The regional educational laboratories.

(C) The Teacher Research Dissemination Demonstration Program.

(D) The **GOALS 2000** *Community Partnerships Program.*

(E) The existing National Diffusion Network and its Developer-Demonstrator and State Facilitator projects.

(F) Such other programs, activities, or entities the Secretary determines are consistent with purposes for which the Dissemination Office is established.

(c) Identification of Programs, calls for the assistant secretary to work closely with the institutes and (A)–(F) above to identify successful programs, and

(3) through cooperative agreements, review for possible inclusion in the system educational programs administered by the Departments of Health and Human Services (particularly the Head Start program), Labor, and Defense, the National Science Foundation, the Department of the Interior (particularly the Office of Indian Education Programs), and any other appropriate Federal agency; and

Maximize collaboration and partnershipping with other federal agencies. Forget the "entire village"; under Title 10 it's going to take an entire federal bureaucracy to raise a child.

(4) provide for an active outreach effort to identify successful edu-

> *cational programs through cooperative arrangements with State and local education agencies, teachers and teacher organizations, curriculum associations, foundations, private schools, institutions of higher education, and other entities that could enhance the ability of the Secretary to identify programs for possible inclusion in the dissemination program.*

Notice who's to be included in an *"active outreach effort"*: *"teacher organizations"* (**the NEA and AFT**); *"curriculum associations,"* e.g., the Association for Supervision and Curriculum Development—**an NEA spinoff**, as well as individual curriculum area organizations (**such as those that developed the standards**); *"foundations,"* like Carnegie Foundation for the Advancement of Teaching, and other liberal ones **interested in promoting their agendas through education**; *"institutions of higher education"* (**state universities and teaching colleges already tied into the reform effort—such as the twenty-three OERI satellite centers**). ORAD knows who to call on to deliver. *"Active outreach"* to the contrary, this is education's "old boy network."

The next sections deal with setting up a panel (or panels) to evaluate programs submitted to the secretary. They are to consider:

> *(A) whether, based on empirical data, which may include test results, the program is effective and should be designated as exemplary and disseminated through the national dissemination system; or*

Remember testing may have nothing to do with academics. The criterion for validation is *"whether . . . the program is effective,"* i.e., does it work?

> *(B) whether there is sufficient evidence to lead a panel of experts and practitioners to believe that the program shows promise for improving student achievement and should be designated as promising and disseminated through the national dissemination system while the program continues to be evaluated.*

Translation: "We aren't sure if this works, but we'll go on using it experimentally anyway." In fact, the law states under (4) Requirements Regarding Panels:

> *(A) A panel shall not eliminate a program from consideration under this subsection based solely on the fact that the program does not have one specific type of supporting data, such as test scores.*

In order to ensure the widest adoption of *"exemplary or promising"* programs at the state and local level, section ***(e) Dissemination of Exemplary and Promising Programs,*** charges the assistant secretary with utilizing the capabilities of: ERIC, the NDN, the RELs, entities established under the ***GOALS 2000*** Community Partnerships Program, department-supported technical assistance providers, the National Library of Education, electronic networking, and other public and private nonprofit entities, including education associations and networks.

The "trickle down" of federal programs into classrooms will be greatly accelerated as this is fully activated.

Section **(f) Educational Resources Information Center Clearinghouses**, (ERIC), reauthorizes the existing sixteen clearinghouses which store in a database and disseminate (for a fee) books, periodicals, reports, and other materials relating to education. The activities of ERIC are to be coordinated with those of the institutes and all other entities within the DOE. Cooperative agreements are to be set up with the Departments of Defense, HHS, Interior, and other federal departments and agencies to insure that all education-related reports, studies, and other resources produced directly or by grant or contract are made available to ERIC. **(See glossary: ERIC.)**

Section **(g) Dissemination through New Technologies**, authorizes the assistant secretary to award grants or contracts for new materials, programs, and resources utilizing *"new technologies."* ORAD is to establish an electronic network to link all of the offices of the DOE, the institutes, the **National Center for Education Statistics**, the National Library of Education, and those under contract with the DOE that are engaged in R&D, dissemination, or technical assistance. This electronic network is to build upon existing networks, and have, at a minimum, the capability to support electronic mail and file transfer services, be linked to state and local education agencies, institutions of higher education, museums, libraries, and others through the Internet and the National Research and Education Network, and be provided to those under contract to the DOE and educational institutions at no cost other than the necessary hardware. **(See glossary: NCES.)**

The use of the Internet should be a boon to researchers and others wishing access to information on education issues. Dealing with the DOE at the present time is a very time-consuming experience.

(C) Information Resources, lists the information that ORAD "may make available" through this electronic network:

> *(i) information about grant and contract assistance available through the Department of Education;*
>
> *(ii) an annotated directory of current research and development activities and projects being undertaken with the assistance of the Department of Education;*
>
> *(iii) information about publications published by the Department of Education and, to the extent feasible, the full text of such publications;*
>
> *(iv) statistics and data published by the National Center for Education Statistics;*
>
> *(v) syntheses of research and development findings;*
>
> *(vi) a directory of other education-related electronic networks and databases, including information about the means by which such networks and databases may be accessed;*
>
> *(vii) a descriptive listing of materials and courses of instruction provided by telecommunications partnerships assisted under the Star Schools program;*
>
> *(viii) resources developed by the Educational Resources Informa-*

> *tion Center Clearinghouses;*
>
> *(ix) education-related software (including video) which is in the public domain;*
>
> *(x) a listing of instructional materials available through telecommunications to local education agencies through the Public Broadcasting Service and State educational networks; and*
>
> *(xi) such other information and resources the Assistant Secretary considers useful and appropriate.*

In section **(E) Training and Technical Assistance**, ORAD is charged with training contractors and grantees to participate in the electronic network and, upon request, to work with the National Science Foundation to provide assistance to state and local educational agencies, the Department of the Interior's Office of Indian Education Programs, tribal departments of education, state library agencies, libraries, museums, and other educational institutions in obtaining access to the Internet and the National Research and Education Network.

Section **(h) Regional Educational Laboratories for Research, Development, Dissemination, and Technical Assistance**, reauthorizes the ten existing Regional Educational Labs (RELs) and makes provision for the **possible creation of two additional ones.** A sum of *"not less than $2,000,000 annually"* would be required to fund any additional lab created and there are various other stipulations regarding establishing new labs. Under (3) Duties, the labs list as their *"central mission and primary function"* to *"promote the implementation of broad-based systemic school improvement strategies,"* such as to:

> *(A) develop and disseminate educational research products and processes to schools, teachers, local educational agencies, State educational agencies, librarians, and schools funded by the Bureau, as appropriate, and through such development and dissemination, and provide technical assistance, to help all students meet standards;*

The key phrase is *"to help all students meet standards,"* (the new OBE content and performance standards).

(B) develop a plan for identifying and serving the needs of the region by conducting a continuing survey of the educational needs, strengths, and weaknesses within the region, including a process of open hearings to solicit the views of schools, teachers, administrators, parents, local educational agencies, librarians, and State educational agencies within the region;

You can contact your nearest lab to see how your needs are being identified and served. **(See glossary: RELs.)**

(C) provide technical assistance to State and local educational agencies, school boards, schools funded by the Bureau, as appropriate, State boards of education, schools, and librarians;

(D) facilitate school restructuring at the individual school level, including technical assistance for adapting model demonstration grant programs to each school;

The labs function as the intermediary change agent between Washington and the local district/school level. They're field offices charged with facilitating systemic change/restructuring and with keeping a watchful eye on compliance *("help all students meet standards")*.

(E) serve the educational development needs of the region by providing education research in usable forms in order to promote school improvement and academic achievement and to correct educational deficiencies;

(F) facilitate communication between educational experts, school officials, and teachers, parents, and librarians, to enable such individuals to assist schools to develop a plan to meet the National Education Goals;

Schools must meet the NEGs or the labs will prod them to *"correct educational deficiencies."*

(G) provide training in—

(i) the field of education research and related areas;

(ii) the use of new educational methods; and

(iii) the use of information-finding methods, practices, techniques, and products developed in connection with such training for which the regional educational laboratory may support internships and fellowships and provide stipends;

(H) use applied educational research to assist in solving site-specific problems and to assist in development activities;

R&D applied to local problems

(I) conduct applied research projects designed to serve the particular needs of the region only in the event that such quality applied research does not exist as determined by the regional education laboratory or the Department of Education;

Lacking a suitable project, the local REL will design and conduct an educational experiment for your area.

(J) collaborate and coordinate services with other technical assistance providers funded by the Department of Education;

(K) provide support and technical assistance in—

(i) replicating and adapting exemplary and promising practices;

Recall the difference between *"exemplary"* and *"promising."* One has been shown to get results; the other hasn't.

(ii) the development of high-quality, ***challenging*** *curriculum frameworks;*

Tied to the national content standards set for each subject area.

(iii) the development of valid, reliable assessments which are linked

> *to State, local, or Bureau-funded content and student performance standards and reflect recent advances in the field of educational assessment;*

State and local standards will be tied to the national. It's semantic deception to suggest that autonomous state or local control over standards exists once a state has taken federal money under *P.L. 103-227.*

> *(iv) the improvement of professional development strategies to assure that all teachers are prepared to teach a* ***challenging*** *curriculum;*

Fine tuning teacher training to assure that all are teaching the *"challenging"* curriculum. **"Challenging"** used again and again in *GOALS 2000* is never once defined. Some possibilities are: it's **"challenging"** because it **challenges** the old assumptions **(knowledge and facts)**; or **"challenging"** to the teacher because it's a new information base requiring new presentation and evaluation **(OBE)**; or maybe it's **any curriculum designed to "challenge" the fixed attitudes, values, and beliefs of students**. Any of these seem **likelier than "harder, more interesting work." (See chronology: 29.)**

> *(v) expanding and improving the use of technology in education to improve teaching and learning;*

> *(vi) the development of alternatives for restructuring school finance systems to promote greater equity in the distribution of resources; and*

Right now the courts are the primary bulldozers used to level the playing field. In future, will laws be passed to create new (perhaps regional) school districts, to tax us in different ways, or to levy an education tax on businesses? We'll have to await the *"development of alternatives."* **(See chronology: 98.)**

> *(vii) the development of alternative administrative structures which are more conducive to planning, implementing, and sustaining*

school reform and improved educational outcomes; and

This bodes very ill for local control of schools. As things stand now, local school districts with their elected school boards, are still a first line of defense against unwanted changes and restructuring *("implementing and sustaining school reform")*. Once the power of local school districts is consolidated/centralized into the hands of a few unelected (and therefore unaccountable) individuals, and school boards are abolished or reduced to mere tokenism, the federal takeover of our schools will be complete. **(See glossary: PPBS, SBM, TQM, and ISO-9000.)**

(L) bring teams of experts together to develop and implement school improvement plans and strategies.

The RELs will help states put together (and into practice) their SIPs.

Section (4) Networking, calls for the governing boards of the labs to create a strategic plan for the development and coordination of activities undertaken by the RELs, to share resources, and plan joint activities. The labs are additionally charged with collaborating with the institutes and consulting with SEAs and library agencies in their regions in developing plans for serving their regions. They are also to develop strategies to utilize schools as critical components in *"revitalizing rural communities"* and reporting on and disseminating information on overcoming obstacles faced by rural educators and rural schools. They are to identify programs used successfully within their regions and make this information available to the secretary and the network of RELs for possible inclusion in the national dissemination system.

Section (6) Certain Requirements, establishes a governing board for each REL that—

(i) reflects a balanced representation of the States in the region, as well as the interests and concerns of regional constituencies, and that includes teachers and education researchers;

The governing board is to be the *"sole entity"* that:

(I) guides and directs the laboratory in carrying out the provisions

> *of this subsection and satisfying the terms and conditions of the contract award;*
>
> *(II) determines the regional agenda of the laboratory;*
>
> *(III) engages in an ongoing dialogue with the Assistant Secretary concerning the laboratory's goals, activities, and priorities; and*

Other duties include the organization and administration of the lab and its staff, directing the lab toward achieving the NEGs and *"reforming schools and educational systems"* and conducting an ongoing survey of the needs, strengths, and weaknesses within the region, *"including a process of open hearings to solicit the views of schools and teachers."* Each REL's resources are to be allocated *"to and within each state in a manner which reflects the need for assistance, taking into account such factors as the proportion of economically disadvantaged students, the increased cost burden of service delivery in areas of sparse populations, and any special initiatives being undertaken by state, intermediate, local educational agencies, or bureau-funded schools, as appropriate, which may require special assistance from the laboratory."* The assistant secretary is to provide for "independent evaluations" of each REL in the third year it receives assistance under this subsection.

Section (8), Invitation Regarding Competition for Awards of Assistance, covers the awarding of grants. Grants are for not less than a five-year period, require the RELs to submit annual reports to the assistant secretary and do not alter any contracts already in effect before the enactment of ***P.L. 103-227***.

(4) ***GOALS 2000*** **Community Partnerships,** sets up five-year grant programs funded at not less than $1,000,000 per year in *"eligible communities,"* having populations of between 200,000 and 300,000 in which at least half the school-age children have family incomes below the poverty line. There can only be one ***GOALS 2000*** partnership per congressional district. The award will go to a *"learning grant institution"* and will be run by an appointed *"District Education Agent."* This is vaguely reminiscent of the 535 "Break the Mold" schools that were to go into every congressional district under George Bush's ***AMERICA 2000*** plan. These ***GOALS 2000*** community partnerships

will be a proving ground for interweaving the interests of schools with other community agencies. As usual with social engineering programs, this one is being piloted in poverty areas where the government can claim "high need/high risk," and few will object to the possible benefits for disadvantaged students. Subsection (B) states the community partnerships *"may include the participation of human, social service and health care agencies, Head Start and child care agencies, libraries, museums, employment and training agencies, and the State educational agency or tribal department of education."* In other words, the horizontal aspect of lifelong learning. In order to become a ***GOALS 2000*** community, participants must develop a comprehensive plan that will:

> *(A) adopt the National education Goals;*
>
> *(B) identify additional needs and goals for educational improvement within the community;*
>
> *(C) focus on helping all students reach* **challenging** *content and student performance standards;*
>
> *(D) be consistent with the State and local improvement plans for system-wide education improvement developed pursuant to title 3;*
>
> *(E) establish a comprehensive community-wide plan for achieving such goals; and*
>
> *(F) develop a means for measuring the progress of the community in meeting such goals for improvement.*

This, too, is reminiscent of the *AMERICA 2000* communities that were established during the latter part of the Bush/Alexander years **(often in partnership with the local Chamber of Commerce)** and in anticipation of the passage of enabling federal legislation. **(See chronology: 90, 94, 95, 101, and 105; and glossary: Lifelong Learning.)**

These community plans are to be implemented by *"supporting innovation, restructuring, and continuous improvement in educational practice"* by identifying, replicating, evaluating, and disseminating information about effective programs, as well as doing area-specific research to improve student achievement. They are to prepare *"all students to reach* ***challenging*** *standards"* through a variety of training programs for prospective, novice, and experienced teachers. Training is not to be limited to *"subject matter and pedagogical expertise,"* but is also to *"increase the ability . . . to teach effectively at-risk students, students with disabilities, students with limited-English proficiency, and students from diverse cultural backgrounds,"* and *"to enhance teaching and classroom management skills, including school-based management skills, of novice, prospective, and experienced teachers."*

Sections (C) and (D) below are most revealing because they cut right to the heart of what the ***GOALS 2000*** partnershipping programs are all about.

> *(C) promoting the development of an integrated system of service delivery to children from birth through age 18 and their families by facilitating linkages and cooperation among—*
>
> *(i) local educational agencies;*
>
> *(ii) health and social services agencies and providers;*
>
> *(iii) juvenile justice and criminal justice agencies;*
>
> *(iv) providers of employment training; and*
>
> *(v) child care, Head Start, and other early childhood agencies; and*
>
> *(D) mobilizing the resources of the community in support of student learning and high achievement by facilitating effective partnerships and collaboration among—*
>
> *(i) local educational agencies;*
>
> *(ii) postsecondary educational institutions;*
>
> *(iii) public libraries;*
>
> *(iv) parents;*

(v) community-based organizations, neighborhood associations, and other civic and community organizations;

(vi) child care, Head Start, and other early childhood agencies;

(vii) churches, synagogues, and other religious institutions;

(viii) labor organizations; and

(ix) business and industry.

Birth to eighteen, **with the parents but one "caretaker" in a long list of community caretakers**—the parent/caretaker reduced in authority, but still responsible/accountable to the state for the successful delivery of a fully usable human resource.

Each *GOALS 2000* community partnership is to coordinate its activities with *"the National Diffusion Network State facilitators, regional educational laboratories, and other components of the Office to utilize most effectively Federal research, development, and dissemination resources in implementing the community-wide plan."* The assistant secretary is to provide technical assistance in setting up and implementing partnerships. Periodic evaluations of the partnership activities are to include:

(i) the impact of the **GOALS 2000** *Community Partnerships program on children and families within each community, including effects on the extent of educational achievement, rates of school retention and completion, and enrollment in postsecondary educational programs; and*

(ii) whether an intensified effort to apply and utilize educational research within a limited geographic area significantly improves student learning and achievement; and

(D) plan for the expansion of the **GOALS 2000** *Community Partnerships program throughout the remainder of the United States beginning in fiscal year 1999.*

Here is the admission that this is not just for the poor and disadvantaged, but that **your community will be "partnershipped" too (target date FY-1999).** Recall that throughout ***P.L. 103-227***, the words **"all children,"** and **"all"** used in connection with parents and other adults were used more than one hundred times! We had better take seriously that **"all"** means just that—**all!** If you are not in a **"high risk"** group targeted for immediate attention, the government intends to get around to you and your family just as soon as they are able.

Section **(j), Teacher Research Dissemination Demonstration Program**, *"finds"* that there are insufficient linkages between R&D centers such as the RELs, the NDN, ERIC, the comprehensive technical assistance centers funded under the ***ESEA***, and schools and classroom teachers. They maintain that teachers do not have direct access to these information systems and networks, haven't enough time to dialogue with peers about strategies for improving learning, have little control over the in-service education they are offered and are not encouraged to move outside their school buildings to identify and use outside resources. Therefore, this section authorizes the secretary to make grants, contracts, and cooperative agreements that will help teachers, especially new teachers, to "become knowledgeable about, assist in the design and use of, and use, education research, including education research carried out under this section," and to "develop, implement, and evaluate models for creation of teacher research dissemination networks." Use of funds will be:

> *(B) to develop simple formats, both administrative and technological, that allow elementary and secondary education teachers easy access to and use of education research findings;*
>
> *(C) to share strategies and materials;*
>
> *(D) to support professional networks;*
>
> *(E) to survey teacher needs in the areas of research and development; and*
>
> *(F) for other activities . . .*

If more of the programs and materials available through the networks supported real academic learning, this would be a commendable development. However, increased access to the educational networks, will mean that many bad programs will be in more classrooms that much sooner.

PART E—NATIONAL LIBRARY OF EDUCATION

This section establishes within the DOE, a National Library of Education (the Library) to act as a central repository of educational materials, to provide reference services to DOE personnel (first priority), their contractors, grantees, other federal employees, and members of the public. Using modern technology, the library seeks to form a network of national educational resources linking major libraries, schools, and educational centers across the united States.

> *(d) ONE-STOP INFORMATION AND REFERRAL SERVICE.—The Library shall establish and maintain a central information and referral service to respond to telephonic, mail and electronic and other inquiries from the public concerning—*
>
> *(1) programs and activities of the Department of Education;*
>
> *(2) publications produced by the Department of Education and, to the extent feasible, education related publications produced by the Departments of Labor, Health and Human Services, and other Federal departments and agencies;*
>
> *(3) services and resources available to the public through the Office, including the Educational Resources Information Center Clearinghouses, the research institutes, and the national education dissemination system;*
>
> *(4) statistics and other information produced by the National Center for Education Statistics; and*
>
> *(5) referrals to additional sources of information and expertise about educational issues which may be available through educational associations and foundations, the private sector, colleges and univer-*

sities, libraries and bibliographic databases.

The library is to maintain and actively publicize a toll-free telephone number through which public inquiries may be made. The number for general information and statistics is 1-800-424-1616.

The creation of a National Library of Education (with a toll-free number) is a promising development for parents, researchers, and other members of the public who will welcome simplified and inexpensive access to educational materials. After all, these materials are funded with tax dollars and used by your children in the public schools. It's important to have this access.

Reference services will include specialized subject searches; search and retrieval of electronic databases; delivery of documents by mail and FAX; interlibrary loans; research counseling; and bibliographic instruction and other training.

Under subsection (f), **Cooperation and Resource Sharing,** the library is charged with the establishment of information and resource sharing networks among libraries and archives with significant education collections; the development of a union list of education journals held by education libraries throughout the U.S.; the development of directories and indexes to textbook and other specialized collections in education libraries; and cooperative efforts to preserve, maintain and promote access to items of special historical value or interest.

The new library will absorb the existing DOE Research Library, reference and information branches, and will be headed by an executive director appointed by the assistant secretary (A.S.) and paid not less than the minimum rate of basic pay for a GS-15 ($67,941 minimum per annum). The A.S. will also appoint a task force of librarians, scholars, teachers, parents, and school leaders to provide advice on the establishment of the library. This group will report to the A.S. within six months after its first meeting. The A.S. is responsible for creating comprehensive collection development, acquisitions and maintenance, operations, and services policies.

The four brief remaining parts of Section 900, are amendments to other existing laws:

PART F—STAR SCHOOLS

Amends the amount of the ***Star Schools Assistance Act*** to be used for an independent evaluation of the program. **(See Title 2, Section 232(F); and glossary: Star Schools.)**

PART G—OFFICE OF COMPREHENSIVE SCHOOL HEALTH EDUCATION

It is of interest that a "comprehensive" health education office already existed within the office of the secretary under the *ESEA*. Part G amends the *ESEA* by a transfer of this office from the secretary of the Office of Elementary and Secondary Education. It also calls for this comprehensive health education office:

> *To act as a liaison office for the coordination of the activities undertaken by the Office under this section with related activities of the Department of Health and Human Services and to expand school health education research grant programs under this section.*

PART H—FIELD READERS

This amends the ***Department of Education Organization Act*** regarding the allowable rate of pay for field readers. Field readers are nongovernmental individuals hired to review grant applications.

PART I—AMENDMENT TO THE ***CARL D. PERKINS VOCATIONAL AND APPLIED TECHNOLOGY EDUCATION ACT***

Amendments to align this act with *GOALS 2000*. The final subsection on data collection, reflects the interest in cross-referencing of data (in this case collaboration with colleges, universities, and trade schools). **(See also Title 10, Section 1021.)**

> *(d) DATA COLLECTION SYSTEM.—In the development and design of a system to provide data on graduation or completion rates, job placement rates from occupationally specific programs, licensing rates, and awards of high school graduate equivalency diplomas (GED),*

each State board for higher education shall develop a data collection system the results of which can be integrated into the occupational information system developed under this section.

(See chronology: 112, 115, 122, and 128; and glossary: NCES.)

Title 10—
Miscellaneous

In which you will find an odd assortment of "afterthoughts" and amendments (almost half of these to **other legislation**). The sections are:

1. School Prayer
2. Funding for the ***Individuals with Disabilities Education Act.***
3. National Board for Professional Teaching Standards
4. Forgiveness of Certain Overpayments
5. Study of ***GOALS 2000*** and Students with Disabilities
6. Amendments to Summer Youth Employment and Training Program
7. Protection of Pupil Rights
8. Contraceptive Devices
9. Assessments
10. Assessment of Educational Progress Activities (NAEP) and the ***Carl D. Perkins Vocational and Applied Technology Education Act***
11. A "Sense of the Congress" statement regarding the "**Buy America Act**"
12. Gun-Free Schools
13. Tobacco Smoke-Free Schools
14. Grants for Midnight Basketball Leagues

TITLE 10—
MISCELLANEOUS

PART A—MISCELLANEOUS PROVISIONS

Miscellaneous **and** extraneous. Six of Title 10's sections are actually amendments to other education-related legislation. Others appear to have been some legislator's pet project or an attempt to do something for "the folks back home." This is what happens to high priority, fast-track legislation. Like a big ship, it picks up barnacles.

Sec. 1011. School Prayer.

No funds authorized to be appropriated under this Act may be used by any State or local educational agency to adopt policies that prevent voluntary prayer and meditation in public schools.

This section (which was introduced in stronger terms as an amendment to ***GOALS 2000***) made points with some of the constituents back home, but is totally toothless. Schools aren't going to adopt policies to ***"prevent"*** voluntary prayer. In today's hostile climate, prayer is effectively prevented by Supreme Court rulings and the ever present threat of "separation of church and state" lawsuits. The inclusion of the words *"and meditation"* points out a major problem with having a voluntary school prayer amendment (or the teaching of religion in the public schools). In order to be "inclusive," and "multicultural," prayers and teachings must somehow be acceptable to everyone. This would be a difficult task if the only differences to be resolved were among the various denominations and sects of Christianity. Given that Christianity is but one among many religions practiced in the United States, the prospect of settling for a generic "minute of silence" (a compromise that **might** be tolerated) looks like a very hollow victory.

Sec. 1012. Funding for the Individuals with Disabilities Education Act.

This is a "sense of the Congress" statement to the effect that since the passage of the ***Individuals with Disabilities Education Act (IDEA)*** which was committed to forty percent federal funding, but which currently only receives eight percent from that source, the federal government should provide *"adequate resources"* as soon as possible. According to this section, *"it would cost the Federal Government approximately $10,000,000,000 each year to fully fund the **Individuals with Disabilities Education Act.**"*

The amount that's needed should indicate how unrealistic this "(non)sense of the Congress" statement is. This was probably offered as a sop to those pressing for full funding of *IDEA* which has been called the largest unfunded federal mandate on state schools.

Sec. 1013. National Board for Professional Teaching Standards.

This section amends the ***Higher Education Act of 1965*** regarding this board and establishes a matching funds arrangement. The National Board for Professional Teaching Standards (NBPTS) was originally set up in the 1980s by the **Carnegie Foundation for the Advancement of Teaching (CFAT)**. CFAT is one of the leading nongovernmental education change agents. They were busily at work preparing to change teaching standards long before ***AMERICA 2000*** was ever launched. The NBPTS which began as a private enterprise (away from public scrutiny) is now federally recognized and funded. **(See chronology: 87 and 113.)**

Sec. 1014. Forgiveness of Certain Overpayments.

This section pertains to Colfax County, New Mexico, and a payment problem related to the use of faulty data.

Sec. 1015. Study of GOALS 2000 and Students with Disabilities.

This section calls for the National Academy of Sciences or the National Academy of Education to conduct a comprehensive study of the inclusion of children with disabilities in school reform activities assisted under the *GOALS 2000* legislation. Funding for this research is $600,000 for FY-94 and *"such sums as may be necessary"* for FY-95. An interim report of findings and recommendations is to be submitted to Congress within twelve months and a final report not later than twenty-four months. Under study components, the following are listed:

> *(1) an evaluation of the National Education Goals and objectives, curriculum reforms, standards, and other programs and activities intended to achieve those goals;*
>
> *(2) a review of the adequacy of assessments and measures used to gauge progress towards meeting National Educational Goals and any national and State standards, and an examination of other methods or accommodations necessary or desirable to collect data on the educational progress of children with disabilities, and the costs of such methods and accommodations;*
>
> *(3) an examination of what incentives or assistance might be provided to States to develop improvement plans that adequately address the needs of children with disabilities;*
>
> *(4) the relation of the Goals 2000: Educate America Act to other Federal laws governing or affecting the education of children with disabilities; and*
>
> *(5) such other issues as the National Academy of Sciences or the National Academy of Education considers appropriate.*

Doubtless this study will come up with ways to get the federal government to assume more of the funding burden for the *IDEA*. The "findings and recommendations" of this study could be to *IDEA* what the O-T-L standards are to finance and other equity issues. **(See also Section 1012.)**

SEC. 1016. AMENDMENTS TO SUMMER YOUTH EMPLOYMENT AND TRAINING PROGRAM.

This section amends the ***Job Training Partnership Act (20 U.S.C. 1632)*** by beefing up basic and remedial education (including pre-employment and work maturity skills training), academic enrichment, the integration of work and learning, and calls for the establishment of *"linkages"* (i.e., better communication between schools and employers about the needs and performance of student participants).

SEC. 1017. PROTECTION OF PUPILS.

Section 439 of the ***General Education Provisions Act (20 U.S.C. 1232g)*** is amended to read as follows:

PROTECTION OF PUPIL RIGHTS

Section 439. (a) All instructional materials, including teacher's manuals, films, tapes, or other supplementary material which will be used in connection with any survey, analysis, or evaluation as part of any applicable program shall be available for inspection by the parents or guardians of the children.

(b) No student shall be required, as part of any applicable program, to submit to a survey, analysis, or evaluation that reveals information concerning—

(1) political affiliations;

(2) mental and psychological problems potentially embarrassing to the student or his family;

(3) sex behavior and attitudes;

(4) illegal, anti-social, self-incriminating and demeaning behavior;

(5) critical appraisals of other individuals with whom respondents have close family relationships;

(6) legally recognized privileged or analogous relationships, such as those of lawyers, physicians, and ministers; or

(7) income (other than that required by law to determine eligibility for participation in a program or for receiving financial assistance under such program), without the prior consent of the student (if the student is an adult or emancipated minor), or in the case of an unemancipated minor, without the prior written consent of the parent.

(c) Educational agencies and institutions shall give parents and students effective notice of their rights under this section.

(d) ENFORCEMENT.—*The Secretary shall take such action as the Secretary determines appropriate to enforce this section, except that action to terminate assistance provided under an applicable program shall be taken only if the Secretary determines that—*

(1) there has been a failure to comply with such section; and

(2) compliance with such section cannot be secured by voluntary means.

(e) OFFICE AND REVIEW BOARD.—*The Secretary shall establish or designate an office and review board within the Department of Education to investigate, process, review, and adjudicate violations of the rights established under this section.*

Parents take note! Here is some legal protection against objectionable material and intrusive questions/surveys. It should be noted that similar protection was provided under the largely ignored Hatch Amendment. **(See chronology: 69 and 80.)** The problems with this sort of "protection" are many: 1) parents usually do not find out about objectionable material until it has been presented or is ongoing and harm has already been done; 2) the material must be part of a federally funded program, something which is often very difficult to prove; 3) parents must be prepared for a tough, protracted, and probably expensive fight if they challenge what their local school is doing; and 4) the track record of the Department of Education in enforcement has been extremely poor. Few parents have the stamina of Anita Hoge, the mother from Pennsylvania described in ***Educating for the New World Order***, who took on the local school establishment, the state, and eventually the Department of Education. Years after the incident that prompted her investigation, Mrs. Hoge won a great moral victory and her story brought to light many of the abuses rampant in state-run schools. For an eye-opening look at the gathering, storage, and dissemination of intrusive, personal information in the NAEP see **resources: journals:** ***Christian Conscience,*** **"When Johnny Takes the Test."**

The safest thing to do if your children are in the system is to carefully go over with them the seven illegal areas spelled out in Section 1017. Give them examples from each area and make sure that they understand what an intrusive, illegal question looks like and that no matter what the teacher says about confidentiality or incomplete answers affecting test scores, etc., they are NOT to provide such information. Intrusion-proofing your children is a far better strategy than hoping that you will be notified in advance of your rights or that controversial programs are coming. After all, **this law has been in effect since the 1994–95 school year. How many parents have been told about the Protection of Pupil Rights contained in *GOALS 2000*?** Since the whole point is to protect children **before** they are exposed to objectionable material, parents must be preemptive rather than wait to address grievances after the fact. It is hard to be on top of everything that is going on in school, harder still to find out in advance what's coming. One district I am familiar with began the sex ed course the week school opened before most parents had even thought to send notes requesting an "opt-out" for their kids. Of course, opt-outs do not protect children from teachers who infuse objectionable material in wherever they can. **(See glossary: Infusion Model.)**

Sec. 1018. Contraceptive Devices.

The Department of Health and Human Services and the Depart-

> *ment of Education shall ensure that all federally funded programs which provide for the distribution of contraceptive devices to unemancipated minors develop procedures to encourage, to the extent practical, family participation in such programs.*

This watered-down, "compromise" (which started out as an anti-condom distribution amendment to ***GOALS 2000***) typifies what's wrong with the law: federal usurpation of parental authority; condoning and enabling immoral and unsafe behavior that children and parents are left to bear the consequences of; and weasly language ("to encourage, to the extent practical, family participation . . .") that legislators know would never be enforced.

> *SEC. 1019. ASSESSMENTS.*

> *(a) TITLE II.—No funds provided under title II of this Act shall be used to develop or undertake assessments that will be used to make decisions regarding the graduation, grade promotion, or retention of students for 5 years after the date of enactment of this Act.*

No high-stakes (you don't move on or graduate) testing till 1999.

> *(b) TITLE III.—Assessments developed with funds under title III of this Act may be used for decisions regarding graduation, grade promotion, or retention of students only on the condition that students have been prepared in the content for which the students are being assessed.*

If testing is high-stakes, it's only fair that children be taught what they're to be tested on. One of the obvious down sides of this is the amount of class time that will be taken up with "teaching to the test" to ensure students will do well.

> *SEC. 1021. ASSESSMENT OF EDUCATIONAL PROGRESS ACTIVITIES.*

This section amends the ***Carl D. Perkins Vocational and Applied Technology Education Act*** to authorize states or state consortia to use items and data from the **National Assessment of Educational Progress (the NAEP)** to evaluate vocational education courses, subject to a variety of restrictions under which the Commissioner of Education Statistics has determined in writing that use of this data by NAEP will not—

> *(i) result in the identification of characteristics or performance of individual students or schools;*
>
> *(ii) result in the ranking or comparing of schools or local educational agencies;*
>
> *(iii) be used to evaluate the performance of teachers, principals, or other local educators for the purpose of dispensing rewards or punishments; or*
>
> *(iv) corrupt or harm the use and value of data collected for the National Assessment of Educational Progress.*

Some additional limitations are placed on the use of the NAEP when used to evaluate these programs. Given the importance and increased emphasis on vo-tech, prep-tech, and other school-to-work programs under *GOALS 2000*, it's very important that all of these are launched carefully, and equally important that the NAEP not attract hostile scrutiny. **(See chronology: 31, 44, 74, 101, and 122; conclusion: *CAREERS* bill; and glossary: NCES.)**

SEC. 1022. SENSE OF THE CONGRESS.

This says that equipment and products purchased with ***GOALS 2000*** money should be obtained in compliance with the *"**Buy America Act**"* and that anyone violating the "made in America" rule should be ineligible to receive a contract or subcontract provided through this act.

PART B—GUN-FREE SCHOOLS

Sections 1031 and 1032 set up *"Gun-Free Schools."* The curious thing about this is that it's actually an amendment to the ***ESEA***, not a part of this law. This is just another proof of the close link between the *GOALS 2000* and *ESEA* legislation. The new Title VIII of the *ESEA* states that no local educational agency (LEA) can receive *ESEA* money unless they have in effect a policy requiring the expulsion from school for not less than one year of any student who brings a weapon (firearm) to school. This can be modified on a case-by-case basis. If expulsions occur under this new title, the LEA is to provide the state with the name of the school involved, the circumstances surrounding the expulsion, the number of students expelled, and the types of weapons used.

PART C—ENVIRONMENTAL TOBACCO SMOKE

This consists of sections 1041 through 1044 and is actually an entire act, the ***"Pro-Children Act of 1994,"*** tacked onto the *GOALS 2000* legislation. It prohibits smoking in any indoor facility providing day care, education, or library services to children under eighteen years of age if the facility is receiving federal funds. A penalty of $1,000 is to be exacted for each violation. Some exemptions and modification provisions are provided, but this is a no-nonsense regulation stating, in effect, that if you operate a federally-funded facility serving children, smokers had better step outside.

PART D—MIDNIGHT BASKETBALL LEAGUE TRAINING AND PARTNERSHIP

This is the final tacked-on section of the ***GOALS 2000*** legislation and consists of Sections 1051 through 1053. It appropriates $2,650,000 for FY-94 and '95 for grants to carry out MBL programs. The usual grant for any one league is $55,000–$130,000. An additional $100,000 for FY-94 and '95 is appropriated for technical assistance grants (to those with experience and expertise in setting up and operating MBLs, employment, job training, and educational services) and a one-time grant of $250,000 to *"carry out a scientific study of the effectiveness of midnight basketball league programs. . . ."* To assist the secretary in making these grants, an advisory committee is set up consisting of: two individuals who manage or administer MBLs, an appointed representative of DOE, and two representative of the Department of Health and Human Services—one from the Center for Substance Abuse Prevention and one involved in issues relating to high-risk youth. Those receiving grants will be required to make an annual report of their activities.

Midnight basketball leagues (somewhat misnamed because under Section 1053, an MBL can be *"any youth sports program that meets the requirements of a midnight basketball league program . . ."* are one of the crime and other dead-end behavior fighting strategies addressed at "high risk" youth. Section 1051 of ***GOALS 2000*** amends the ***Cranston-Gonzales National Affordable Housing Act*** by adding MBL training and partnership programs. Under program requirements, the following are listed:

> *(A) The program shall establish a basketball league of not less than 8 teams having 10 players each.*
>
> *(B) Not less than 50 percent of the players in the basketball league shall be residents of federally assisted low-income housing or members of low-income families (as such term is defined in section 3(b) of the United States Housing Act of 1937).*
>
> *(C) The program shall be designed to serve primarily youths and young adults from a neighborhood or community whose population has not less than 2 of the following characteristics (in comparison with national averages):*
>
> *(i) A substantial problem regarding use or sale of illegal drugs.*
>
> *(ii) A high incidence of crimes committed by youths or young adults.*
>
> *(iii) A high incidence of persons infected with the human immunodeficiency virus or sexually transmitted diseases.*
>
> *(iv) A high incidence of pregnancy or a high birth rate, among adolescents.*

(v) A high unemployment rate for youths and young adults.

(vi) A high rate of high school drop-outs.

(D) The program shall require each player in the league to attend employment counseling, job training, and other educational classes provided under the program, which shall be held immediately following the conclusion of league basketball games at or near the site of the games and at other specified times.

(E) The program shall serve only youths and young adults who demonstrate a need for such counseling, training, and education provided by the program, in accordance with criteria for demonstrating need, which shall be established by the Secretary, in consultation with the Advisory Committee.

(F) The majority of the basketball games of the league shall be held between the hours of 10:00 p.m. and 2:00 a.m. at a location in the neighborhood or community served by the program.

(G) The program shall obtain sponsors for each team in the basketball league. Sponsors shall be private individuals or businesses in the neighborhood or community served by the program who make financial contributions to the program and participate in or supplement the employment, job training, and educational services provided to the players under the program with additional training or educational opportunities.

(H) and (I) deal briefly with criteria for the MBLs and training and technical assistance.

It's clear from the description that these programs are designed to fight crime, drug use, the spread of sexually transmitted diseases, and teen pregnancies by providing structured activities during the peak hours when young people are tempted to get themselves into trouble. A secondary benefit appears to be job counseling and training. However, having children out in their neighborhoods between the hours of 10:00 p.m. and 2:00 a.m. (and beyond) is a violation of curfew laws which seems to have been overlooked here. One wonders how much effective counseling, job training, and other education can take place during those late hours *"immediately following the conclusion of league basketball games."* Since high incidence of HIV, sexually transmitted diseases, pregnancy, and birth rates are mentioned as part of the participant profile, and since under (G), private sponsors to supplement *"educational services"* are solicited, parents of children participating in these programs would do well to take a close look at who is coming in and what educational services are being provided. The potential is there for organizations with an agenda at odds with Christian values to impact this captive audience.

END—P.L. 103-227

Conclusion

Finally, what is the future of *GOALS 2000*? Despite the broad bipartisan support **AMERICA 2000** and *GOALS 2000* have enjoyed, there is some opposition to this highly controversial legislation and it's not just coming from wideawake parents. The Republican majority who came to Washington in 1995 arrived enthusiastic about defunding *GOALS 2000*. Unfortunately, they have not followed through. There has even been legislation introduced to do away with the Department of Education altogether. One such bill, however, would transfer powers now enjoyed by the DOE over to the Departments of Health & Human Services and Labor **(hardly an improvement—just a reshuffling—and a dangerous one, further legitimizing the labor, education, social services merger we have seen all too clearly in GOALS 2000)**!

Another major bill awaiting final approval that will micromanage society and the economy is **H.R.1617**, ***The Consolidated and Reformed Education, Employment, and Rehabilitation Systems Act (CAREERS)***. The Senate version, **S.143**, is called ***The Job Training Consolidation Act.*** As this goes to press, *CAREERS* has passed in both the House and the Senate and is awaiting conference (where it will be fine-tuned). Only a final vote after the conference remains to start the gears grinding on what one researcher has called "The Great Perpetual Work Force Machine." Unfortunately, many of our "conservative" representatives have supported this bill without (one assumes) closely examining it. *CAREERS* has been promoted as "government downsizing" and "cost effective" because it "repeals" the ***School-to-Work Opportunities Act, P.L.103-239***, and scores of other existing training programs. It "repeals" ***School-to-Work***, however, by consolidating it with all the other major federal training programs then returns the money as block grants to the states. But this is far from a simple consolidation of programs.

CAREERS calls for each state to submit a three-year Strategic Improvement Plan (*a la* the ***GOALS 2000*** SIPS); classifies 16-year-olds as adults (conveniently skirting child labor laws); sets up one-stop career centers; an unemployment compensation system; a national labor market information system with its own database listing available jobs; and a Work Force Development Partnership to administer this new behemoth. Does this sound like a "repeal," or even remotely like "downsizing"? *CAREERS* creates a huge new multilayered bureaucracy and yet another government intrusion into our schools and the economy, cancelling our basic freedom to choose and pursue vocational preferences. If only our representatives would refuse to vote for any bill they have not read in its entirety and are sure they have thought through! *CAREERS* seems to have come directly from the plan of the NCEE to create a seamless web extending from cradle to grave, as outlined in Marc Tucker's letter to Hillary Clinton. **(See glossary: 112; and resources: Christian Conscience: "The Great Perpetual Workforce Machine"; and miscellaneous: Parents Involved in Education.)**

Parents, be **very cautious** about any legislation intended to do away with *GOALS 2000*, other pieces of education legislation, or the DOE. **Bills calling for repeals, abolishing of offices, etc. should be done outright with no transfers of power; and done by "sudden death," i.e., no "sunset" provisions that can be refunded by a different set of legislators a few years down the road.** Get a copy of any bill that's being promoted **(by whatever group)** and **read it for yourself before you endorse it.** Some "conservative" legislators and groups have endorsed really bad legislation.

GOALS 2000 is a fact of American life and likely to remain so. The momentum and resolve of the Republican majority to defund *GOALS 2000* seems to have all but evaporated. Though the federal budget is still not resolved as this goes to press, instead of defunding or repealing *GOALS 2000*, Congress has permitted it to function by funding it at seventy-five percent of its 1995 level through a continuing resolution. Will the continued existence of this new law end up as part of a budget deal with Clinton and the Democrats—a trade for something seen as more important? Time will tell, but that seems probable. The situation reminds me of 1980 when President Reagan came to office having promised to abolish the Department of Education. If campaign promises requiring bold, decisive actions are not taken early on, they usually are not taken at all. Realistically, however, the chances of any repeal of ***GOALS 2000*** or abolition of the DOE while Clinton is in office and has the veto power are practically nil. Because of all the powerful backers and vested interests, repeal would be very difficult even with a sympathetic Senate and a conservative President.

Still, totally **repealing *GOALS 2000* and abolishing the Department of Education is a worthwhile goal for the future**. The less money the federal government has for education programs, the less harm will be done. We need to be sure as time passes that programs and activities under ***GOALS 2000*** are not simply merged into new or existing legislation, or transferred to other federal agencies (with HHS and/or Labor being the most likely).

Getting the federal government completely out of education, out of parental replacement, out of micromanaging the economy and other social engineering should be a priority for Christian parents whether their children are in the state schools or not. With most children from Christian homes still in state schools, it seems a bit ironic that parents with children in Christian schools and especially Christian homeschoolers (those seemingly with the least vested interest in state schools) have been the point men and women in past educational battles and likely will continue to lead as "salt and light" on state school issues and as goads to the legislative conscience.

After reading ***GOALS 2000*** you are aware (if you were not already) that much of what's in this law is firmly in place in the schools—**all our state schools**. Some of it has been there for years, and **what isn't there yet will be.** Nevertheless, despite the ongoing restructuring, **there seems to be a great deal of denial that these changes are occurring close to home.** A frequent comment I hear is: "Well, yes, I'm aware of those bad (fill in the blank) programs. School district (fill in the blank) is doing that and it's awful. But we have a very conservative (fill in the blank) and so we've managed to avoid that. Our local school is actually doing a pretty good job." I hope a close look at the pervasive restructuring effort embodied in ***GOALS 2000*** will have some effect on this "hear no evil/see no evil/speak no evil" syndrome.

GOALS 2000, and the closely allied ***ESEA, School-to-Work,*** and now the ***CAREERS bill*** may be your final wake-up call.

Can the enormous educational bureaucracy be dismantled? Can legislation (some of it in place for years) be defunded or repealed? I don't know, but until that happens (if ever), what should Christian parents do about their own children's education? **Your first responsibility as a parent is to your own children. All other efforts should be subordinate to the assurance your children are getting an academic education in a safe environment that fosters godly character development.**

I believe it's a great mistake to leave your children in state schools thinking you will somehow be able to outguess/outmaneuver the social planners or that because you are smart, dedicated, and feisty you can stay one step ahead of the latest educational fad or bad program. Even if you have a lot of time to expend on research and activism, you should probably ask yourself: Is this a productive way to spend my time? For most people it is not. You have probably noticed that if you manage to put out one brush fire, you're soon facing another somewhere else. It's one battle after another. And it should be clear after reading ***GOALS 2000*** that educational restructuring is far more than OBE, humanistic sex ed, or just another new brush fire. It's more like a fire wall. ***GOALS 2000* is, and was meant to be, start from scratch, top-to-bottom, systemic educational/societal restructuring.**

Parents, I ask with a sense of real urgency, that you consider whether you really want to take the chance that your children will **not be harmed** by leaving them in state schools. Many parents say: "Well, I went through the public schools and I turned out O.K." That would probably have been my response a few years ago, too. My thought now is: First, don't be so sure that your education was not in some/many respects deficient. Many homeschooling parents (myself included) have discovered this after we began teaching our own children using traditional academic materials. Also, a fully operational ***GOALS 2000*** school bears little resemblance to the schools you and I attended.

So what are your choices? What alternatives are out there for Christian parents?

Charter schools, as we have seen, are not really a "choice," they are simply state schools set up and run a little differently, subject to less red tape. But they are *GOALS 2000* schools. Schools that don't meet the basic criteria don't get chartered. Many of these will replicate the schools set up as "design team winners" by the New American Schools Development Corporation in 1992 under the *AMERICA 2000* plan. Enough time has passed on these "break the mold" schools to see which are viable models. **Expect to see many charter schools opening in the next few years. (See chronology: 110.)**

"Choice" in the form of vouchers, tuition tax credits, and other plans for parents to get some money back when they place their children outside the system should, in my opinion, be avoided. **Let your common sense and not your desire for monetary advantage lead you on this one.** I know that **"choice"** is a rallying cry of many Christian and conservative organizations, but how quickly they overlook what has always been true: **what the government funds, it controls.** Wouldn't it be pretty irresponsible for the government to hand out money without demanding some accountability? Accountability would most likely take the form of mandatory testing, requiring the use of the state's (*GOALS 2000*) curriculum, etc. The attractiveness and apparent ease of getting federal dollars at first **(the bait)**, soon followed by regulations and restrictions **(the switch)** would effectively obliterate the differences that make Christian schools and homeschooling a distinctive type of education. **Sooner or later the government will probably give parents vouchers or tax credits.** This will be touted as a great victory for Christians, conservatives, and other groups who have asked the government to return some of **their** money to spend as they choose on education. **The government would be smart to do this. It's the surest way to "level" private, Christian, and homeschools, too.**

Christian schools (carefully screened—because they have their problems, too!) are the first choice for many families where both parents work, or for single parents. Private schools are, of course, expensive and many parents (even if they can afford this choice) don't take it because they view it as paying twice: once through taxes and again through tuition. My answer to this is that you must look at the hidden but true cost of submitting your children to thirteen (or more) years of "free" government education. Godly grandparents or other relatives may wish to help their families by providing tuition money now (rather than leaving everything in an inheritance later).

Increasing numbers of parents have opted to put the enormous amounts of energy involved in constantly policing their schools, keeping up with the latest government directives and trying to shield their children from harm, into the **more positive and rewarding task of assuming direct responsibility for educating their own children.** These parents have sent the clearest kind of message to Washington and to their state capitals by simply never entering their children, or withdrawing them from the state schools, creating instead their own learning environment at home. An estimated 1 million parents nationwide (probably a low estimate) are currently doing this. Homeschooling is legal in all fifty states and would be an even more popular choice if parents only knew how "do-able" it is.

It's certainly lots easier to homeschool in the 1990s now that so many families have blazed the trail, fighting the precedent-setting legal battles and establishing numerous local support groups and other assistance such as state conferences and curriculum fairs. Curriculum materials are available in a great variety of formats and prices. A fairly elaborate outlay for a year at home is almost certainly going to cost far less than a year's tuition in a private school. **(See resources: Homeschooling.)**

We should thank God with the flood of socialistic legislation engulfing this nation that we do still have the opportunity to educate our own children or place them where we feel a proper job will be done. Every family must, of course, **seek the Lord's wisdom** in this. But unless you are directed specifically to leave your children in the system, now (or at the close of this school year) is the time to do as Paul advised the Corinthians (2 Corinthians 6:14–18) ". . . come out from among them, and be ye separate. . . ."

The most effective way to protect your children and to send the social engineers unmistakably clear messages is by giving the state empty school desks instead of your children. Imagine what might happen if a sufficient number of parents simply did that!

I'll close with some prophetic words from Martin Luther:

> I'm much afraid that schools will prove to be great gates of hell unless they diligently labor in explaining the Holy Scriptures, engraving them in the hearts of youth. I advise no one to place his child where the Scriptures do not reign paramount. Every institution in which men are not increasingly occupied with the Word of God must become corrupt.

Author's Note: As this was going to the printer, word came that the House and Senate finally agreed upon a budget, voting for the ***Balanced Budget Downpayment Act, Number 2*** (April 25, 1996). This was signed by President Clinton the following day.

Where is ***GOALS 2000*** in all this? According to an article entitled **"To Placate Conservatives, Measures Alter *GOALS 2000*,"** by Mark Pitsch that appeared in the May 1, 1996, issue of ***Education Week***, the following modifications have been made (my comments follow in parentheses):

- The National Education Standards and Improvement Council (NESIC) is formally abolished. (This had never been funded.)
- School districts in states that have chosen not to participate in ***GOALS 2000*** can apply for aid on their own if their SEA approves. (This opens the door for the holdout states to come on board.)
- States are no longer required to submit State Improvement Plans, but must still draft plans based on challenging standards and aligned assessments and must promise that money will be spent properly. (Most of the states having taken ***GOALS 2000*** money have already done their SIPs.)
- Provisions specifying composition of state and local panels charged with drafting SIPs and LIPs are deleted. (Since most state and local plans have already been done or extensively worked on, this will change little or nothing.)
- States are no longer required to have opportunity-to-learn standards or strategies. (A good move, but since ***GOALS 2000*** has been in effect for two years, states that have submitted their SIPs have already formulated O-T-L strategies. At least now they will not be enforceable by the federal government.)
- New language states that no district, state, or school "shall be required . . . to provide outcome-based education or school-based health clinics." (Of course, nothing **prevents** states from moving forward with these—or prevents the federal government from using leverage to encourage states in that direction.)
- New language also states that ***GOALS 2000*** will not "require or permit any State or federal official to inspect a home, judge how parents raise their children, or remove children from their parents." (This must have been a response to the inclusion of the ***PAT*** program in the law. Please note this wording **does not forbid** such action either.)

In a phone call to the House Appropriations Subcommittee on Labor, HHS, and Education, I was told that under this FY-96 budget, ***GOALS 2000*** is given $350 million (as compared to approximately $378 million in last year's budget.)

To sum up where we are with ***GOALS 2000***, Secretary Riley's assistant, Michael Cohen, comments in the ***EW*** article about the appropriation and new language:

> "We're comfortable with it, and we signed on to it. There isn't anything . . . that undermines or in any way alters the fundamental goals of the program."

Glossary Entries

Community Action Toolkit

Delphi Technique

Distance Learning

Educational Resources Information Center (ERIC)

Facilitator/Facilitation

Higher Order Thinking Skills (HOTS)

Infusion Model

ISO 9000

Lifelong Learning

NASDTEC—OBE Standards for Teachers

National Center for Education Statistics (NCES)

National Diffusion Network (NDN)

Opportunity-to-Learn Standards (O-T-L)

Parents as Teachers (PAT)

Partnerships

Planning, Programming, Budgeting System (PBBS)

Regional Educational Laboratories (RELs)

Site-Based Management (SBM)

Star Schools

Total Quality Management (TQM)

United Nations Educational, Scientific and Cultural Organization (UNESCO)

U.S./Soviet Agreements

Whole Language

Glossary

Community Action Toolkit

In an article **"Kits to String Parents Along"** in the ***Washington Times*** (10/25/94) Robert Holland has critiqued the Community Action Toolkit. Prepared by the National Education Goals Panel, with distribution in late 1994, the CAT is a five-pound assortment of materials designed to "sell" ***GOALS 2000*** at the local level. By charging $37.00 apiece for the material, the panel claims the government will reclaim its costs for printing and distribution of these blatant propaganda kits. Included are: arguments in favor of ***GOALS 2000***, prewritten letters-to-the-editor, and entire speeches to use in promoting federal education goals. Use of "facilitators" to guide public meetings in reaching phony consensus on agendas preset by the "facilitator" is promoted. Educators are warned to avoid the terms "self-esteem," "outcomes," or "outcome-based education." A "troubleshooting" guide is included to identify "resistance" in the community with tips for successfully dealing with opponents. One section presents case histories showing how opponents can be neutralized, or co-opted.

Delphi Technique

Greek history records the oracle at Delphi (8th C. B.C.–4th C. A.D.). At the temple of Apollo in Delphi, a priestess, Pythia, spoke oracles which were interpreted by a priest. These oracles answered public, as well as private questions, and were used to determine the plans of the ancient Greeks. According to researcher and writer, Don Bell, the Delphi Technique was developed by Olaf Helmer and Theodore Gordon in an experiment carried out during 1963 and 1964 by the **Rand Corporation.** An account of this is given in Helmer's book, ***Social Technology***. It was originally a method of **forecasting technological developments by obtaining a consensus of opinions among experts**. Those using the technique soon realized that rather than just "**predicting**" what might happen in the future, it was possible to expand this technique to help bring about **planned change.** The Rand Corporation has developed many guides for use of the Delphi strategy, including in the educational setting.

Distance Learning

DL is information coming from a "distance" through technology (as opposed to live in the classroom). The distance could be as close as a camera/TV hookup to another classroom down the hall, or as far away as a program coming via satellite from Russia. Technologies employed in distance learning include: satellite, cable, fiber optics, open broadcasts, microcomputers, the Internet, digital compression, interactive videodiscs, faxes, and telephones.

Educational Resources Information Center (ERIC)

ERIC is a database of education information headquartered in the U.S. DOE and operated by OERI. It contains more than 850,000 abstracts of documents and journal articles on education research and practice. ERIC attempts to collect and disseminate **all existing information** on the development of children from birth through early adolescence, with emphasis on education theory, research, and practice. They provide reference and referral services, on-line searches, and tips on research strategy. **Clearinghouses** specializing in various subject areas are scattered across the country and include: adult, career, and vocational education; assessment and evaluation; community colleges; counseling and student services; disabilities and gifted education; educational management; elementary and early childhood education; higher education; information and technology; languages and linguistics; reading, English, and communication; rural education and small schools; science, mathematics, and environmental education; social studies/social science education; teacher and teacher education; and urban education. There are also eight Adjunct Clearinghouses: art education; Chapter l (compensatory education); clinical schools; consumer education; ESL literacy education; law-related education; test collection; and U.S.–Japan studies. ERIC is open to the public. A call to **1-(800)-LET-ERIC** will get you into the system.

Facilitator/Facilitation

The New Lexicon Webster's Dictionary defines *facilitate* as "to make easy or easier." An educational facilitator is an advance man who smooths the way for change. While appearing to be just a neutral moderator interested only in seeing that meetings run smoothly, **facilitators have a hidden, preset agenda for specific, planned change.** An example of "facilitation" that parents might encounter (or have already) would be serving on a committee or panel whose task is to, e.g., "set the direction of the district/school for the twenty-first century." The meetings will be led by a **"facilitator"** (or team) who is, in reality, the **"change agent bringing the preset agenda** of where **they/those they report to** want the district/school to go." Guided by the maxim, "Who frames the question wins the argument," all discussion, starting with the assumptions and questions that are posed about the task are being skillfully led or "facilitated" by this person. **Opposition is at first encouraged** to "smoke out" the resistance. Once this has been done, the opposing individual (or individuals) is neutralized by a variety of techniques (whatever is seen as most effective in that particular setting) including: **isolation** ("You seem to be the only one who feels that way"); **ridicule** ("Mrs. Brown has brought statistics from her Christian magazine"); **ignoring** the dissenter while appearing to be fair ("Your ideas will be printed in a minority opinion to the committee's report"); **ostracizing** (facilitator makes it obvious the dissenter is a total pain in the neck and impediment to progress); or **expulsion** from the meeting/group. The latter is not typically done as the illusion of this being a democratic process involving a broad section of the community is important in "selling" the final product (the preset agenda) to those who didn't participate in the "process." All of the facilitator's efforts are directed at arriving at a contrived "consensus" from the group that lines up with the original preset agenda. Some personalizing touches by participants are usually included in the final plan so that they feel "ownership." **Because of the time they've invested and the fact that their suggestions (those not at odds with the main objectives) are often included, participants are fooled into thinking this is really their own creation and they will usually defend the consensus product quite vigorously.** Because this is a technique for effecting planned change, (as is Delphi) many people refer to the above scenario/facilitation process as the Delphi technique, as in, "I was Delphied on that committee."

Higher Order Thinking Skills (HOTS)

HOTS is but the latest name for the amalgamation of two dangerous concepts, one a hierarchy of thinking skills; the other a methodology for ascending its steps. The hierarchy is Benjamin Bloom's taxonomy of thinking skills (taught as received truth to education majors) in which Bloom has ordered the steps so that **knowledge/facts/memorization is on the bottom** (lowest order thinking skill) and **judging/valuing/creativity is on the top** (the highest order). It is probably from Bloom's taxonomy that HOTS derives its name. The second concept, the methodology, is an apparent retread of "values clarification," now called "critical thinking skills." (Other names generally utilizing "thinking skills" are also used in various programs.) Those familiar with values clarification will recall that VC is a "no absolutes" system in which paradigm shifts in thinking are brought about by: 1) challenging the old assumptions/beliefs so as to cause one to let go of them (that's what "critical thinking" is—being **"critical"** of every assumption and idea presented); 2) introducing new assumptions/values to replace the ones that have been rejected; and 3) causing the person thus manipulated to feel "ownership" of the new beliefs because he has been (skillfully led) through a "process" of "objectively" examining "all" the possibilities and has chosen those he likes best. The federal laboratories (the RELs) have a newsletter, ***Human Intelligence***, devoted to disseminating information on HOTS. Of eighty-nine member organizations listed on their ***Human Intelligence International Network***, twenty-eight (one-third) were identifiable as engaged primarily in **psychological research**. This makes sense when you realize that HOTS has everything to do with the affective (feeling) domain and little to do with cognition. **HOTS** is to attitudes, values, and beliefs what **Delphi/facilitation** is to planned change.

Infusion Model

My *NLWD* tells me that an infusion is "something blended or mixed in," or "a liquid resulting from infusing, e.g. tea." Tea is a perfect example of an infusion. You start with a cup of hot water and a tea bag.

Moments after putting the bag in the cup, the water begins to take on the color, then the flavor, and finally the aroma of the tea leaves because it is being infused with the essence of the tea and the longer you leave the bag in the water, the stronger the infusion will be. Another name for the infusion model is the "infusion grid." Just think of a grid being deeply embedded in something and you have the picture. So how does "infusion" work in education? Infusion in the classroom involves taking a subject—it could be anything—but usually is something where the teacher hopes to affect a change in students' attitudes, values, and beliefs. That topic is then introduced in every conceivable way a subject can be brought up—ideally **across the entire curriculum**—so that **saturation** occurs and students can see **this topic fits in everywhere.** It's often quite a stretch to "infuse" the curriculum and teachers have to get really inventive as topics are imbedded in some rather unlikely subject areas.

For example, a high school math teacher tells how math concepts provide a model for discussions of social justice. After showing on a horizontal line positive and negative numbers and using the signs for greater than, less than, and equal to, he rotates the number line vertically so that the greater numbers are above the lesser. He states: "The ideas that greater is up and lesser is down are well-developed in high school students. The word 'positive' implies up while 'negative' suggests down. 'Upper class' and 'low life' are vertical concepts. Once the trichotomy foundation is laid, [greater than, less than, equal to] connecting the idea to tolerance comes naturally. Typically, I select a day when there is a news item involving intolerance to call a 'time out for tolerance' and broaden the discussion of what it means to be 'greater than,' 'less than,' or 'equal to.' . . . To link our ideas of social justice with mathematical concepts, I ask 'In what ways do we use numbers to identify the differences between us? We talk about how we sometimes use differences in income, age, or grade levels to rank human beings. People whose incomes are higher on the number line, for instance, are typically treated with more importance in our society. Their incomes are 'greater than' and they are treated 'better than.'"

I have used this example from a math class because if you can do this with math, imagine how much easier it is with the classes that naturally generate a lot of discussion such as English, history, social sciences, civics, etc.

Here's another one taken from a state curriculum framework for social studies. Under **"applications"** for **science** is the following suggested activity: "Research the impact that various interest groups (e.g. Act-Up, National Organization for Women, UNICEF) have had on science-related discoveries, inventions, or cures. Join or contribute to one of these organizations and keep a journal recording your activities, feelings, and achievements." This is a **science** application?

Jan Mickelson in his article **"Perversity in Diversity"** that appeared in *Christian Conscience* in February 1995, says of infusing gay rights into the schools: ***"The Iowa Human Growth and Development Manual*** also calls for **infusing** and **integrating** sex education across the curriculum. Of course, when sexuality is taught in math, science, literature, and every other subject, this makes it nearly impossible for parental notification to take place, thus ensuring that parents cannot pull their children out of classes covering offensive or explicit material." He then gives examples of discussion or information topics from Project 21 (a homosexual advocacy group) that ended up in a Des Moines proposal to teach about homosexuality.

ISO 9000

Read the Total Quality Management (TQM) entry first. No discussion of TQM would be complete without mentioning **ISO 9000**. ISO is an acronym rearranging the letters in the International Organization for Standardization. ISO 9000 was launched in 1979 by the Technical Committee 176 and grew out of a **perceived** need to set international minimum standards for manufacturing companies to establish control methods for product quality and for maintaining product uniformity and predictability. Thirty countries participated in this process and created, **by consensus,** the ISO 9000 standards which were issued in 1987. Although voluntary, **over fifty countries have adopted ISO 9000 as a national standard**. ISO 9000 certification, a fairly involved process, is becoming more and more desirable and even necessary, as companies increasingly trade overseas with clients seeking some assurance of quality control and who are demanding that their suppliers have ISO registration. Lewis and Smith in their book, ***Total Quality in Higher Education,*** list the **nine goals of an integrated ISO**

9000 based total quality system as: **1)** Listen to the voice of the customer. **2)** Focus on the needs of the market. **3)** Achieve top quality performance in all areas, not just in the product or service. **4)** Establish simple procedures for quality performance. **5)** Continually review processes to eliminate waste. **6)** Develop measures of performance. **7)** Understand the competition and develop a competitive strategy. **8)** Ensure effective communication. **9)** Seek continuous improvement. The authors state that the education and training **"markets"** have not yet felt the competitive pressures experienced in automobile manufacturing, process industries, and electronics where TQM has been widely applied. They comment: "However, as the worldwide privatization trend continues, it is likely that training and education will become more competitive. Particularly with the aid of high-tech media, customers will less and less frequently automatically turn to the nearest local provider of training or education. It is, therefore, reasonable to expect that providers of training and education will increasingly find themselves competing in terms of quality, satisfaction, and price. Mandatory total quality and ISO 9000 could well be on the way. Today's choice may be tomorrow's mandate."

Over two hundred colleges, universities, and community colleges are reported to be involved in TQM. How many elementary and secondary schools and districts are also involved in TQM is unknown, but judging from the number of articles in professional journals and training workshops and materials currently available, interest in TQM is definitely high. The September 1994 ***Quality Systems Update*** (a global ISO 9000 information service) carried an article about the Lancaster, Pennsylvania, school system in the process of restructuring with ISO 9000. The article states: "Dr. Robert Shekletski, superintendent of the School District of Lancaster, says he expects to accomplish two ambitious goals by September 1997—a complete organizational restructuring of the school district and ISO 9000 registration. If successful, Lancaster would be the first school district in the United States to hold a quality management certificate. . . . 'Our whole system is going to change,' Shekletski said. 'Organization structure will change. Instead of grade levels, we will have instructional levels without grades. We will integrate curriculum and transfer decision making power to individual schools. This may not sound like much for business, but no other school district is going the full nine yards [restructuring] from top to bottom.' Lancaster's detailed implementation plan includes **more than 1,000 individual steps** on the road to registration, but said Shekletski, 'Our audit team has not run into an obstacle we haven't been able to overcome. The principles [of TQM] are absolutely transferable." If successful in their certification bid, the nineteen schools in Lancaster will join three ISO 9000 certified businesses in Lancaster and 238 others throughout the state.

Lifelong Learning (LL)

The School Policy Institute has extensively researched the UNESCO connection to lifelong learning and other school restructuring efforts. **(See resources: Videos.) LL** is the unifying principle/control mechanism underlying ***GOALS 2000***. More importantly, it's the underlying concept in the global master plan to track "human capital" and as such will play a large part in uniting the world's economies, governments, and religions. If the world is "to be as one," there needs to be an efficient record keeping system to see that this is happening, on schedule, and in a planned and orderly way. **LL** will do this very effectively. It gives the government access to its citizens from birth (in some places this already occurs prenatally) and provides a rationale/excuse to set up a data collection system (individual electronic dossiers) to track each person throughout their lifetime. Utilizing **OBE** and **HOTS** (which are perfect and logical companions to LL because **the new paradigm is work force training and other social engineering, not education**) each little unit of human capital gets a carefully controlled amount of "education/training" with a large dose of attitude adjustment. Citizen/workers are plugged into LL as soon as their existence comes to the attention of the government and from that time forward, they're a "work in progress," ever learning—what the government permits them to learn; ever evolving—into what the state needs. **UNESCO** determined in 1970 that lifelong education would be the master concept for the restructuring of schools throughout the world and in 1971 commissioned a study, ***Towards a Conceptual Model of Lifelong Education*** by New Zealander George W. Parkyn. He describes lifelong learning as being both **vertical** (extending over the entire lifespan of each individual) and **horizontal** (the partnershipping/coordination of schools with social and health care services, businesses, and cultural institutions) so that no matter where an individual turns, all information and services are integrated. The *GOALS 2000* legislation is replete with examples of both. **Lifelong learning may be viewed as a practical outworking of PPBS—and as a blueprint for global enslavement.**

National Association of State Directors of Teacher Education and Certification (NASDTEC)

A draft copy, dated June 1993, of the *NASDTEC Outcome-Based Standards: Promoting Systemic Change in Teacher Education and Certification* (outcome-based teacher education standards for the high school level), states that "since NASDTEC outcomes are role performances, **they assume that content knowledge has been mastered** in order to demonstrate a role performance in the school setting. . . . The focus is on what the beginning teacher should be able to do, **think, and feel**; not on what the prospective teacher should study." (Emphasis added.) This document states NASDTEC's efforts are linked to those of the National Council for the Accreditation of Teacher Education and the **National Board for Professional Teaching Standards**. The work of OBE guru Bill Spady is referenced under **"Underlying Assumptions of Outcome-Based Standards."** Twelve outcome areas suggested by NASDTEC for teacher evaluation are: **readiness for high school** (identified directly from the National Education Goal of School Readiness); **student development; curriculum** (assumes alignment with NEG); **instruction** (assumes alignment with NEG); **assessment** (for systematic feedback, adjustment, meeting standards, and continuous improvement); **school improvement** (Total Quality Management); **support services** (coordination of services, especially for "at risk" students); **youth service** (socialization of children); **home, school, and community** (partnershipping); **technology; resource management** (project management techniques); and **workplace know-how** (necessitated by SCANS). Teachers will prepare portfolios of their work in any of these areas (or additional ones) required by the state in which they are seeking licensure. As with all OBE, **these new standards tell us: "In the new framework, the outcomes are held constant and time and licensure are the variable entities."**

National Center for Education Statistics (NCES)

NCES is part of the Department of Education's Office of Educational Research and Improvement (OERI) and is the primary education data collection and analysis arm of the federal government. Their activities and publications are numerous. At the elementary and secondary level, these include studies and surveys such as: the **Common Core of Data (CCD)** which lists and provides descriptive statistics on schools and school districts; the **Schools and Staffing Survey (SASS)** and **SASS Teacher Follow-up Survey** (used to project teacher demand); **Private School Survey** (similar to the CCD); **National Household Education Survey** (done by phone on various topics); **Current Population Survey** (monthly household survey on school enrollment and educational attainment); and a **Fast Response Survey System** (to collect issue-oriented data quickly). Other services at the elementary and secondary level are **School District Mapping** (using Bureau of the Census demographic data); a **National Data Resource Center** (special statistical tabulations and analyses of data); and the **National Cooperative Education Statistics System** which serves as a vehicle for NCES and the states to collaborate in developing the infrastructure for electronic data transmission for a variety of education purposes. **The National Forum on Education Statistics** plans and carries out much of the cooperative system's work and supports such projects as the **Internet Demonstration Project** (using the Internet for data reporting and access) and the **SPEEDE/ExPRESS (electronic transmission of student transcripts)**. The forum will consider data policy issues regarding privacy, access, and the criteria for consistency of identifying data items. Then there are NCES's **Longitudinal Studies** (where a group of students is followed over time). There are five of those, with plans for more. There's a whole series of surveys and studies on **postsecondary education,** including the **adult education component of the National Household Education Survey,** implemented in 1991 "as a result of the national education goals and the concern about America's ability to compete in a global economy." NCES also collects data on **vocational education** and **libraries** (public school and college). And, of course, they're involved in the **National Assessment of Educational Progress, the NAEP.** According to ***Programs and Plans of the National Center for Education Statistics, 1995:*** "NAEP was begun in 1969 and has periodically assessed students aged 9, 13, and 17 and at various grade levels. . . . The subject areas have included: reading, writing, mathematics, science, citizenship, U.S. history, geography, social studies, art, music, literature, computer competence, and career and occupational development. From time to time NAEP has conducted special assessments in other educational areas such as health, energy, consumer math, and young adult literacy. NAEP has also collected **background information from students, teachers, and administrators, and has related these data to student achievement.** Performance data are reported for the nation, and for various subgroups categorized by **variables such as region, gender, race/ethnicity, parental education, type of school, and type and size of community.**" This source also tells us that NAEP ". . . is mandated by Congress (*GEPA 406*)," and that "in 1988 Congress amended this legislation to establish the National Assessment Governing Board (NAGB). . . . The Board is composed of national and local elected officials, chief state school officers, classroom teachers, local school board members, and leaders of the business community, and others. Specifically it has been charged by Congress to perform the following duties: select subject areas to be assessed; identify appropriate achievement goals for each age group; develop assessment objectives; design the methodology of the assessment; and produce guidelines and standards for national, regional, and state comparisons. . . . **The current legislation requires assessment in reading and mathematics at least every two years, in science and writing at least every four years, and in history or geography and other subjects selected by the Board at least every six years.**" NCES also compiles **international education statistics.** According to ***Programs and Plans of the NCES***, "NCES is actively involved with the **Organization for Economic Cooperation and Development (OECD)**, based in Paris, France, and with the **International Association for Evaluation of Educational Achievement (IEA)**, based in the Hague, the Netherlands. NCES, along with the National Science Foundation, also supports the **Board on International Comparative Studies in Education at the National Academy of Sciences.**" Surveys and studies resulting from these collaborations include the **OECD International Education Indicators Project (INES)**; the **IEA Reading Literacy Study**; the **Third International Mathematics and Science Study**

(TIMMS); and the **International Adult Literacy Survey**. Many of their publications are for sale from the Government Printing Office. To get more information about Internet and other electronic access, call 1-800-424-1616.

National Diffusion Network (NDN)
The **NDN** is a program within the Department of Education, run by the Office of Educational Research and Improvement (OERI). It was formed in 1974 out of a reorganization of the administration of Title III of the *ESEA*. **NDN** is a computerized databank containing curricular programs that have been approved ("validated") by an appointed review board. The term **"validated" simply means that the program has been shown to work,** so whether its purpose is psychological manipulation or the teaching of fractions, **it works.** Since the creation of the cabinet level Department of Education, the DOE has been charged by law with the task of disseminating information on proven research—or what works. Each state has an **NDN "facilitator"** to help school districts match NDN programs to local needs.

Opportunity-to-Learn Standards
The *GOALS 2000* legislation defines O-T-L standards as: "*. . . the criteria for, and the basis of, assessing the sufficiency or quality of the resources, practices, and conditions necessary at each level of the education system (schools, local educational agencies, and states) to provide all students with an opportunity to learn the material in voluntary national content standards or state content standards.*" Once these standards have been determined, the stage is set for any school or district that feels it has been shortchanged in any way to sue the state. Some have dubbed O-T-L, "opportunity-to-litigate." If a suit brought under O-T-L is successful, the state will have to make the "resources, practices, and conditions" just as good in school A as they are in school B. Someone (the taxpayer, of course) is going to have to pay for this, so new taxes will be levied or new tax funding formulas imposed. Because of the enormous expense involved in bringing these suits, not to mention upgrading substandard schools or entire districts, O-T-L standards amount to a legal maneuver to **level the schools**. Some schools may improve but others will go down as their funding is reduced to achieve "equity."

Parents as Teachers (PAT)

We are all indebted to Laura Rogers, a Missouri researcher, who first sounded the alarm on PAT. **(See resources: The Florida Forum.)** The PAT program began in Missouri in 1981 as a voluntary pilot project called, "New Parents as First Teachers." It was brought into four school districts at a cost of $30,000 each. The (stated) rationale behind the program was that it would help disadvantaged "at-risk" children by screening them for developmental delays. Four years later, **Missouri mandated PAT's availability for all schools and all children.** The cost then rose to $9.1 million and involved 53,000 families. A year later (1990) 100,000 Missouri children were in the program and the cost had escalated to $15 million. At the time of passage of the ***GOALS 2000*** legislation (1994), PAT (though often by a different name) was in **more than forty states**, and a number of foreign countries. The generous start-up funding for PAT in ***P.L. 103-227*** all but assures that **it will soon be in place in all fifty states.** PAT recruits at prenatal clinics or in hospitals before new parents have brought their baby home. Parents are enticed with free developmental screenings and the prospect of "timely information on each stage of their child's development and ways to encourage development and learning." The program works by assigning all parents and children a state **"certified parent educator" (CPE).** This state employee assigns the child a computer code classification and **initiates a computer file that the state can use to track that child for the rest of his/her life.** There are **twelve classification codes**, indicating some specific **"at-risk"** category; the thirteenth category is **"other"** for the CPE to fill in. **There are no codes for normal!** Here are Missouri's **twelve risk factor definitions: 1)** Illness or handicapping condition at birth; **2)** Signs of failure to thrive; **3)** Delay in any area of development, detected through observing or screening; **4)** Inability of parent to cope with inappropriate child behavior; **5)** Low functioning parent: Is the parent too ill, too heavy, too tired, or too depressed to get up and regularly deal effectively with the child? **6)** Inability of parent to relate or connect with child. **7)** Overindulgent or undue spoiling; **8)** Does the child have too many toys? Or not enough? **9)** Low level of verbal response or communication with the child; **10)** Negative or hostile behavior toward the child; **11)** Undue stress that adversely affects the family's functioning. **12)** Indication of child abuse: Are there indications on the child's body or in his behavior or in the parent's statement that abuse may be happening? **13)** Other (that wonderful catchall!). Number twelve should be of particular concern to Christian parents as spanking is considered abusive. After the initial screening, the program is carried out through a combination of visits to the home by the CPE and group meetings. Eight to ten annual home visits are recommended. **Parents are not aware that this "helpful" person who is visiting them with parenting tips, information on free or low-cost medical care, etc. is also writing up a report on what she observes at each home visit.** Parents who do not go along with the recommendations of the CPE can find they have been reported to child protective agencies for neglect or abuse. Some parents have had their children removed from their homes as a result. Prior to inclusion of the PAT legislation into ***GOALS 2000***, PAT was already functioning with a grant from the U.S. Department of Education as an **NDN** program. **PAT provides a perfect point of entry into lifelong learning because it appears on the surface to be helpful and is, therefore, readily accepted by many unsuspecting parents.** That's why the government has pushed it so hard despite growing parental concern and opposition.

Partnerships

Partnerships are a **key concept** in ***GOALS 2000***. Partnerships between: the school and home, the school and business, the school and social service agencies, the school and health care providers, and, of course, partnerships between various governmental agencies so that their boundaries blur and lines of authority become much more coordinated. What is the purpose of all these partnerships? Those involved in partnerships would say cost effectiveness, less duplication of effort, and better service. **However, few parents have considered the legal contractual nature of partnerships (equal jurisdiction or joint ownership)—or that they may be held liable if they fail to hold up their end of the partnership. The state of Virginia is now requiring parents to sign a "Parental-Responsibility Contract." Parents who don't comply face a $50 fine. Partnerships are essential to a centrally controlled state where keeping track of each individual as he moves through the various stages of his life is required. Lifelong learning**

demands the tight coordination of services that people need over the course of a lifetime; services such as education, health care, and jobs. This is the **horizontal aspect of lifelong learning** described by Parkyn in his 1971 UNESCO study, ***Toward a Conceptual Model of Lifelong Education.*** In this study Parkyn describes the horizontal integration of lifelong education as: "coordination of effort between the formal education system itself and the external world—between schools, libraries, museums and other agencies of culture—all places of culture and productive enterprise." Carefully controlling and coordinating everything a person is taught or comes in contact with that may impact his thought formation or acquisition of skills will certainly prove less haphazard than just letting each person pursue his own interests. **Partnerships give legitimacy to the idea that things which are no business of governmental agencies are their business**, e.g., partnerships between the home and a school or social service agency giving that entity the "right" to enter your home, do surveillance, collect data on you, and refer you (or turn you in) to some other agency they partnership with. The more partnerships the government manages to tie together, the more of a **net** you, as an individual, are entangled in.

Planning, Programming, Budgeting System (PPBS)

This understanding of PPBS comes from the work of researcher and writer **Don Bell.** The precursor to PPBS was its English version, **Political and Economic Planning (PEP)**. PEP was employed in England by the inner circle of Fabian Socialists prior to the 1930s and was instrumental in turning that country toward socialism. At the same time PEP was being tried out in England, a similar, but cruder and coercion-based version, the familiar **Five-Year Plan**, was being used in the Soviet Union. Early attempts to bring PPBS into our government (during the Roosevelt years) were interrupted by World War II. The postwar Marshall Plan was another early foray into PPBS. In 1956, President Eisenhower set up the Commission on National Goals **(goals being essential to a PPB system)** and in 1961, following suggestions of the **Rand Corporation**, President Kennedy launched PPBS in the **Department of Defense (DOD)** under **Robert Strange McNamara. Charles J. Hitch** is the name most associated with the development of the American version of PPBS. He worked for thirteen years at the **Rand Corporation**, then joined McNamara to install PPBS in the DOD. The Vietnam War was one of the first large-scale PPBS endeavors. **PPBS was clumsy, costly, and ineffective,** and no more successful in industry than it was in managing the Vietnam War. McNamara used it at Ford to develop the Edsel and huge losses were reported at Litton Industries (and elsewhere) after instituting PPBS. Nevertheless, because it was considered **so effective administratively**, in 1965 President Johnson initiated PPBS throughout the entire legislative branch. Later it was put into **all branches of the federal government.** A key point about running the government by PPBS is that it is **government by appointed—not elected**—officials. Appointed officials issue orders to elected officials (those accountable to you) who in turn carry out the orders **or else** (they lose their funding/jobs). In 1970, President Nixon upgraded the Bureau of the Budget into the **Office of Management and Budget** and gave **OMB** complete control over PPBS throughout the government. **PPBS has become a worldwide movement** through, among other strategies, having its adoption a condition of loans or giveaways by the World Bank. (**McNamara** became head of the **World Bank** after leaving the DOD. Most people think of him as the master strategist of the Vietnam War, but his most enduring accomplishment is as a popularizer and purveyor of PPBS. In 1972 an International Institute of Applied Systems Analysis (another name for PPBS) was established in Austria with twelve nations participating, including the United States and the Soviet Union. **PPBS** (under many names and variations) has become the **dominate organizational/restructuring/reengineering model** for most of corporate America and in many institutions and organizations.

This quick history of PPBS is essential to understand where it came from and its worldwide diffusion. So **what exactly is a Planning, Programming, Budgeting System?** The **"B"** in PPBS would seem to indicate that it is an accounting system. However, as seen above, as an accounting system, it was a failure from the beginning. PPBS has been described as **applied scientific socialism, used to control what people produce, what they consume, how they spend their work and leisure time, what they think, and how they react to various stimuli.** The concept, applied to education, is: if you know what you have to start with (young, impressionable child)—and you know what you want to end up with (citizen/worker for a centrally planned global economy), it's possible to design a system that will achieve that outcome. PPBS begins with **"Planning"** or **the setting of goals and objectives. Goals are general, timeless, and long-range** (e.g. the eight National Education Goals). **Objectives are specific, short-range, measurable ways in which individuals are to think, feel, and act as a result of the goals** (the setting of standards and "benchmarks" called for in *GOALS 2000* by which progress toward attaining the goals will be measured.) The next "P," **"Programming,"** refers to the types of activities and measurements needed to bring about the policy requirements of the first "P," Planning. **"Programming" would include the new curricula being developed, the experimental and "validated" programs of the OERI designed to move students from point A to Z, as well as the new OBE-performance assessments. "Budgeting" is the wherewithal meted out to those programs that are meeting the planned objectives** (and withheld from those that are not). **PPBS is a continuous loop**, renewable/reviewed/refunded every three, five, or seven years so that basic assumptions/goals can be recalibrated.

Regional Educational Laboratories (RELs)

The U.S. Department of Education maintains ten **RELs** ("labs") in scattered geographic areas—all under the jurisdiction of OERI. The labs function as field offices of OERI, assisting the states under their jurisdiction in finding and implementing educational resources (such as the "validated" programs of the NDN) suited to their needs. They also generate and oversee research projects, print publications, and provide training programs to teachers and administrators. Each lab puts out a catalog of its publications. Under *GOALS 2000* the regional labs are charged with designing appropriate materials for their clients if suitable ones cannot be found. **The ten regions are:**

1. The **Northeastern Region** (Maine, New Hampshire, Vermont, Massachusetts, Rhode Island, Connecticut, New York, and Puerto Rico and the Virgin Islands) served by **the Education Alliance for Equity and Excellence** at Brown University in Providence, Rhode Island.

2. **The Mid-Atlantic Region** (New Jersey, Pennsylvania, Delaware, Maryland, and Washington, D.C.) served by the **Center for Research in Human Development and Education** at Temple University in Philadelphia.
3. **The Appalachia Region** (Virginia, West Virginia, Kentucky, and Tennessee) served by the **Appalachia Educational Laboratory (AEL)** in Charleston, West Virginia.
4. **The Southeastern Region** (North Carolina, South Carolina, Georgia, Florida, Alabama, and Mississippi) served by the **Southeastern Regional Vision for Education (SERVE)** in Greensboro, North Carolina.
5. **The Southwestern Region** (Arkansas, Louisiana, Oklahoma, Texas, and New Mexico) served by the **Southwest Educational Development Laboratory (SEDL)** in Austin, Texas.
6. **The Central Region** (North Dakota, South Dakota, Nebraska, Kansas, Missouri, Colorado, and Wyoming) served by the **Mid-Continental Regional Educational Laboratory (McREL)** in Aurora, Colorado.
7. **The Midwestern Region** (Minnesota, Wisconsin, Michigan, Ohio, Indiana, Illinois, and Iowa) served by the **North Central Regional Educational Laboratory (NCREL)** in Oak Brook, Illinois.
8. **The Northwestern Region** (Alaska, Washington, Oregon, Idaho, and Montana) served by the **Northwest Regional Educational Laboratory (NWREL)** in Portland, Oregon.
9. **The Western Region** (California, Nevada, Utah, and Arizona) served by the **Far West Laboratory for Educational Research and Development (FWL)** in San Francisco, California.
10. **The Pacific Region** (Hawaii, American Samoa, Commonwealth of the Northern Mariana Islands, Federated States of Micronesia, Kosrae, Pohnpei, Chuuk and Yap, Guam, Republic of the Marshall Islands, and the Republic of Palau) served by the **Pacific Regional Educational Laboratory (PREL)** in Honolulu, Hawaii.

Site-based Management (SBM)

SBM goes by various names, "local control council," "shared decision making board," and others implying a new seat of power and a new form of management for individual schools. Control over local education differs from state to state, but the usual chain of command is an elected school board for each district. These accountable citizens (accountable precisely because they have been elected) hire the superintendent, and within the guidelines of the many state and federal mandates, choose curriculum and set policies for the district. The superintendent, in turn, oversees the work of the central office and exerts real power through the hiring of teachers and other staff and by the control of money and information filtered down to individual schools and principals in his district. Proponents of SBM usually point to the district level as too far removed from the day-to-day realities of what each school needs to empower principals, teachers, and parents to do their jobs effectively. But even those enthusiastic about SBM identify many obstacles to effective functioning. For example, participants must be clearly informed as to the parameters of their power and know how they are constrained by contractual agreements, by district, state, and federal policies, procedures, and/or accountability provisions (no small constraints!). Proponents further point out that if SBM teams are not provided the resources they need, such as time to meet, technical assistance, and funding, they are likely to end up frustrated by the time-consuming character of the process. This is especially true for teachers, as the demands of the classroom compete with SBM responsibilities. Members dealing with the frustration of fiscal and regulatory constraints, may well feel they have only modest influence on marginal matters. An SBM team is typically composed of the school's principal, a majority of teachers, a few parents, and in high schools a couple of students. In this **new management model**, the principal is, *de facto*, the CEO; the teachers, who are the majority, have the deciding vote; and parents and students, who are not education "experts," assume the role of advisors. Even if a team is functioning well, **a question that must be asked is: Do we want decisions affecting the philosophical direction of the school, e.g., mission statements, curriculum, special courses, workshops for teachers, etc., being decided by those who are not elected and therefore not**

accountable to us? In a worst case scenario, the SBM becomes an end-run around the school board, with the teachers who are appointed (or voted on internally), the union activists, who are in a position to bring in programs and curriculum that would not have been likely under board scrutiny. SBM has caught on in a big way for three reasons. One, it's an increasingly familiar way to run things, as many organizations and businesses have begun using a similar management model. Two, it appears to be a move in the right direction—away from central control; and three, it holds out the promise of continuous quality improvement. **(See Total Quality Management.)**

Star Schools

A relatively new program, the Star Schools Program **(SSP)** was set up in 1988 under ***P.L.100-297***. SSP is one of the largest networks of public and private sector partners engaged in helping the education "community" through technical and other assistance to **get on and make effective use of the information superhighway.** It's another program of the DOE administered by OERI. This one is a grant program; the DOE makes awards to "telecommunications partnerships." Partners include local school districts, state departments of education, public broadcasting, and other public and private organizations. The following information is taken from a DOE brochure, ***Star Schools Program***. The original function of the program was to provide distance learning to small rural schools; it has since been expanded to include schools in large urban areas. More than five thousand schools have been served by the SSP. A wide range of technologies (satellite, open broadcasts, cable, fiber optics, microcomputers, digital compression, interactive video, faxes, telephones, and the Internet) are employed in the program and offerings run the gamut from video field trips and instructional modules to semester or year-long courses. Other uses are **staff development**: teachers and other staff can participate in teleconferences and communicate with colleagues in other places; **classes for parents**: several projects provide programming to "help parents" help their children to have greater success in school; a special **demonstration project**: a statewide project has been funded through the **Iowa Distance Education Alliance** "to develop a two-way, full-motion, interactive fiber optic telecommunications network. When operational, the system will link all of Iowa's ninety-nine counties, bringing together public colleges and universities and secondary schools throughout the state. Although limited to Iowa participants, it will serve as a demonstration model." **A formal evaluation of the Star Schools Program is currently being conducted by the Southwest Regional Lab in Austin, Texas.** From another DOE information packet on SSP, we learn: "The Star Schools Program is **a national study of the change process, documenting the role of technology and telecommunications in school reform at both the local and state level and examining alternative assessment strategies through technology."**

Total Quality Management (TQM)

This understanding of TQM comes, in part, from the work of Lewis and Smith (see bibliography). TQM, the latest management strategy to impact education, goes by many names: Continuous Quality Improvement, Process Quality Management, Quality Assurance, etc., and while each application of the "total quality" idea may differ in emphasis, most share common characteristics. Where did this latest management fad come from and what is its history? The name most associated with TQM is **W. Edwards Deming**, a Ph.D. in physics, who worked for Bell Labs in the 1930s. Deming borrowed from, expanded upon, and popularized the ideas of an older co-worker, Walter Shewhart, who worked on the problem of statistical process control. Both men were called on by the government to aid in the war effort, establishing quality guidelines for defense contractors. After the war, under the leadership of General Douglas MacArthur, **quality control tools and techniques were chosen as the approach to turn around the devastated Japanese economy.** Lewis and Smith explain that in 1950, Deming began a series of lectures to Japanese management on "Elementary Principles of Statistical Control and Quality." The Japanese embraced both the man and his principles. The rest, as they say, is history. Japan's highest quality award is called the Deming Prize. (The U.S. now has its counterpart, the **Malcolm Baldridge National Quality Award.**) The quality movement which lay dormant in the U.S. at the very time it was taking off in Japan was eventually carried back to America by Deming and other quality gurus such as Joseph Juran, Kaoru Ishikawa, Armand Feigenbaum, and Philip Crosby, each with his own spin on achieving total quality. Since TQM was developed for the business world, specifically for industry, how is it being applied in education? **TQM, like PPBS, is foremost a management/control system**. Whereas PPBS originated as an accounting system, the emphasis in the TQM model is on **quality of product and customer satisfaction**. There are many ways to "do" TQM. The following is a possible four-step adaptation. **Like PPBS, TQM begins with strategy management/planning**. Senior management takes the lead in the strategic phase, but everyone is involved through a variety of team-building, brainstorming, and consensus activities. The outcome of this phase is a vision (ideal, long-range), a mission (achievable, mid-range), guiding principles or values (ideals), and goals and objectives (achievable, short-range). "Ownership" of the strategy is achieved when everyone acknowledges the focus and that it will help the organization move in a common direction. The three–five year plan that typically emerges from this process is very similar to the first P in a PPBS. **The second stage in setting up TQM is process management** or planning/coordinating the discrete operations that will ensure customer satisfaction, eliminate waste, redundancy, and bottlenecks, and establish a common language and process for documenting activities. **The third stage is project management**. At this point, **teams (always an integral part of TQM efforts)** are formed to organize and carry out programs. Teams develop the schedules, tracking mechanisms, performance indicators, and other control systems for the projects. Stages two and three resemble the second **P** in PPBS. **The fourth stage in TQM is personal management**. Each employee is guided through a process of developing a personal mission and vision, compatible with the organizational vision and is expected to develop procedures for managing and controlling his/her own individual tasks. This (theoretically) empowers each employee to implement continuous quality improvement in his own work performance and at the points of interface with the other three management aspects of TQM.

Since TQM has become an increasingly popular management strategy in schools, especially with site-based teams, what are some of the problems/concerns about TQM in the educational setting? According to William Berkson's article, **"Mastery Learning and 'Total Quality,'"** ***in Education Week,*** March 24, 1995, TQM and OBE (here referred to as mastery learning) are highly compatible. He states: "Mastery learning provides a basis for TQM in schools because of its focus on the individual steps that lead to the final 'product' of the educated student. In mastery learning, a skill or a body of knowledge is broken down into steps or units, and a standard of mastery or quality is set up for each unit." Berkson's assumption is that **the student is the "product"** in TQM. Since quality of product is key to TQM, how "quality" is to be measured is also of great importance. **Customer satisfaction** is another of the primary indicators of the success of any TQM effort. So a question that must be asked is: **Who is seen as the customer?** The student? The parents? Institutions of higher education? The workplace? Society as a whole? All, some, or none of the above? Since TQM aims for a standardized, "quality" product, **how quality/standardization is determined and by whom becomes of great importance.** In reality though, hasn't ***GOALS 2000*** already answered these questions? In the aftermath of this law, is any TQM team free to engage in the four-step process (or any other TQM variant) independent of the law's requirements.

In writing about quality, Deming stresses respect for people and the need to drive out fear (eliminating competition as a motivator). When applied in an educational setting, that means eliminating the A,B,C,D,F grading system and probably grade levels as well. It is apparent how compatible this control system is with OBE, the nongraded classroom, group learning, and other related classroom fads. TQM is not a short-term, quick-fix solution; it becomes the way you do business. Imagine the frustration and daily pressure of forever working in teams, arriving at decisions by consensus, and being in a constant self-evaluation mode. The Japanese call it ***kaizen***: a never-ending cycle of self-improvement. The ability to spot problems, respond quickly, and change direction, heralded as one of TQM's greatest strengths also represents its greatest danger in the educational setting. In a society that has abandoned absolutes, favors affective training over education, and where change is the norm, TQM provides the perfect control system for bringing in the "total quality" flavor of the month.

UNESCO

UNESCO stands for United Nations Educational, Scientific, and Cultural Organization. It's a specialized agency of the UN, headquartered in Paris. UNESCO began in 1946 with twenty member states and now has 171 members. Describing their mission in a brochure, ***What Is UNESCO?*** we read: "UNESCO's Constitution says that 'since wars begin in the minds of men, it is in the minds of men that the defences of peace must be constructed.' Building these defences through international cooperation remains UNESCO's top priority."

UNESCO lists the following as priorities:

- **Education:** literacy, **teacher training,** education for refugees, and the **recognition of university diplomas (a world convention for this purpose is planned), drug abuse education,** AIDS prevention, education for peace and international understanding, nutritional, and **vocational and technical education.** The **1990** Jomtiem, Thailand, **Conference on Education for All** is mentioned. They state their educational program "aims to give everyone access to quality education that will lay the foundations for **lifelong learning** . . ." with each member country ". . . taking into account **a common core of ideas that are universal in their application**." They ask: "What kind of education should we provide for today's children who will be living and working in the twenty-first century? . . . To prepare them for **the increasingly interdependent and rapidly changing world** they are about to enter, [UNESCO] seeks to foster cooperation in order to adapt educational content and methodologies to society's needs in the decades to come."
- **Science and Technology:** the Intergovernmental Oceanographic Commission (with priority given to the World Climate Research Programme); Man and the Biosphere (begun in the 1970s). ***What Is UNESCO? (WIU)*** states: "UNESCO is now placing particular emphasis on raising world consciousness to the threat of environmental degradation"; the International Geological Correlation Programme, "some fifty projects covering all spheres of geology and geophysics worldwide"; the International Hydrological Programme "to promote rational use and management of the earth's water re-

sources, demands on which are expected to double within thirty years." They are also concerned with man-made and natural disasters.

- **Culture:** UNESCO's International Fund for the Promotion of Culture supports a variety of art and artists. UNESCO also "... helps in **defining national strategies and options for the development of human resources and strengthening national research and training capabilities in the area of future-oriented studies in order to better anticipate social, economic and cultural changes and their impact on development."** ***WIU*** tells us that we are currently in "the United Nations Decade for Cultural Development (1988–97)." As part of this effort to "protect" the world's natural and cultural heritage, "by December 1988, 108 countries had ratified **'The World Heritage Convention'** to safeguard sites. . . ." More than 315 sites, including **Monticello** and **the University of Virginia** "... all outstanding and all **endangered,**" are included.

In an article on the UN by William Perry Pendley appearing in the ***Washington Times*** (11/7/95), Perry had this to say: "In an audacious attempt to kill a proposed Montana mine—even before the Environmental Impact Statement has been completed—Bruce Babbitt's Department of the Interior asked the World Heritage Center of the UN Educational Scientific and Cultural Organization (UNESCO) to come to the United States to place Yellowstone National Park on an international 'Endangered Heritage List.'" Another article appearing in the ***Wisconsin Report*** (12/21/95) tells us that: "The following properties [fifteen in the U.S., including the two above and 454 elsewhere] have been approved by the World Heritage Committee to be included in UNESCO's World Heritage List."

In addition to the three areas mentioned in UNESCO's name, they are involved in two additional areas:

- **Communication**: Their primary arm is the International Programme for the Development of Communications which has aided establishment of news agencies in Africa and Latin

America, financed training of journalists, etc. Help is also given to Third World countries for communications infrastructures and to computerize information services.

- **Social and Human Sciences**: "Current work is directed towards the fundamental application of social sciences, clarifying concepts, exploring the relationship with natural sciences and interdisciplinary research. While continuing work on racial discrimination, apartheid, and human rights teaching, UNESCO has undertaken studies on problems of development and sociocultural environment, including research on youth . . ." ("Youth Shaping the Future," an international youth clearinghouse and information service is in the works) ". . . and on the status of women. Studies are conducted on demographic changes and sociocultural transformation on a global scale. Activities also include helping to build up social science institutions." "Cooperation with the United Nations Fund for Population Activities (UNFPA) has led to a technical assistance programme which benefits developing countries in the areas of population education and communication."

UNESCO is headed by an elected director-general (six-year term) and a 51-member executive board. Many member countries have UNESCO national commissions to link their country's chief educational, scientific, and cultural institutions with UNESCO headquarters. Some maintain their own permanent delegations in Paris, as well. Additionally, more than five hundred international nongovernmental organizations (NGOs) have working and mutual information arrangements with UNESCO. A **very important** part of UNESCO's work is sponsorship of international conferences and the generation of many publications. These fall into three categories: documentaries/analyses; theoretical works "aimed at stimulating reflection on contemporary and world problems and future orientations," and specialized and general journals. Two of the latter are: ***The UNESCO Courier*** and ***UNESCO Sources*** (monthly news).

The above summary is extracted from two official UNESCO publications (both titled ***What Is UNESCO?***). This information has been provided to show the enormous range of areas they are involved in and to suggest the power they have achieved through the wide dissemination and influence of their many international projects, published works, conferences (especially through the sponsorship and promotion of international "conventions," many of which are later signed and ratified by member nations)—and perhaps just as importantly through years of networking with governmental organizations and NGOs.

The United States officially withdrew from UNESCO in 1984, and though we no longer support them financially, their influence on U.S. education continues undiminished. UNESCO states its mission as building peace through international cooperation, but from their earliest days opponents suspected that **greasing the skids for world government was the primary agenda.** A ***Saturday Review*** article of March 23, 1953, (favoring UNESCO) had this to say: "If UNESCO is attacked on the grounds that it is helping to prepare the world's people for world government, then it is an error to burst forth with apologetic statements and denials. Let us face it; the job of UNESCO is to help create and promote the elements of world citizenship. When faced with such a 'charge,' let us by all means affirm it from the housetops." **UNESCO represents, at the highest level, the integration of education with science, technology, culture, and mass communications to provide the comprehensive (horizontal) aspect of lifelong learning.**

U.S./Soviet Agreements

This understanding of the U.S./Soviet exchanges comes from the work of Charlotte Iserbyt **(see resources)**. Cultural, scientific, and educational exchanges between the U.S. and the Soviet Union are nothing new. In fact they predate UNESCO (the UN agency dedicated to cooperation in these areas) by more than a decade. As far back as 1933, the Institute of International Education (established in 1919 with a **grant from the Carnegie Endowment for International Peace**) conducted a summer school teacher exchange program in the Soviet Union (then under the tyrannical Stalinist regime). Teachers who attended the University of Moscow Summer School were issued certificates which entitled them to an annual salary increase when they got back to their teaching posts in the U.S. Again in 1958, during the Krushchev era, official U.S./Soviet exchanges (and again with the heavy involvement of the **Carnegie Corporation**) were set up. In 1977 an exchange called the American-Soviet Textbook Study Project was begun, but along with other agreements was suspended in 1979 by President Carter when the Soviet Union invaded Afghanistan. As the memory of this incident and other Cold War atrocities and affronts faded during the Reagan-Gorbachev years, the **Carnegie Corporation** once again (1985) entered into negotiations with the Soviets for the exchange of curricula and teaching materials for elementary and secondary schools. **Carnegie's role** in setting up the exchange was explained by Dr. David Hamburg, president of the Carnegie Corporation in an interview in the ***Los Angeles Times*** on June 12, 1987, when he spoke of **"the special position of privately endowed foundations that can operate in areas government may prefer to avoid."** These negotiations culminated in a formal agreement between the **Carnegie Corporation,** the Soviet Institute of Informatics, and the Soviet Academy of Sciences. The agreement stipulated that we would provide the Soviets with computer hardware (in short supply in the Soviet Union) and specialists to show them how to use it. In return, the U.S. was to receive curriculum software, jointly developed, for use in restructuring our elementary schools. Incredible as this arrangement with our Cold War enemy sounds, such is the power of influential foundations. Because all of this was negotiated privately, away from public scrutiny, hardly anyone knew about this exchange until well after it had become a *fait accompli.* Even when the exchanges came to light, the media did not publicize this amazing and disgraceful arrangement. One of the few voices sounding the alarm was former Maryland congresswoman Helen Bentley, who said in the October 8, 1987, ***Dundalk Eagle,*** in **"What Can the Russians Teach Our Children?"**: "I am increasingly concerned over the tendency of government to hand over to private agencies and groups the power to create programs and schemes which have the force of government behind them **without the responsibility or safeguards** inherent in programs directly sponsored by the government. Interestingly enough, it is illegal for the federal government to develop curriculum for local schools, **but this quasi-legal** arrangement with the Carnegie Corporation and Soviet Academy of Sciences skirts the intent of that law—giving us no recourse, as citizens, to control the content of the curriculum." (Emphasis in the original.)

Approximately one month later (November 21, 1985) in a separate but related agreement, U.S. Secretary of State George Shultz and Soviet Foreign Minister Eduard Shevardnadze signed a 41-page general agreement covering a broad range of exchanges and cooperative projects in the education, scientific, and cultural fields. **This is an agreement impacting U.S. education but entered into by our State Department—to be implemented by the U.S. Information Agency—and it is still in effect!** The agreement calls for (among other things) the exchange of students, graduate students, teachers, professors, specialists, and delegations in various fields of education, as well as the organization of educational lectures, seminars, and symposia. Visiting Russian teachers and students have been much in evidence in the U.S. since this second agreement was signed. The media has printed and shown on TV many pictures of smiling exchange students and teachers with heartwarming stories of new friendships between individuals and the two countries. Few Americans are aware of the "story behind the story."

Whole Language

This understanding of WL comes from the work of Dr. Samuel Blumenfeld, internationally respected author and authority on phonics and related reading issues **(see resources)**. WL may have actually begun in New Zealand (where it has been utilized for many years), but through the networking of international educators, WL has become the dominant reading movement not only in New Zealand, but in Australia, Canada, the U.S., and other parts of the English-speaking world. What is it? One of the problems is that, like other educational fads, WL has numerous definitions. Perhaps looking for a moment at what it replaces will be helpful. Since the 1930s the dominant reading strategy in the U.S. has been **a method originally designed for use with the deaf,** the look-say method (a.k.a. whole word, sight method, word recognition, total word configuration, word memory, and others). Look-say was taught with basal readers having a limited vocabulary (e.g. the old "Dick and Jane" series), complemented by workbooks where children circle things and fill in blanks.

The look-say method begins with the child memorizing a core list of sight words. Memorization is based on the shape or configuration of the written word (what the printed word "looks like") and this is the basic problem. English is a language with a phonetic alphabet, based on the spoken sounds of the twenty-six letters of the alphabet, plus the forty-four irreducible sounds made when these twenty-six symbols are combined. Other languages work differently. Early civilizations used pictographs where the symbol looked like the thing it represented. Then came ideographs that do not look like the thing they represent. Chinese is an ideographic system. But even Chinese has added the use of some ideographs as sound symbols to enable them to write foreign words. Look-say views English as ideographic writing; it treats English as though it were Chinese! As Blumenfeld puts it: "The idea that written words in English can be viewed as ideographs negates all of the advantages of alphabetic writing which is a purely sound-symbol system enabling the reader to read any word after having developed an automatic association between letters and sounds. The great advantage of alphabetic writing is that it permits us to do much more with much less." Given the nature of the English alphabet, the **logical** way to teach reading is utilizing phonics. **Phonics instruction begins with introducing the twenty-six letters of the alphabet. The children then learn the sounds the letters stand for in an intensive manner, using drills, flashcards, and word families. Next the forty-four sounds of English and their spelling forms are taught in a sequential and systematic way, generally beginning with the simplest (short vowels and consonants) and ending with long vowels and their various spellings. This is intensive, systematic phonics.** The purpose is to help the child become an accurate, independent, phonetic reader who can "sound out" any word (however strange or of whatever length) he encounters. By contrast, in the look-say method after the child has memorized a list of words by sight, he is then introduced to beginning consonant letters in order to reduce totally wild guessing. He's then taught "word attack" strategies for figuring out the text such as picture clues, context clues, and phonetic clues. The use of **phonetic clues** is why teachers will often tell parents: "We use a variety of techniques, including phonics." **But this isn't teaching phonics**; it's using phonics as only one among a number of **guessing strategies** and it's too little, too late. **The awkwardness of look-say with its many "attack" strategies, and the fact that it works against our phonetic alphabet instead of with it, tends to produce inaccurate, subjective readers, whereas intensive, systematic phonics, the logical system for English, produces accurate, objective readers.**

What does a WL classroom look like? Blumenfeld describes a typical one. Gone are the old "Dick and Jane" basal readers and the accompanying workbooks. In their place children are given "real literature" (children's books), and few could argue this is an improvement. The teacher "primes the pump" by doing a lot of reading to the children, the idea being that children are first drawn into the stories and then want to start reading on their own. The "teaching" of reading, as such, is passe. **It is somehow assumed that if children are surrounded by books, read to, and immersed in literature, they will teach themselves to read—through something like the process of osmosis.** Children may be in small groups reading to each other or stretched out on the floor reading alone, so the atmosphere is decidedly more homelike. All of the old look-say "word attack" guessing strategies are encouraged to help the children get the general sense of the text. In this regard, **WL is but another retread of look-say, but worse because of the further de-emphasis on accuracy.** There are "critical thinking" discussions about what has been read. **Creativity and personal interpretations of the text, not literal interpretation, are encouraged.** Other children may be working at composing their own stories, dictating them, or writing them out, using what is called **"invented spelling" (guessing)**. Writing is encouraged from the beginning before any mastery of reading, spelling, punctuation, or grammar has been attained. **Creativity is in; accuracy is out.** The idea is that the technical part of writing can be cleaned up later when the child is interested in and ready for such things. Part of the WL philosophy is that writing encourages the desire to read. The atmosphere is relaxed, creative, and decidedly nonjudgmental. In the words of Blumenfeld:

> And so, it is not difficult to understand why so many teachers find whole language preferable to the workbook-oriented basal programs. They are not pleased with the results they get from the basals and

> the children are bored. And suddenly there is whole language which promises fun and joy and liberation and empowerment. The belief system tells you that children learn to read by reading. No need to teach them to read. They can do it themselves. The classroom becomes a joy-filled community where everyone helps everyone else. Competition is replaced by cooperation. You don't even have to teach spelling. Children invent their own spelling and eventually correct themselves. **There is no such thing as a reading error, only a "miscue."**

Perhaps in the midst of the widespread euphoria over WL, we would do well to ask what kind of readers/thinkers this system produces? Looking at the underlying **philosophy and political agenda** behind WL is perhaps the best way to see what kind of readers/thinkers this method is **intended to produce**.

Blumenfeld points out that John Dewey was behind the change in the 1930s from phonics to look-say. In Dewey's scheme of things far too much emphasis was put on teaching reading. He favored the "**socialization**" of the child in a child-centered classroom with lots of real-life experiences, simulations, and "learning by doing," and since his political agenda was the transformation of America into a collectivist society, **activities which moved children in the direction of socialism were, in fact, what he ultimately meant by "socialization."** Like other socialists, he frequently referred to his brand of socialism as "democracy," or "democratic ideals," misleading terms, but better accepted by the general public. In his book ***Democracy and Education,*** Dewey says: "The notion that the 'essentials' of elementary education are the three R's mechanically treated, is based upon ignorance of the essentials needed for realization of democratic ideals." Blumenfeld counters this with: "Isn't it interesting that the three R's 'mechanically treated' produced our highly literate Founding Fathers who could write a Declaration of Independence and create a free society where literacy became virtually universal?" Dewey's contributions are frequently acknowledged in the writings of WL advocates. This country's leading WL guru is Kenneth Goodman, a professor of language, reading, and culture at the University of Arizona in Tucson. Goodman has referred to reading as a **"psycholinguistic guessing game."** A few statements from Goodman and others (as quoted in the ***Blumenfeld Education Letter (BEL)*** are real eye-openers as to the philosophy and agenda, totally unknown to most teachers and parents, behind WL:

"Whole Language: What's New?" in ***The Reading Teacher***, November 1987:

> Whole language views the learner as profoundly social. Thus practice congruent with whole language includes participating in a community of readers during small group literature study, peer writing workshops, group social studies projects with built-in plans for collaborative learning. . . . (***BEL***, Vol. 6, No. 2, p. 4, Feb. 1991)

Phi Delta Kappan, January 1989, (an article by Frank Smith):

> Literacy is power. Literacy can do more than transform thought; it can transform the world. Literacy can raise social consciousness and provide a means for the expression and fulfillment of this consciousness. . . . Paulo Freire's pedagogic technique raises social consciousness not as a way of using literacy but as a means of acquiring it. [According to Blumenfeld, Paulo Freire is a leading Marxist theoretician who has used adult literacy campaigns in the Third World to foment Marxist revolution. Freire used a form of "critical consciousness" which he called conscientization, to awaken critical thinking in the minds of the oppressed.] (***BEL***, Vol. 6, No. 6, p. 2, June 1991)

"The Politics of Whole Language," an article by Bess Altwerger and Barbara Flores in ***The Whole Language Catalog*** (ed. by Kenneth and Yetta Goodman and Lois Bird):

> The traditional approach to teaching reading works effectively as this sorting mechanism, virtually assuring that one group of children—usually the poor and minorities—don't win or earn that admission ticket. Whole language teaching is subversive, in the best sense of the word, because it seeks to restore equality and democracy to our schools, to our children, and in essence, to our society. . . . Whole language puts power for learning, decisionmaking, and problem-solving back into the hands of teachers and students. It

> creates active learners; it empowers all of us to act upon and transform our environments and society in general. We are not just asking for a change in the teaching of reading, but a radical change in the social and political structure of schooling and society. (*BEL*, Vol. 7, No. 8, p. 7, Aug. 1992)

Also in his article in ***The Whole Language Catalog***, Professor Henry A. Giroux writes:

> In the most general sense, literacy can be defined in pedagogical terms that adapt people to existing configurations of power, as in the advocacy of functional literacy. . . . In the most emancipatory sense, literacy is a political and pedagogical process of naming the world, which is biographical, historical and collective. . . . In short, literacy is about the issues of politics, power, and possibility. One of the most important projects for teachers in the next decade will be the development of a critical literacy that incorporates the politics of cultural diversity with a view of pedagogy that recognizes the importance of democratic public life. . . . Eurocentric culturally dominated curricula must be rejected as resistant to seeing schools as places for educating students to be critical citizens in a vital, democratic society. On the other hand, progressive views of literacy must openly acknowledge their own politics and commitment to pedagogical practices that deepen the goals of democratic struggle and cultural justice. . . . Whole language has done much to provide educators with both a language of critique and possibility, particularly in terms of its emphasis on the necessity for teachers to incorporate into their teaching the voices that students bring with them to the classroom. (*BEL*, Vol. 7, No. 8, p. 6, Aug. 1992)

Again from Goodman writing in ***The Whole Language Catalog***:

> Whole language classrooms liberate pupils to try new things, to invent spellings, to experiment with a new genre, to guess at meanings in their reading, or to read and write imperfectly. Our research on reading and writing has strongly supported the importance of error in language development. Miscues represent the tension between

> invention and convention in reading. . . . In whole language classrooms risk-taking is not simply tolerated, it is celebrated. Learners have always been free to fail. ["Miscues" and "risk-taking" are Goodman's euphemisms for error.] (*BEL*, Vol. 7, No. 8, pp. 1–2, Aug. 1992)

Goodman's last sentence is ironic because according to Blumenfeld, **fail they do**. Professor Jeanne S. Chall, who runs a reading lab at Harvard University's Graduate School of Education (and one of the very few respected reading authorities opposed to WL) said in the ***Washington Post*** on November 29, 1986: "I see the failures from it already. Children are coming into the lab who were in [whole language] classes." I would add to Chall's statement my own experience with a favorite young relative who has been in a WL language classroom since first grade. His oral reading in first grade revealed many of the problems Blumenfeld speaks of with those whose first exposure to reading is some variant of look-say: changing words, adding words, and skipping words. None of this, however, seemed to bother him and he had excellent "self esteem" about his reading ability. His mother was assured that by second or third grade he would be ready to "clean up" the invented spelling, and other mistakes. But in fifth grade, I was still receiving notes from this ten-year-old that would have been barely acceptable from a second grader if judged by any objective standards of spelling, punctuation, and grammar. Sad, but like millions of other American children, he's a victim of **educational malpractice**.

WL is now a reality in most of America's classrooms. It began coming in in the late 1970s, picked up steam in the 1980s, and is in place almost everywhere by the mid 1990s. Most teachers and parents who enthusiastically embrace it as a refreshing break with the past and as a new way to get children interested in reading, writing, and reflecting on these two activities are totally unaware of the roots of WL or that almost all arguments about its merits reflect either the basic philosophy of Dewey and the "progressivists," or the political agenda put forward by its most left-leaning advocates. **WL is also being promoted because it's a hand-in-glove fit with other current classroom fads such as the child- or learner-centered classroom, holistic education, OBE, cooperative learning, the ungraded class-**

room, the self-esteem movement, critical thinking (using literature as the vehicle to get into the affective domain), the "infusion" model of global or peace education currently being called "multiculturalism," and academic equity/leveling of students (dumbing them down).

Bibliography

"Applying TQM in the Classroom." ***Total Quality and Site-Based Management Journal,*** January/February 1993.

Barton, David. ***America: To Pray or Not to Pray.*** Aledo: Specialty Research Associates, 1988.

Bauer, Gary L. ***When All Else Fails, Restructure: Interpreting the New SAT Scores.*** (Perspective series). Washington, D.C.: Family Research Council, 1995.

Baumeister, Roy F., Boden, Joseph M., and Smart, Laura. **"Relation of Threatened Egotism to Violence and Aggression: The Dark Side of High Self Esteem."** ***Psychological Review,*** Vol. 103, No. 1, p. 5–33, 1996.

Bell, Don. ***"Proofs of a Conspiracy."*** A Special Edition (32 pages) of ***The Florida Forum*** reprinting twenty articles from the ***Don Bell Reports*** 1972–94. Seventeen articles are from Bell's 1972 series: ***"Proofs of a Conspiracy to Build a Total, Managed Global Society."*** Highland City: The Florida ProFamily Forum, Inc., 1994.

Bergmann, Sherrel, and Rudman, Gerald J. ***Decision-Making Skills for Middle School Students.*** Washington, D.C.: National Education Association of the United States, 1985.

Berkson, William. **"Mastery Learning and 'Total Quality.'"** ***Education Week,*** March 24, 1995.

Berthoud, John E. ***Who Got It Right? What Proponents and Opponents of the Creation of the Department of Education Promised and Predicted.*** Arlington: The Alexis de Tocqueville Institution, 1996.

Blumenfeld, Samuel L. *The Blumenfeld Education Letter.*
"The 'Whole Language' Fraud," Vol. 4, No. 3, March 1989
"What's Wrong with Whole Language?" Vol. 6, No. 2, February 1991
"The Political Agenda Behind Whole Language." Vol. 6, No. 6, June 1991
"'The Whole Language Catalog' or a Review of the Fetish of the Whole," Vol. 7, No. 8, August 1992

__________ **"The 'Whole Language' Boondoggle."** ***Practical Homeschooling,*** pp. 41–44, Fall 1993.

Boyer, Ernest L. ***Ready to Learn: A Mandate for the Nation.*** Princeton: The Carnegie Foundation for the Advancement of Teaching, 1991.

Brown, Jerome O., Levans, Katherine, and Simonton, Chey. ***The People vs. the Educational Confederacy: Educational Restructuring on Trial.*** (82-page transcript of 4-video set). Rollingbay: School Policy Institute, 1995.

Carle, Erica. ***The Hate Factory.*** Milwaukee: Erica Carle Foundation, 1972.

Carnegie Council on Adolescent Development. ***Turning Points: Preparing American Youth for the 21st Century: the Report of the Task Force on Education of Young Adolescents.*** Washington, D.C.: Carnegie Council on Adolescent Development, 1989.

Chambers, Claire. ***The Siecus Circle: a Humanist Revolution.*** Belmont: Western Islands, 1977.

Clinton, Hillary Rodham. ***It Takes a Village and Other Lessons Children Teach Us.*** New York: Simon & Schuster, 1996.

Coleman, James S. ***Parental Involvement in Education.*** "Policy Perspective Series." Washington, D.C.: U.S. Department of Education, 1991.

Commission on Global Governance. ***Our Global Neighborhood: The Report of the Commission on Global Governance.*** New York: Oxford University Press, 1995.

Committee for Economic Development. Research and Policy Committee. ***Putting Learning First: Governing and Managing the Schools for High Achievement.*** New York: Committee for Economic Development, 1994.

———— ***The Unfinished Agenda: A New Vision for Child Development and Education.*** New York: Committee for Economic Development, 1991.

Council for Basic Education. ***History in the Making: An Independent Review of the Voluntary National History Standards.*** Washington, D.C.: Council for Basic Education, 1996.

David, Jane L. ***Restructuring in Progress: Lessons from Pioneering Districts.*** Washington, D.C.: National Governor's Association, 1989.

Diegmueller, Karen. **"14-State Reform Project Releases Draft Standards."** ***Education Week,*** November 22, 1995

Educational Excellence Network and Education Policy Committee. ***Looking Back, Thinking Ahead: American School Reform 1993–1995.*** Indianapolis: Hudson Institute, 1994.

Educational Leadership. **"Improving School Quality."** Vol. 50, No. 3, November 1992, pp. 3–44. Twelve articles on Total Quality Management in education.

———— Vol. 51, No. 1, September 1993, pp. 58–69. Six articles on Total Quality Management in education.

Eurich, Nell P. ***The Learning Industry: Education for Adult Workers.*** Princeton: The Carnegie Foundation for the Advancement of Teaching, 1990.

Ferguson, Marilyn. **The Aquarian Conspiracy.** Los Angeles: J. P. Tarcher, Inc., 1980.

Fields, Melanie K., Leslie, Sarah H., and Hoge, Anita B. **"When Johnny Takes the Test."** *Christian Conscience,* September 1995.

Finn, Chester E., Jr., Bierlein, Louann A., and Manno, Bruno V. ***Charter Schools in Action: A First Look.*** Washington, D.C.: Hudson Institute: Educational Excellence Network, 1996.

Finn, Chester E., Jr. and Ravitch, Diane. ***Education Reform 1994–1995.*** (A report from the Educational Excellence Network to its Education Policy Committee and the American people.) Indianapolis: Hudson Institute, 1995.

Gabler, Mel and Norma. ***What Are They Teaching Our Children?*** Wheaton: Victor Books, 1985.

Gardner, Howard. ***Frames of Mind: The Theory of Multiple Intelligences.*** New York: Basic Books, 1983.

Greenawalt, Charles E. ***Charter Schools: A National Innovation for Pennsylvania***. Harrisburg: The Commonwealth Foundation for Public Policy Alternatives, 1995.

Grossman, Stephen R. **"Why TQM Doesn't Work . . . and What You Can Do About It."** ***Industry Week,*** January 3, 1994. (Reprinted in ***Wisconsin Report,*** March 10, 1994.)

Hitchcock, James. ***What Is Secular Humanism?*** Harrison: RC Books, 1982.

Hoge, Anita. **"Womb to Tomb: The New Social Technologies."** ***Christian Conscience,*** March 1995.

Holland, Robert. **"Kits to String Parents Along."** ***The Washington Times,*** October 25, 1994.

Hornbeck, David W., and Salamon, Lester M. (eds.). ***Human Capital and America's Future.*** Baltimore: The Johns Hopkins University Press, 1991.

Iserbyt, Charlotte T. ***Back to Basics Reform or . . . Skinnerian International Curriculum?*** Upland: The Barbara M. Morris Report, 1985.

Jennings, John F. (ed.). ***National Issues in Education: Elementary and Secondary Education Act.*** Bloomington: Phi Delta Kappa, International and the Institute for Educational Leadership, 1995.

———— ***National Issues in Education: GOALS 2000 and School-to-Work.*** Bloomington: Phi Delta Kappa, International and the Institute for Educational Leadership, 1995.

Johnston, William B. and Packer, Arnold H. ***Workforce 2000: Work and Workers for the 21st Century.*** Indianapolis: Hudson Institute, 1987.

Kagan, Spencer. **"Group Grades Miss the Mark."** ***Educational Leadership,*** pp. 69–71, May 1995.

Kane, Cheryl M. ***Prisoners of Time—Research.*** Washington, D.C.: National Education Commission on Time and Learning, 1994.

Kochhar, Carol A., and Erickson, Maureen R. ***Business-Education Partnerships for the 21st Century: A Practical Guide for School Improvement.*** Gaithersburg: Aspen Publishers, Inc., 1993.

Lewis, Bettye. **"The Great Perpetual Workforce Machine."** ***Christian Conscience,*** December 1995.

Lewis, Ralph G., and Smith, Douglas H. ***Total Quality in Higher Education.*** (Total Quality Series.) Delray Beach: St. Lucie Press, 1994.

Lodge, George C. ***Managing Globalization in the Age of Interdependence.*** San Diego: Pfeiffer & Co., 1995.

Lyman, Lawrence, Foyle, Harvey C., and Azwell, Tara S. ***Cooperative Learning in the Elementary Classroom.*** (Developments in Classroom Instruction Series.) Washington, D.C.: National Education Association, 1993.

Malen, Betty, Ogawa, Rodney T., and Kranz, Jennifer. **"Site-Based Management: Unfulfilled Promises."** ***The School Administrator,*** February 1990.

Marshall, Jennifer A. ***GOALS 2000: The Case for Repeal.*** (Insight series). Washington, D.C.: Family Research Council, 1995.

Marzano, Robert T., Pickering, Debra, and McTighe, Jay. ***Assessing Student Outcomes: Performance Assessment Using the Dimensions of Learning Model.*** Alexandria: Association for Supervision and Curriculum Development, 1993.

Mickelson, Jan. **"Perversity in Diversity."** ***Christian Conscience,*** February 1995.

Mitchell, James E. **"Coaxing Staff from Cages for Site-Based Decisions to Fly."** ***The School Administrator,*** February 1990.

Mojkowski, Charles, and Bamberger, Richard (ed.) ***Developing Leaders for Restructuring Schools: New Habits of Mind and Heart.*** A Report of the National LEADership Network Study Group on Restructuring Schools. Washington, D.C.: The Institute for Educational Leadership, 1991.

Morris, Barbara M. ***Change Agents in the Schools.*** Upland: The Barbara M. Morris Report, 1979.

__________ ***The Great American Con Game.*** Upland: The Barbara M. Morris Report, 1986.

NASDTEC Standards Committee. ***NASDTEC Outcome-Based Standards: Draft of Outcome-Based Teacher Education Standards for the High School Level.*** 1993.

National Board for Professional Teaching Standards. ***Toward High and Rigorous Standards for the Teaching Profession***. 3rd edition. Detroit, National Board for Professional Teaching Standards, 1991.

The National Center on Education and the Economy's Commission on the Skills of the American Workforce. ***America's Choice: High Skills or Low Wages!*** Rochester: National Center on Education and the Economy, 1990.

The National Commission on Excellence in Education. ***A Nation At Risk: The Imperative for Educational Reform.*** Washington, D.C.: Government Printing Office, 1983.

"NEA Plays Key Role in UN Agency Founding." ***NEA Today,*** February 1993.

National Education Association. ***Student Portfolios.*** (Teacher-to-Teacher Series.) Washington, D.C.: National Education Association of the United States, 1993.

National Education Goals Panel. ***The National Education Goals Report: Building a Nation of Learners.*** Washington, D.C.: National Education Goals Panel, 1995.

National Endowment for the Humanities. ***National Tests: What Other Countries Expect Their Students to Know.*** Washington, D.C.: National Endowment for the Humanities, 1991.

Ohio, State of. ***School-to-Work: The State of Ohio's Application for a School-to-Work Opportunities Act Implementation Grant.*** Columbus: Office of the Governor, June 1995.

Parkyn, George W. ***Towards a Conceptual Model of Lifelong Education.*** Paris: UNESCO, 1973.

Pendley, William Perry. **"Enlisting UN in the War on the U.S. West?"** ***The Washington Times,*** November 7, 1995.

Philadelphia Futures. ***Shaping the Future: Philadelphia's Public School Partnerships.*** Philadelphia: Philadelphia Futures, Spring 1995.

Price, Joyce. **"Millions from Medicaid Help Fund School Systems."** ***The Washington Times,*** January 2, 1996.

Public Education Network. **"The Medicaid Factor."** ***Education Update,*** February 21, 1995.

Public Law 103-229. ***GOALS 2000: Educate America Act.*** Washington, D.C.: U.S. Government Printing Office, 1994.

Public Law 103-239. ***School-to-Work Opportunities Act of 1994.*** Washington, D.C.: U.S. Government Printing Office, 1994.

Public Law 103-382. ***Improving America's Schools Act of 1994.*** Washington, D.C.: U.S. Government Printing Office, 1994.

The Robert Muller School. ***The Robert Muller School World Core Curriculum Manual.*** Arlington: The Robert Muller School, 1986.

"School System Working to Implement ISO 9000." ***Quality Systems Update,*** Vol. 4, No. 9, September 1994. (Reprinted in ***Wisconsin Report,*** May 11, 1995.)

Schlafly, Phyllis. **"Are All Children Really at Risk?"** ***The Washington Times,*** October 6, 1995.

Schmoker, Mike. **"Unlocking the Potential for Success."** ***The Oregonian,*** January 9, 1994. (Reprinted in ***Wisconsin Report,*** January 27, 1994.)

Sommerfield, Meg. **"Clinton Calls for National Education-Techology Effort."** ***Education Week,*** September 27, 1995

Sowell, Thomas. ***Inside American Education: The Decline, the Deception, the Dogmas.*** New York: The Free Press, 1993.

Sykes, Charles J. ***Dumbing Down Our Kids.*** New York: St. Martin's Press, 1995.

Thompson, Jean. **"Officials Assess Lessons of EAI."** ***The Sun,*** November 26, 1995

United Nations. ***Basic Facts About the United Nations.*** New York: United Nations Department of Public Information, 1993.

__________ ***What is UNESCO?*** Paris: UNESCO Publishing, Promotion and Sales Division, 1992.

United States Department of Education. ***All About ERIC.*** Washington, D.C.: USDOE, 1991.

__________ ***America Goes Back to School: A Place for Families and the Community. Partner's Activity Guide.*** Washington, D.C.: USDOE, 1995.

__________ ***AMERICA 2000: An Education Strategy.*** Washington, D.C.: USDOE, 1991.

__________ ***GOALS 2000: A World Class Education for Every Child: An Invitation to Your Community.*** Washington, D.C.: USDOE. n.d.

__________ ***Office of Educational Research and Improvement: Who We Are and What We Can Do For You.*** Washington, D.C.: USDOE, n.d.

__________ ***Programs and Plans of the National Center for Educational Statistics 1995 edition.*** Washington, D.C.: USDOE, 1995.

__________ ***Star Schools Program.*** Washington, D.C.: USDOE, n.d.

__________ ***Strong Families, Strong Schools: Building Community Partnerships for Learning.*** Washington, D.C.: USDOE, 1994.

_________ *A Teacher's Guide to the U.S. Department of Education.* Washington, D.C.: USDOE, 1993

_________ *World Class Standards for American Education.* Washington, D.C.: USDOE, 1992.

United States Department of Education. Office of Educational Technology. *Making It Happen: Report of the Secretary's Conference on Educational Technology.* Washington, D,C.: USDOE, 1995.

United States Department of Education and United States Department of Health and Human Services. *Together We Can: A Guide for Crafting a Profamily System of Education and Human Services.* Washington, D.C.: U.S. Government Printing Office, 1993.

United States Department of Health and Human Services. *Creating Caring Communities: Blueprint for an Effective Federal Policy on Child Abuse and Neglect.* (Executive Summary.) Washington, D.C.: U.S. Government Printing Office, 1991.

United States Department of Labor. *Learning a Living: A Blueprint for High Performance/A SCANS Report for AMERICA 2000.* Washington, D.C.: U.S. Government Printing Office, 1992.

_________ *SCANS Blueprint for Action: Building Community Coalitions.* Washington, D.C.: U.S. Government Printing Office, 1991.

_________ *What Work Requires of Schools: A SCANS Report for AMERICA 2000.* Washington, D.C.: U.S. Government Printing Office, 1991.

United States General Accounting Office. Health, Education, and Human Services Division. *Charter Schools: New Model for Public Schools Provides Opportunities and Challenges.* Washington, D.C.: U.S. Government Printing Office, 1995.

Viadero, Debra. **"In Reorganization of Research Effort, E.D. Seeks Proposals for 7 New Centers."** *Education Week,* November 26, 1995.

"Virginia's Parental 'Contract' Draws Challenge in Court." *Education Week* (News Roundup), September 27, 1995.

Vold, Edwina Battle (ed.). ***Multicultural Education in Early Childhood Classrooms.*** (NEA Early Childhood Series.) Washington, D.C.: National Education Association of the United States, 1992.

Warren, Donald R. ***To Enforce Education: A History of the Founding Years of the United States Office of Education.*** Detroit: Wayne State University Press, 1974.

Waters, Betty. **"Local High School Students Required to Wear Badges."** ***Tyler Telegraph,*** August 13, 1995.

Wolf, Wayne. **"The Myth of Local Control: The Reality of Site-Based Decision-Making."** ***Iowa Report,*** January 1993.

Resources

Available from **The Florida Forum, Inc.**, P.O. Box 1059, Highland City, Florida 33846-1059. Prices include shipping and handling:

The Florida Forum. Newsletter primarily on educational issues. National in scope. 4 times a year. $25.00/yr.

Bell, Don. ***"Proofs of a Conspiracy."*** 32-page tabloid. Compilation of articles from the ***Don Bell Reports*** dealing with preparatory steps leading the U.S. into the NWO. 1–3 cys/$2.50 each.

Cuddy, Dennis. ***A Chronology of Education with Quotable Quotes***. Covers the years from about 1790 to the present. Almost 700 entries. $15.95.

__________ ***The Grab for Power: A Chronology of the NEA.*** 29-page thumbnail sketch of the NEA from its beginning to the present time. $3.25.

__________ ***The Road to Socialism and the New World Order***. 80-page booklet outlining socialist inroads into U.S. government and institutions. $6.75.

Lyon, Billy. ***Connections and Conflicts of Interest.*** 8-page tabloid showing many business/education linkages. $.25 + a legal-sized SASE.

Rogers, Laura. ***Is "Parents as Teachers" Replacement of Parents in the Brave New World Order?*** 8-page tabloid of articles by the mother who first sounded the alarm on PAT. $.25 and a legal-sized SASE.

Florida Forum carries other education-related materials. Write for their listing.

- - - - -

Outcome-Based Education:

OBE: The Education Reform Agenda, a compilation of good articles on (mostly) OBE is available for $17.50. Order from Free World Research, Box 458, Farnhamville, Iowa 50539. Back issues of *Free World Research Report* (1993 through October 1994) are also available. Write for a free list of articles carried during that period.

Georges, Jeannie. ***The Media Bypass Manual On: Outcome-Based Education and Higher Order Thinking Skills.*** 19 pages $3.95 per copy or 10 copies for $10.00. from Media Bypass Magazine, P.O. Box 5326, Evansville, Indiana 47716.

Gotcher, Dean. The following pamphlets provide a **philosophical/ biblical** overview of **OBE**:

- ***Brief Evaluation of Process Education***
- ***Scriptures Concerning Process Education***
- ***OBE and Lessons from History***
- ***Taxonomy of Educational Objectives***

Each pamphlet is $.50 + a legal-sized SASE. Available from the Institution for Authority Research, 5436 S. Boston Place, Tulsa, Oklahoma 74105. (918) 742-3855.

Dean Gotcher is adjunct faculty at ORU and is available for consulting and speaking on current concepts and directions in education.

Iserbyt, Charlotte. ***Back to Basics Reform or . . . OBE . . . Skinnerian International Curriculum.*** $7.00. Order from Charlotte Iserbyt, 1062 Washington St., Bath, Maine 04530. (207) 442-7899. Mrs. Iserbyt has other materials, including videos on OBE. Contact her for a complete listing or for availability as a conference speaker.

McLemore, Judy. ***Outcome-Based Education: Another View.*** Excellent short article on OBE. $1.00 from Alabama Research Associates, Route 5, Box 100, Rogersville, Alabama 35652.

Schlafly, Phyllis. ***What's Wrong with Outcome-Based Education?*** With the usual Schlafly succinctness, a terrific 10-point summary. (See entry under "journals/newspapers" for ordering information).

- - - - -

The following resources are available from **Citizens for Academic Excellence,** P.O. Box 1164, Moline, Illinois 61265:

Patrick, James, compiler and editor. ***Research Manual: America 2000/ Goals 2000—Moving the Nation Educationally to a "New World Order."*** Over 800 pages of important articles and source material on school restructuring. This contains the entire text of ***P.L.103-227 (GOALS 2000)*** accompanied by Rev. Patrick's critique, as well as parallel passages from Vladimir Turchenko's ***The Scientific and Technological Revolution and the Revolution in Education.*** $23.50 This research you will not want to miss!

__________ ***Addendum to Research Manual.*** For those who already own the first edition of the ***Research Manual*** which did not contain the text of the ***GOALS 2000*** law, this is the entire text of ***P.L.103-227,*** Patrick's critique, and the Turchenko excerpts only. $8.00

Foundations of Liberty series ($2.50 each):

- ***Choice in Education.*** More than a dozen articles.
- ***Tuition Tax Credits: A Responsible Appraisal.*** Reprint of Barbara M. Morris's classic, out-of-print, 90-page book.
- ***Public Education—Its Philosophy.*** Articles on the problem and some solutions.

Miscellaneous

Guzman, Ingrid. ***Parent Police: The UN Wants Your Children.*** 47 pages.

Analysis of the ***UN Convention on the Rights of the Child.*** 47 pages. $5.49. Available from Huntington House, P.O. Box 53788, Lafayette, LA 70507. 1-800-749-4009.

Iserbyt, Charlotte. ***Soviets in the Classroom: America's Latest Education Fad.*** (Still in effect!) Order from Charlotte Iserbyt, 1062 Washington St., Bath, Maine 04530. $1.00 + SASE.

Kauser, Janson. ***Social Service Gestapo: How the Government Can Legally Abduct Your Child.*** 46 pages. Written by a municipal court judge. How the legal process works, and how parents can protect their families. $5.49. Available from Huntington House, P.O. Box 53788, Lafayette, LA 70507. 1-800-749-4009.

McLemore, Judy. Research papers:

- ***Cooperative Learning.*** $1.00 + SASE
- ***DARE: Drug Abuse Resistance Education.*** $5.00
- ***Educational Restructuring.*** $10.00

Available from Alabama Research Associates, Route 5, Box 100, Rogersville, Alabama. Send $1.00 and a SASE for a complete listing of other topics.

Parents Involved in Education. ***America or Amerika?***, a 58-minute video on **H.R.1617,** ***CAREERS*** (school-to-work). $17.50. Large package of supporting documents for $20.00. PIE also carries the NCEE's out-of-print ***The Human Resources Development Plan for the United States*** (the plan referenced in the Marc Tucker letter to Hillary Clinton—**chronology entry 112**). $15.00. (All prices are a suggested donation to cover copying and shipping costs.) Order from: Parents Involved in Education, P.O. Box 3004, Palm Desert, California 92261. FAX (619) 564-5344

Stuter, Lunn. ***Putting the Puzzle Together***. A multipart expose on educational restructuring, the Industrial Areas Foundation, and work force training/school-to-work. A variety of brochures are also available, including *The Hegelian Principle in Education; What's Wrong with Consensus?* and *What is Outcome-Based Education?* (2-part brochure on recognizing it in your school). Contact Mrs. Stuter, P.O. Box 345, Nine Mile Falls, Washington 99026 to order. (509) 468-9217.

- - - - -

Journals/Newsletters

The Blumenfeld Education Letter. Monthly.

Dr. Blumenfeld believes that state schools put children at risk spiritually, morally, physically, and intellectually and he develops this premise in his well researched and written newsletter. $36.00/yr.; $18.00/6 mos.; $9.00/3 issues. A list of back issues is available upon request, as well as a free information packet with ordering information on Blumenfeld's books and other materials. Contact the Paradigm Company, P.O. Box 45161, Boise, Idaho 83711. (208) 322-4440.

Wisconsin Report, a weekly newsletter covering many issues (including education) of interest to Christian conservatives. Order from *Wisconsin Report,* P. O. Box 45, Brookfield, Wisconsin 53008. (414) 782-4832. $20.00/yr.; $32.00/lst class. *WR* carries a small selection of books and reprints. Because Chambers of Commerce were active in promoting *AMERICA 2000*, I recommend:

The Chamber of Commerce: Its Power and Goals. $1.00

Christian Conscience, a monthly journal of articles (mostly education) is an excellent newcomer, taking on cutting edge and controversial developments in education in the Christian community. Available from Iowa Research Group, P.O. Box 17346, Des Moines, Iowa 50317. $28.00/yr. Free sample issue sent upon request and/or a list of articles appearing in back issues—include a SASE. Back issues (to January 1995) are available for $3.50. Two that provide essential information relative to *GOALS 2000* are: *"When Johnny Takes the Test"* (on the NAEP), available as a reprint for $1.00 + a SASE, and *"The Great Perpetual Workforce Machine"* (on school-to-work and lifelong learning) in the December 1995 issue.

The Florida Forum. (See first entry.)

Phyllis Schlafly Report, a monthly newsletter covering a variety of subjects of interest to conservatives; education is a frequent topic. $20.00/yr. from Eagle Forum, Box 618, Alton, Illinois 62002. Back copies of issues are available: 2 for $1.00. Especially recommended are:

- ***Are All Our Children "At Risk"?***
- ***Let's Abolish the Department of Education***
- ***How Liberals Are Rewriting History***
- ***What's Wrong with Outcome-Based Education?***
- ***The New World Order Wants Your Children***
- Fliers: ***Drug Education*** and ***Nosy Questions***

Eagle Forum also carries ***Child Abuse in the Classroom.*** Paperback is $8.00. 30-minute video is $21.95. Cassette soundtrack of the video is $5.00. Add $2.00 for shipping. Write for a complete listing of other materials.

Mother's Heart. Mostly education. Research and analysis on the impact of educational reform on families and society. Documentation packets also available. About 2 issues a year. $10.00. Send a SASE for list of available packets and back issues to Mother's Heart, c/o Melanie Fields, 14 Pocohontas Path, Front Royal, Virginia 22630.

The Traditional Educator. Written by Jed Brown, a former school teacher and curriculum consultant, **TTE** is a look at current educational restructuring from a traditionalist view. $12.00 for 12 issues. Order from School Policy Institute, P.O. Box 4572, Rollingbay, Washington 98061. (360) 598-2753. Jed Brown is currently running for state superintendent of public instruction in Washington and is a popular lecturer.

\- - - - -

Videos

The School Policy Institute has also put out a valuable set of four half-hour videos and an accompanying transcript (useful for documentation). The emphasis is on the **international connection, the illegality of what is being done (and accompanying deception)** and the **educational malpractice** perpetrated in the name of educational restructuring. The four video set is $22.00. The transcript is $13.00. Videos and transcript are $30.00. Audio tape version is $15.00. Add $5.00 S&H to any order. Order from School Policy Institute, P.O. Box 4572, Rollingbay, Washington 98061. (360) 598-2753. See also "journal" entry: ***The Traditional Educator.***

People for Responsible Educational Policy (PREP), the New Hampshire group largely responsible for N.H.'s refusal of ***GOALS 2000*** money also has a set of four videos. All are taped commentaries by PREP founder Eleanor Campbell. The topics are: 1) ***GOALS 2000***; 2) **PPBS-TQM for the Public Schools**; 3) **OBE**; and 4) **Humanism—the Religion of the Public Schools.** Prices are: $15.00 for one, 2 for $25.00, 3 for $37.00, or 4 for $45.00. Order from People for Responsible Educational Policy, P.O. Box 129, 33 Hayward Road, Plainfield, New Hampshire 03781. PREP has a free book list which will be sent upon request.

Parents Involved in Education. A video on school-to-work. (See entry under "miscellaneous."

- - - - -

Books

Cuddy, Dennis. ***Now Is the Dawning of the New Age New World Order.*** Dr. Cuddy has a Ph.D. in history and is a former senior associate at the U.S. Department of Education. He brings out many interesting historical threads woven into the present/coming NWO. Education is covered in several chapters. $17.00. Order from Southwest Radio Church, 1-800-652-1144.

Duffy, Cathy. ***Government Nannies: The Cradle-to-Grave Agenda of GOALS 2000 and Outcome-Based Education.*** Analysis and lots of examples and stories of what's going on in towns and schools across America. Interesting thoughts on the history, purposes, and necessity of state schools. $17.95 Order from Noble Publishing Associates, 1-800-225-5259.

Eakman, Beverly. ***Educating for the New World Order.*** Published in 1991, this expose of illegal testing, data collection, and social engineering in our public schools has become a best seller. $21.95. Order from Halcyon House, 1-800-827-2499.

Michaelsen, Johanna. ***Like Lambs to the Slaughter.*** A former occultist writes about the inroads of the occult into the media, children's literature, toys, and the classroom. $12.99. Order from Harvest House Publishers, 1-800-547-8979.

- - - - -

Access to Homeschooling

If you have made this decision (or are considering it), you will have a number of concerns. Among them:

1. The legal requirements in your state.
2. What curriculum to use.
3. The support of other families in your area who homeschool. (Most people find this helpful, especially as they start out.)

Regarding curriculum, there's a great variety on the market and each child and parent/teacher has different requirements, so I will only suggest that you begin talking to families that homeschool, attending curriculum fairs, and reading books on homeschooling. One of the perennial favorites for curriculum is Mary Pride's ***The Big Book of Home Learning.*** Originally a single title, this has expanded to four volumes: Vol. 1: Getting Started; Vol. 2: Preschool and Elementary; Vol. 3: Teen and Adult; and Vol. 4: Afterschooling. Cathy Duffy has also done a two-volume set, ***Chrsitian Home Educators' Curriculum Manual.*** These are available from: Great Christian Books, 229 South Bridge Street, P.O. Box 8000, Elkton, Maryland 21922-8000. 1-800-775-6422. Ask for their homeschooling catalog which contains a huge selection of materials, all at discounted prices.

To find out what the legal requirements are in your state, as well as to locate a local support group, contact the appropriate group listed below. If you are writing, including a SASE. (Be sure to ask about their annual convention/curriculum fair as these are a great way to look over materials to be sure they're right for you before purchasing.)

Christian State Homeschool Organizations:

Alabama: Christian Home Education Fellowship of Alabama, Box 563, Alabaster, AL 35007 / Telephone: 664-2232.

Alaska: Alaska Private and Home Education Association, Box 141764, Anchorage, AK 99514 / Telephone: 696-0641.

Arizona: Arizona Families for Home Education, Box 4661, Scottsdale, AZ 85261 / Telephone: 941-3938.

Arkansas: Arkansas Christian Home Educators Association, Box 4025, N. Little Rock, AR 72190 / Telephone: 758-9099.

California: Christian Home Education Association of California, Box 2009, Norwalk, CA 90651 / Telephone: 1-800-564-2432.

Colorado: Christian Home Educators of Colorado, 1015 S. Gaylord, #226, Denver, CO 80209 / Telephone: 388-1888.

Connecticut: The Education Association of Christian Homeschoolers, 25 Field Stone Run, Farmington, CT 06032 / Telephone: 1-800-205-7844.

Delaware: Delaware Home Education Association, Box 1003, Dover DE 19903 / Telephone: 234-9044

Florida: Florida at Home, 4644 Adanson, Orlando, FL 32804 / Telephone: 740-8877.

Georgia: Georgia Home Education Association, 245 Buckeye Lane, Fayetteville, GA 30214 / Telephone: 461-3657.

Hawaii: Christian Homeschoolers of Hawaii, 91-824 Oama Street, Ewa Beach, HI 96706 / Telephone: 689-6398

Idaho: Idaho Home Educators, Box 1324, Meridian, ID 83680 / Telephone: 323-0230.

Illinois: Illinois Christian Home Educators, Box 261, Zion, IL 60099 / Telephone: 670-7150.

Indiana: Indiana Association of Home Educators, 408 S. 9th St., Noblesville, IN 46060 / Telephone: 770-0644.

Iowa: Network of Iowa Christian Home Educators, Box 158, Dexter, IA 50070 / Telephone: 1-800-723-0438.

Kansas: Christian Home Education Confederation of Kansas, Box 3564, Shawnee Mission, KS 66203 / Telephone: 755-2159.

Kentucky: Christian Home Educators of Kentucky, 691 Howardstown Road, Hodgenville, KY 42748 / Telephone: 358-9270.

Louisiana: Christian Home Educators Fellowship of Louisiana, Box 74292, Baton Rouge, LA 70874 / Telephone: 775-9709.

Maine: Homeschoolers of Maine, HC 62, Box 24, Hope, ME 04847 / Telephone: 763-4251.

Maryland: Maryland Association of Christian Home Educators, Box 3964, Frederick, MD 21705 / Telephone: 663-3999.

Massachusetts: Massachusetts Homeschool Organization of Parent Ed., 15 Ohio St., Wilmington, MA 01887 / Telephone: 658-8970

Michigan: Information Network for Christian Homes, 4934 Cannonsburg Rd., Belmont, MI 49306 / Telephone: 874-5656.

Minnesota: Minnesota Association of Christian Home Educators, Box 188, Anoka, MN 55303 / Telephone: 717-9070.

Mississippi: Mississippi Home Education Association, 109 Reagan Ranch Road, Laurel, MS 39440 / Telephone: 649-6432.

Missouri: Missouri Association of Teaching Christian Homes, 307 E. Ash St., #146, Columbia, MO 65201 / Telephone: 443-8217.

Montana: Montana Coalition of Home Educators, Box 43, Gallatin Gateway, MT 59730 / Telephone: 587-6163.

Nebraska: Nebraska Christian Home Educators Association, Box 57041, Lincoln, NE 68505 / Telephone: 423-4297.

Nevada: Home Education and Righteous Training, Box 42264, Las Vegas, NV 89116. (No phone given.)

New Hampshire: Christian Home Educators of New Hampshire, Box 961, Manchester, NH 03105 / Telephone: 569-2343.

New Jersey: Education Network of Christian Homeschoolers, 120 Mayfair Lane, Mt. Laurel, NJ 08054 / Telephone: 273-4447.

New Mexico: New Mexico Christian Home Educators, 5749 Paradise Blvd., NW, Albuquerque, NM 87114 / Telephone: 879-1772.

New York: Loving Education at Home, Box 88, Cato, NY 13033 / Telephone: 346-0939.

North Carolina: North Carolinians for Home Education, 419 N. Boylan Ave., Raleigh, NC 27603 / Telephone: 834-6243.

North Dakota: North Dakota Home School Association, 4007 N. State Street, Bismark, ND 58501 / Telephone: 223-4080.

Ohio: Christian Home Educators of Ohio, Box 262, Columbus, OH 43216 / Telephone: 474-3177.

Oklahoma: Christian Home Education Fellowship of Oklahoma, Box 471363, Tulsa, OK 74147 / Telephone: 583-7323.

Oregon: Oregon Christian Home Education Association Network, 2515 NE 37th, Portland, OR 97212 / Telephone: 288-1285.

Pennsylvania: Christian Home School Association of Pennsylvania, Box 3603, York, PA 17402 / Telephone: 661-2428.

Rhode Island: Rhode Island Guild of Home Teachers, Box 11, Hope, RI 02831 / Telephone: 821-1546.

South Carolina: South Carolina Home Educators Association, Box 612, Lexington, SC 29071 / Telephone: 951-8960.

South Dakota: West Dakota Christian Home Schools, Box 528, Black Hawk, SD 57718 / Telephone: 923-1893.

Tennessee: Tennessee Home Education Association, 3677 Richbriar Court, Nashville, TN 37211 / Telephone: 834-3529.

Texas: Home-Oriented Private Education for Texas, Box 59876, Dallas, TX 75229 / Telephone: 358-2221.

Utah: Utah Christian Home Schoolers, Box 3942, Salt Lake City, UT 84110 / Telephone: 255-4053.

Vermont: Christian Home Educators of Vermont, 214 N. Prospect, #105, Burlington, VT 05401 / Telephone: 658-4561.

Virginia: Home Educators Association of Virginia, Box 1810, Front Royal, VA 22630 / Telephone: 635-9322.

Washington: Washington Association of Teaching Christian Homes, N. 2904 Dora Road, Spokane, WA 99212 / Telephone: 922-4811.

West Virginia: Christian Home Educators of West Virginia, Box 8770, S. Charleston, WV 25303 / Telephone: 776-4664.

Wisconsin: Wisconsin Christian Home Education Association, 2307 Carmel Ave., Racine, WI 53405 / Telephone: 637-5127.

Wyoming: Homeschoolers of Wyoming, 339 Bicentennial Court, Powell, WY 82435 / Telephone: 754-3271.

- - - - -

Access to Legislation

To get **information on bills, call LEGIS (202) 225-1772.** With minimal information, you can access bills in a number of ways: e.g., you know the bill's name, but not its number; you know who sponsored the bill and what it's about, but not the name or number. It's helpful to get the report(s) that often accompany a bill, too. LEGIS can tell you if reports exist and their numbers.

If a bill originates in the **House** and you know the bill number, you can call the House Documents Room **(202) 225-3456** to (sometimes) **get a free copy.** Under a **restrictive new policy** (July 1995) only 150 copies of **certain** House bills are being made available to the public. The way this was explained to me is: if "they" expect a bill to be "hot," they're only giving the House Documents Room 150 copies. With all the possible ways the government might save money, **this policy looks very suspicious to me.** Perhaps if enough people called their congressman to complain, this might be changed. If you cannot obtain a bill from the number above, there are four other possibilities: 1) Call your congressman or senators. 2) If you have Internet access, I'm told the text of bills is available: *http://thomas.loc.gov* (assumes a lot!). 3) Government Depository Libraries should have a copy (inconvenient!). 4) Buy from the Government Printing Office (202) 512-1808 (expensive!). **I hope many will complain about this policy which limits our access to proposed House-generated legislation.** Since we pay for what goes on in Washington (and then have to live under laws passed), I think we should at least be able to see what Congress is up to, don't you?

Senate bills cannot be ordered over the phone, but may be ordered by **FAX: (202) 228-2815.** You can also order up to six bills per request in writing from: Senate Documents Room, SH-B 04, Washington, D.C. 20510. Include a gummed, self-addressed label. Senate bills are still available (as far as I know) in reasonably generous quantities to the public.

David Benoit

Did you know that every day, thousands of children are molested by adults? To this question most of you would answer, "Yes, I knew that." But did you know that most child abusers are introduced to these innocent children by unsuspecting parents? That's right. Child molesters have an uncanny way of convincing parents that their child would be perfectly safe with them. They may be friends, day care workers, baby-sitters, educators, and even family members.

Who's Watching the Playpen? is not a book about child molestation. It is a book about the subtlety of the ungodly. *Who's Watching the Playpen?* is not a book about fear; it's a book about courage and hope.

This book is designed to give parents information needed in order to stand guard over the souls of their children. The greatest deterrent to a child molester is the presence of a well-informed parent. The Bible says, "I have not given you the spirit of fear but of power and of love and of a sound mind" (2 Tim. 1:7).

So now, let's give fair warning to those who may have their sights set on our children. *We are watching the playpen!*

ISBN 1-57558-000-4 • 195 pages

This live presentation featuring David Benoit is a must view for Sunday school classes, churches, Christian school classes, as well as Bible study groups. There are only a handful of speakers who can expose the deception of the one-world government and their plot to capture the hearts of the youth.

Hitler thought it was amusing that by the time the parents found out about his plot to convert their children's will for the Nazi Party, it was too late. Hitler had stolen the children right from under the noses of the unsuspecting parents.

Today, the Antichrist is doing the same thing. You owe it to yourself as a pastor, teacher, parent, or grandparent, to know the content of this powerful presentation.

This video covers the newest material dealing with the New Age movement, and how it affects our children. See how education and entertainment are indoctrinating our society to accept the philosophies of the New Age.

ISBN 1-57558-002-0 • 150-minute VHS video

PSYCHOLOGY:
Pied Piper of New Age

Louise S. Idomir

Psychology: Pied Piper of New Age unmasks the mystique of psychology and exposes it for what it is. Completely objective and documented, it addresses such questions as:

Why is psychology so appealing?

•••

What does it really teach?

•••

Can its teachings be verified or validated scientifically?

•••

Are its "truths" and values the same as those of Secular Humanism?

•••

Is there a psycho-New Age connection?

•••

What are the techniques most commonly used by professionals in therapy and training sessions?

•••

Are they safe?

•••

Is there evidence of psychological/New Age infiltration into the Church?

•••

Why has our educational system become ineffective?

•••

What is the original and real meaning of many words and phrases in common usage in today's society?

•••

Is "Christian psychology" a legitimate term?

ISBN 1-879366-90-8 • 180 pages

TOWARD A NEW WORLD ORDER

THE COUNTDOWN TO ARMAGEDDON

Donald S. McAlvany

It is scary to hear the President of the United States, the president-dictator of Russia, and the head of the Eastern Establishment, who has for years controlled the Council on Foreign Relations and founded its stepchild, the Trilateral Commission, all promoting the same thing—the New World Order!

How can a committed communist, an arch capitalist, and the head of the freest and richest nation on earth have the same vision for our world? The communist is an atheist, consequently, he doesn't believe in God. The capitalist worships money and power, and the President of the United States claims he is a Christian.

Either these three men do not mean the same thing by the New World Order, or there is a conspiracy to lead the people of this world into a one-world government that needs to be exposed!

From all indications, this world is rapidly moving to the very times our Lord and His disciples predicted would exist at the end of this age. Is the New World Order the means of bringing the world toward the one-world government of the last days?

ISBN 0-9624517-9-7 • 375 pages

AFTER THE EMPIRE

THE FALL OF THE SOVIET UNION AND BIBLE PROPHECY

Mark Hitchcock

The Soviet Union has fallen, but what is happening *After the Empire?*

- Militant Islam is surging in the Middle East.
- The former Russian republic still has great military power and still has a vested interest in the Middle East.
- The fall of the Soviet Union has spawned the creation of 15 newly independent nations.
- Six of these new nations are Moslem nations with a total population of 60 million.
- These new Moslem nations have nuclear weapons in their control.
- Turkey and Iran are developing close ties with these newly independent Moslem nations.

After the Empire is a fascinating overview of contemporary events that shows how, in light of the fall of the Soviet Union, the nations in Ezekiel 38 and 39 are coming together in preparation to invade Israel as Ezekiel predicted 2,600 years ago!

ISBN 1-879366-30-4 • 150 pages

Why So Many CHURCHES?

N. W. Hutchings

Brother Hutchings became interested in why those who profess the Name of Jesus Christ as Savior and Lord believe differently on hundreds of doctrinal issues, when it is obvious that all cannot be right.

After an appraisal of the entire spectrum of denominational differences, the author reduces the many ecclesiastical variances to one common denominator: the Gospel of the Kingdom committed to Peter to preach to the Circumcision (Israel) and the Gospel of sovereign Grace committed to the Uncircumcision (Gentiles).

If you have ever wondered why there are so many denominations and sects, and why church memberships cannot agree on even simple doctrinal differences like baptism, then you will want to read and study this book.

ISBN 1-879366-28-2 • 200 pages

. . . COMING SOON . . .

The Great Pyramid

—Prophecy In Stone—

N. W. Hutchings

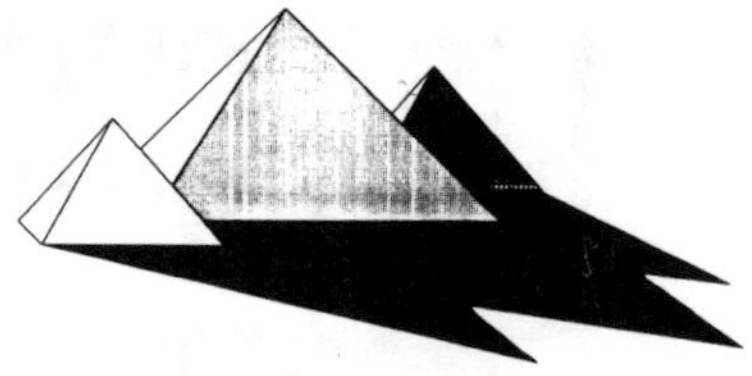

"Great in counsel, and mighty in work: for thine eyes are open upon all the ways of the sons of men: to give every one according to his ways, and according to the fruit of his doings: Which hast set signs and **wonders in the land of Egypt**, even unto this day. . ." (Jer. 32:19).

The wonders of God enumerated in the scriptures are countless and beyond comprehension. Everything we see and touch was created by God. Life in every form is a wonder. Man, who was created in the image of God, may bring forth wonders limited to three dimensions like the Tower of Babel. But even in some of the so-called physical wonders of man, God's presence is made known, as in the wonders of Egypt.

Man in his own wisdom has catalogued the greatest seven wonders of man who lived in the ancient world. By the ancient world, we set this era as being before Christ was born. Some recognized authorities on such matters disagree as to which is the greatest seven man-made wonders of the ancient world. However, all agree that the Great Pyramid of Giza is the greatest wonder of man's accomplishment.

ISBN 1-57558-007-1